# GREEK & ROMAN PHILOSOPHY

"Written by an expert in the field, *Greek and Roman Philosophy* skillfully guides the reader through this fascinating but labyrinthine topic. The scope of this book is immense, and Brookins masterfully curates the material to allow for meaningful understanding. The work is clearly organized, and the summaries, annotated bibliographies, notes on primary sources, definitions of key terms and concepts, and evaluation of scholarship make this work ideal for those coming to the topic with minimal prior knowledge. This work will make classroom teaching and learning easier, and Brookins is to be thanked for this helpful survey."

**—Sean A. Adams, professor of New Testament and Ancient Culture, University of Glasgow**

"Timothy Brookins' *Greek and Roman Philosophy: A Survey for Students of the New Testament* is an indispensable resource that bridges complex domains—ancient classical, Hellenistic, and 'popular' philosophy alongside early Christian studies—with clarity and captivating depth. Brookins offers a thorough and systematic overview of Greek and Roman philosophical traditions, skillfully contextualizing their ideas within the world that shaped and engaged with the New Testament. Enhanced by stimulating tables, appendices, bibliographies, and maps, this work is an invaluable tool for anyone seeking a deeper understanding of the intellectual environment of the New Testament."

**—Athanasios Despotis, professor of New Testament Faculty of Protestant Theology, University of Bonn**

"Timothy Brookins's *Greek and Roman Philosophy* should be the first book off the shelf for anyone looking for a survey of the Greek and Roman philosophical traditions. This is especially the case for serious students of the New Testament since—as Brookins puts it—early Christianity 'was able to flower and propagate only by competing with these intellectual traditions.' Whereas Socrates reportedly brought philosophy down from heaven to earth, this book brings it down from the ivory tower to the classroom, the coffee house, and the bedside table."

**—Joseph R. Dodson, The Craig L. Blomberg Chair of New Testament, Denver Seminary**

"For students with little or no training in ancient philosophy, making sense of Plato, Aristotle, the Stoics, and the Epicureans (among other names and schools) is a daunting task. Brookins has provided us with a masterful treatment of ancient philosophy, and even explored some of its relationship to the New Testament and early Christianity, in a manner that is both comprehensive and readable. I highly recommend it for both professors and students!"

**—Joshua W. Jipp, professor of New Testament Trinity Evangelical Divinity School**

"This is a clear, simple, and helpful introduction to Graeco-Roman philosophy for students and scholars better versed in the New Testament and early Christianity. The author has already contributed to interrelating these in his books on Paul and Stoicism. It is important that scholars in the New Testament and ancient Christianity and religions be familiar with ancient philosophy, and vice versa, given that they cannot be studied without one another. Patristic philosophy and philosophical theology build precisely on this interrelation: in the New Testament and Patristic period, philosophy and theology were not separate disciplines as in the post-Cartesian and post-Kantian thought."

**—Professor Ilaria L.E. Ramelli, Stanford University**
**Sacred Heart University, Angelicum,**
**University of Bonn, University of Cambridge**

"Brookins does here for a new generation what Malherbe's *Moral Exhortation: A Greco-Roman Sourcebook* did for the previous generation: He provides a summary and synthesis of ancient philosophy geared specifically toward the study of the New Testament and early Christianity. Working succinctly and accurately, Brookins provides a birds-eye view of the philosophical schools, figures, developments, and topics (including all *topoi*, unlike Malherbe's volume), alongside clear visuals and the curated bibliographies needed for inquiring students. This introduction to the scholarship and key issues provides a much-needed service for theology and religious studies students, who inevitably find their time for Classics limited. I can't wait to use this in my classes!"

**—Annalisa Phillips Wilson, affiliated lecturer**
**University of Cambridge**

# GREEK & ROMAN PHILOSOPHY

*A Survey for Students of the New Testament*

TIMOTHY A. BROOKINS

**Greek and Roman Philosophy**
**A Survey for Students of the New Testament**



Hendrickson Publishers
3 Centennial Drive
Peabody, Massachusetts 01960
www.hendricksonpublishers.com

ISBN 978-1-68307-415-1 (print)
ISBN 979-8-4005-1235-3 (Kindle ebook)
ISBN 979-8-4005-1236-0 (epub)
ISBN 979-8-4005-1237-7 (Apple epub)



*Printed in the United States of America*

*First Printing — May 2025*

Library of Congress Control Number: 2024952851

# Contents

## Part 4. Christianity and Philosophy



## Appendixes

# Illustrations

Tables



Figures

# Acknowledgments

I have many people to thank for their assistance over the course of this project. Several read earlier versions of chapters and offered helpful feedback or suggestions for revision. These include Chris Atkins, Joseph Dodson, Gary Hartenburg, Jason Maston, Adam White, and Richard Wright. I'm grateful to my colleagues at Houston Christian University for bearing with me. I must also thank the acquisitions editor at Hendrickson, Jonathan Kline, for initiating the conversations that led to this project. I also thank my editorial director, Patricia Anders, for her hard work and her patience with me throughout the process as I kept my door shut to buckle down. I greatly benefited from the class I taught at HCU on Greek and Roman Philosophy in the summer of 2023, which led me to revise my outline substantially and helped me better synthesize and articulate the content by talking through it with students. For the many tables and charts that appear in the book, I'm especially grateful to Marc Hinds at Hinds Designs for his needed skills and gracious employment.

This work has found much of its inspiration in the work of others. No one has done more to stimulate research on the Greco-Roman philosophical traditions in biblical studies than Abraham Malherbe, who inspired a generation of students to carry on his line of research. Over the past several decades, the prolific publications of Troels Engberg-Pedersen have given constant impetus to this area of study. I've been especially encouraged to continue in this direction by two contributors among the newer generation who share this interest and who are producing high-quality work of their own—my friends Joey Dodson and Max Lee, to whom I dedicate this book.

# Abbreviations

## Primary Source Literature

Apuleius

| | |
|---|---|
| *Flor.* | *Florida* |

Aratus

| | |
|---|---|
| *Phaen.* | *Phenomena* |

Aristotle

| | |
|---|---|
| *Cael.* | *Heavens* |
| *Eth. Eud.* | *Eudemian Ethics* |
| *Eth. Nic.* | *Nicomachean Ethics* |
| *Metaph.* | *Metaphysics* |
| *Pol.* | *Politics* |
| *Rhet.* | *Rhetoric* |
| *Top.* | *Topics* |

Augustine

| | |
|---|---|
| *Civ.* | *The City of God* |

Aulus Gellius

| | |
|---|---|
| *Noct. Att.* | *Attic Nights* |

Cicero

| | |
|---|---|
| *Acad.* | *Academica* |
| *Brut.* | *Brutus* |
| *Fam.* | *Letters to Friends* |
| *Fat.* | *On Fate* |
| *Fin.* | *On Ends* |
| *Inv.* | *On Invention* |
| *Nat. d.* | *On the Nature of the Gods* |
| *Off.* | *On Duties* |
| *Or.* | *On the Orator* |
| *Top.* | *Topics* |
| *Tusc.* | *Tusculan Disputations* |

Clement of Alexandria

| | |
|---|---|
| *Strom.* | *Miscellanies* |

Dio Chrysostom
*Or.* *Orations*

Diogenes Laërtius
*Vit. phil.* *Lives of Eminent Philosophers*

Epictetus
*Diatr.* *Diatribes*

Epicurus
*Ep. Idom.* *Epistle to Idomeneus*
*Ep. Men.* *Epistle to Menoeceus*
*Kur. dox.* *Kuriae Doxae*

Galen
*De puls. diff.* *On the Differences of Pulses*

Gregory of Nazianzus
*Or.* *Orations*

Hesiod
*Theog.* *Theogony*

Horace
*Sat.* *Satires*

Irenaeus
*Haer.* *Against Heresies*

Jerome
*Jov.* *Adversus Jovinianum libri I*
*Vir. ill.* *Lives of Illustrious Men*

Josephus
*Ag. Ap.* *Against Apion*
*Ant.* *Jewish Antiquities*
*Vit.* *The Life*

Justin
*1 Apol* *First Apology*
*2 Apol.* *Second Apology*
*Dial.* *Dialogue with Trypho*

Justinianus
*Dig.* *The Digest*

Juvenal
*Sat.* *Satires*

Lactantius
*Inst.* *The Divine Institutes*

Lucian

| | |
|---|---|
| *Alex.* | *Alexander the False Prophet* |
| *Bis. acc.* | *The Double Indictment* |
| *Dem.* | *Demonax* |
| *Eun.* | *The Eunuch* |
| *Fug.* | *The Runaways* |
| *Gall.* | *The Dream,* or *The Cock* |
| *Herm.* | *Hermotimus* |
| *Iupp. conf.* | *Zeus Catechized* |
| *Par.* | *The Parasite* |
| *Peregr.* | *The Passing of Peregrinus* |
| *Vit. auct.* | *Philosophies for Sale* |

Lucretius

| | |
|---|---|
| *Rer. nat.* | *On the Nature of Things* |

Musonius Rufus

| | |
|---|---|
| *Diatr.* | *Diatribes* |

Origen

| | |
|---|---|
| *Cels.* | *Against Celsus* |
| *Ep. Greg.* | *Epistle to Gregory* |

Philo

| | |
|---|---|
| *Aetern.* | *On the Eternity of the World* |
| *Cher.* | *On the Cherubim* |
| *Praem.* | *On Rewards and Punishments* |
| *Plant.* | *On Plantings* |
| *Prob.* | *That Every Good Person Is Free* |
| *Sobr.* | *On Sobriety* |
| *Spec.* | *On the Special Laws* |

Philodemus

| | |
|---|---|
| *Lib.* | *On Frank Speech* |

Philostratus

| | |
|---|---|
| *Vit. Apoll.* | *On the Life of Apollonius* |
| *Vit. Soph.* | *Lives of the Sophists* |

Plato

| | |
|---|---|
| *Apol.* | *Apology* |
| *Crit.* | *Critias* |
| *Gorg.* | *Gorgias* |
| *Phaed.* | *Phaedo* |
| *Phaedr.* | *Phaedrus* |
| *Rep.* | *Republic* |
| *Soph.* | *Sophist* |
| *Tim.* | *Timaeus* |

Pliny

| | |
|---|---|
| *Ep.* | *Epistles* |
| *Nat.* | *Natural History* |

Plutarch

| | |
|---|---|
| *Cat. Maj.* | *Cato the Elder* |
| *Mor.* | *Moralia* |
| *Quaes. conv.* | *Table Talk* |
| *Sull.* | *Sulla* |

Ps.-Cicero

| | |
|---|---|
| *Rhet.* | *Rhetorica ad Herennium* |

Ps.-Plutarch

| | |
|---|---|
| *Lib. ed.* | *On Educating Children* |

Quintilian

| | |
|---|---|
| *Inst.* | *Institutio Oratoria* |

Seneca

| | |
|---|---|
| *Ep.* | *Moral Epistles* |
| *Ben.* | *On Benefits* |
| *Const.* | *On the Constancy of the Wise Man* |
| *Ira* | *On Anger* |
| *Ot.* | *On Leisure* |
| *Tranq.* | *On Tranquility of the Soul* |
| *Vit. Beat.* | *On the Happy Life* |

Sextus Empiricus

| | |
|---|---|
| *Contra Log.* | *Against the Logicians* |
| *Math.* | *Against the Mathematicians* |
| *Pyr.* | *Outlines of Pyrrhonism* |

Stobaeus

| | |
|---|---|
| *Anth.* | *Anthology* |

Strabo

| | |
|---|---|
| *Geogr.* | *Geography* |

Suetonius

| | |
|---|---|
| *Aug.* | *Divus Augustus* |

Tacitus

| | |
|---|---|
| *Agr.* | *Agricola* |

Tatian

| | |
|---|---|
| *Or. Graec.* | *Oration Against the Greeks* |

Tertullian

| | |
|---|---|
| *An.* | *The Soul* |
| *Pall.* | *The Pallium* |
| *Praescr.* | *Prescription Against Heretics* |

THEON

| | |
|---|---|
| *Prog.* | *Progymnmasmata* |

XENOPHON

| | |
|---|---|
| *Apol.* | *Apology of Socrates* |
| *Mem.* | *Memorabilia* |

## Papyrological and Epigraphical Sources

| | |
|---|---|
| *IG* II$^{2}$ | *Inscriptiones Graecae II et III: Inscriptiones Atticae Euclidis anno posteriores.* 2nd ed., Parts I–III, ed. Johannes Kirchner. Berlin 1913–1940. |
| *IG* IV$^{2}$ | *Inscriptiones Graecae IV = Inscriptiones graecae Aeginae, Pityonesi, Cecryphaliae, Argolidis*, ed. Max Fraenkel. "Corpus inscriptionum graecarum Peloponnesi et insularum vicinarum," 1. Berlin 1902. |
| *IG* V | *Inscriptiones Graecae, V,2. Inscriptiones Arcadiae*, ed. Friedrich Hiller von Gaertringen. Berlin 1913. |
| *IPrusaOlymp* | *Die Inschriften von Prusa ad Olympum.* 2 vols., ed. Thomas Corsten. "Inschriften griechischer Städte aus Kleinasien," 39–40. Bonn 1991–1993. |
| *IvO* | *Die Inschriften von Olympia*, eds Wilhelm Dittenberger, and Karl Purgold. "Olympia," 5. Berlin 1896. |
| *IKorinthKent* | *Corinth*, Vol. VIII, part III, *The Inscriptions 1926–1950*, ed. J. H. Kent. Princeton: American School of Classical Studies at Athens, 1966. |
| *IKorinthMerritt* | *Corinth VIII,1. The Greek Inscriptions 1896–1927*, ed. Benjamin D. Meritt. Cambridge, MA 1931. |
| *SEG* | *Supplementum epigraphicum graecum.* Vols. 1–11, ed. Jacob E. Hondius. Leiden 1923–1954. Vols. 12–25, ed. Arthur G. Woodhead. Leiden 1955–1971. Vols. 26–41, eds. Henry W. Pleket and Ronald S. Stroud. Amsterdam 1979–1994. Vols. 42–44, ed. Henry W. Pleket, Ronald S. Stroud, and Johan H.M. Strubbe. Amsterdam 1995–1997. Vols. 45–49, ed. Henry W. Pleket, Ronald S. Stroud, Angelos Chaniotis, and Johan H. M. Strubbe. Amsterdam 1998–2002. Vols. 50– , ed. Angelos Chaniotis, Ronald S. Stroud, and Johan H. M. Strubbe. Amsterdam 2003– |
| *PIR*$^{2}$ | *Prosopographia Imperii Romani Saec I. II. III.* 2nd ed. Berlin 1933–2015. |
| *P.Herc.* | *Catalogo dei Papiri Ercolanesi*, compiled under the direction of M. Gigante at Centro Internazionale per lo Studio dei Papiri Ercolanesi (Naples 1979) and Manuale di papirologia ercolanese, by M. Capasso (Lecce 1991 = Università degli Studi di Lecce, Dipartmento di Filologia Classica e Medioevale, Testi e Studi 3). |

## Secondary Literature

| | |
|---|---|
| *ANF* | *Ante-Nicene Fathers* |
| DK | Diels, Hermann, and Walther Krantz, eds. and trans. *Die Fragmente der Vorsokratiker: Griechisch und Deutsch.* 7th ed., 3 vols. Berlin: Weidmann, 1954. |
| *GRA* | Harland, Philip A. *Greco-Roman Associations: Texts, Translations, and Commentary.* Vol. 2. North Coast of the Black Sea, Asia Minor. BZNT 204. De Gruyter, 2014. |
| LCL | Loeb Classical Library |
| LS | Long, A. A., and David N. Sedley. *The Hellenistic Philosophers.* 2 vols. Cambridge: Cambridge University Press, 1987. |
| *SVF* | von Arnim, Hans. *Stoicorum Veterum Fragmenta.* 4 vols. Leipzig: Eubner, 1903; repr. 1964. |

# 1

# Introduction

This book offers a survey of the Greek philosophical tradition from its inception in the Classical period until the final stages of its evolution beginning in the first part of Late Antiquity (ca. 550 BCE–ca. 300 CE). The book has been written, however, with an underlying interest in the relevance of Greek philosophy to the early Christian movement, especially the New Testament. That our understanding of early Christianity is hereby illuminated has long been recognized. For although Christianity is rooted in and ineradicably attached to Judaism, its shoots quickly extended outward into the Greco-Roman world, where it was able to flower and propagate only by competing with the intellectual traditions of the Greek-speaking world, and above all, the philosophical traditions. A knowledge of these traditions, therefore, is an essential complement to the study of Second Temple Judaism for serious students of the NT and early Christianity. It is the purpose of this book to offer such an introduction.

To begin, the present chapter traces the stages of modern research on Greco-Roman philosophy and the New Testament and provides an overview of the volume. The remainder of the book traces the history of Greek philosophy chronologically (chapters 2–15), before returning in the final two chapters to the matter of philosophy and early Christianity (chapters 16–17).

## Greek Philosophy and Early Christianity

The extent to which Greek philosophy impacted early Christianity, or to what extent they engaged each other, has long been an interest of modern scholarship. The following sections provide an overview of the history of inquiry into this area of study.

### *The Religionsgeschichtliche Schule*

The first wave of interest in this interface traces back to the so-called *Religionsgeschichtliche Schule*, or history of religions (HOR) school, associated with the University of Göttingen in the late nineteenth and early twentieth centuries. Represented by such scholars as Wilhelm Bousset, Johannes Weiss, and Rudolf Bultmann, the HOR school scoured the sources for parallels between Christian belief and Greek philosophy and religion, endeavoring thereby to demonstrate that Christianity had a fundamental genealogical relationship with Greco-Roman thought. While the comparative efforts of the HOR school helped highlight certain areas of "uniqueness" in Christianity, the overwhelming conclusion—or presupposition—of the HOR school was that Christianity was not a revealed religion but naturally derived from antecedent pagan beliefs.

## *The Corpus Hellenisticum Project*

New life was breathed into this line of inquiry in 1910 with the inauguration of the *Corpus Hellenisticum* (CH) project.[1] Founded under the aegis of C. F. Georg Heinrici (d. 1915) in the early twentieth century, the CH group produced a number of contributions, each utilizing various lexical, stylistic, historical, philosophical, and religious data from the wider Jewish-Hellenistic matrix to help better interpret the NT. Noteworthy were Weiss's commentary on 1 Corinthians, Windisch's commentary on 2 Corinthians, and several volumes (e.g., Dobschutz; Lietzman; Dibelius) focused on literary and rhetorical conventions employed in the NT and the teachings of Hellenistic moral philosophers.[2] Languishing somewhat in the middle of the century, the CH project was revived again in the 1960s and '70s under the oversight of W. C. van Unnik in Europe and Hans Dieter Betz in the United States.

The final goal of the CH project, as van Unnik describes, was an ambitious one: "To investigate everything that has been preserved from Greek and Roman antiquity as to its significance for the proper understanding of the NT."[3] Cataloguing parallels as comprehensively as possible,[4] contributors went on to evaluate these parallels with an eye to their relevance to interpretation of the NT. The short-lived monograph series *Studia ad Corpus Hellenisticum Novi Testamenti* (issuing only two volumes) served as an outlet for these findings.[5] Through the 1980s, most of this work centered on comparison with Stoicism, although certain works took up comparison with Epicureanism, Pythagoreanism, and Cynicism as well.[6]

---

1. For a history of the *Corpus Hellenisticum* project, see W. C. van Unnik, "*Corpus Hellenisticum Novi Testamenti*," *JBL* 83 (1964): 17–33; and Abraham J. Malherbe, "Hellenistic Moralists and the New Testament," *ANRW* (1989): 2.26.1:267–333, esp. 272–76. Van Unnik acknowledges this project as a reboot of J. J. Wettstein's much earlier *Novum Testamentum Graecum* (1751–1752), the text-critical apparatus of which included parallels from Jewish-Hellenistic and pagan material to elucidate the meaning of NT terminology.

2. Johannes Weiss, *Der Erste Korintherbrief*, KEK (Göttingen: Vandenhoeck & Ruprecht, 1910); Hans Windisch, *Der zweite Korintherbrief* (Göttingen: Vandenhoeck & Ruprecht, 1914); Ernst von Dobschütz, *Die urchristlichen Gemeinden* (Leipzig: J. C. Hinrichs'sche Buchhandlung, 1902), 277–84; Hans Lietzman, *An die Romer* (Tübingen: J. C. B. Mohr, 1906); and Martin Dibelius, *An die Kolosser, an die Epheser, an Philemon* (Tübingen: J. C. B. Mohr, 1913).

3. Van Unnik, "*Corpus Hellenisticum*," 23.

4. Between 1973 and 1981, Pieter W. van der Horst published several articles that listed parallels but included no evaluation: "Macrobius and the New Testament: A Contribution to the Corpus Hellenisticum," *NovT* 15 (1973): 220–32; "Musonius Rufus and the New Testament," *NovT* 16 (1974): 306–15; "Hierocles the Stoic and the New Testament: A Contribution to the Corpus Hellenisticum," *NovT* 17 (1975): 156–60; and "Cornutus and the New Testament: A Contribution to the Corpus Hellenisticum," *NovT* 23 (1981): 165–82.

5. Gerd Petzke, *Die Traditionen über Apollonius von Tyana und das Neue Testament*, SCHNT 1 (Leiden: Brill, 1970); and Gerard Mussies, *Dio Chrysostom and the New Testament*, SCHNT 2 (Leiden: Brill, 1970).

6. Norman W. De Witt, *St. Paul and Epicurus* (Minneapolis: University of Minnesota Press, 1964); David L. Balch, "The Neo-Pythagorean Moralists and the New Testament,"

In the last quarter of the twentieth century, by far the most influential scholar associated with the CH project was Abraham Malherbe. Malherbe was a key player in the founding of the Hellenistic and Moral Philosophy and Early Christianity section at the annual meeting of the Society of Biblical Literature (SBL), and many of the most important contributors in that era completed their doctoral work under his oversight (including Ronald Hock, David Balch, Stanley Stowers, Benjamin Fiore, and John Fitzgerald). Malherbe turned attention to Paul and the "popular" philosophers or "hellenistic moralists," which he closely identified with the Cynic tradition.[7] A hallmark of Malherbe's comparative work was its balanced consideration of similarities and differences. His purpose was not to show how Paul was like others, but how Paul employed contemporary traditions to original ends.

Between 1994 and 2001, Troels Engberg-Pedersen edited two volumes dedicated to an exploration of Paul within his Hellenistic context.[8] Shaping the essays herein were the convictions that (1) Paul was a co-player *in* his context, not a unique object standing out splendidly *against* it, and that (2) both Judaism and Hellenism were ideological constructs. Thus Paul was neither Jewish nor Hellenistic, per se; rather, he stood *beyond* the Judaism-Hellenism divide.[9] In at least one place, Engberg-Pedersen describes this work as a renewal of the old *Religionsgeschichtliche Schule*.[10] While the essays in these volumes often balance emphasis on Paul's similarities with his Hellenistic counterparts on the one hand, and acknowledgment of differences on the other, the essays' primary aim was to highlight similarities and thereby counterbalance scholarship that, in the editor's view, had given (to preserve a tension in the terms of the project) too much emphasis to Paul's continuity with Judaism.[11]

---

*ANRW* (1992): 2.26.1:380–411; F. Gerald Downing, *Cynics, Paul, and the Pauline Churches* (London: Routledge, 1988); and *Cynics and Christian Origins* (Edinburgh: T&T Clark, 1992).

7. Abraham J. Malherbe, *Moral Exhortation: A Greco-Roman Sourcebook*, Library of Early Christianity (Philadelphia: Westminster Press, 1986), esp. 11–16; *Paul and the Popular Philosophers* (Minneapolis: Fortress, 1989), which builds on *Paul and the Thessalonians: The Philosophic Tradition of Pastoral Care* (Minneapolis: Fortress, 1987) and consists almost entirely of essays published earlier (1968–1986); "Hellenistic Moralists and the New Testament," 2.26.1:267–333; a posthumous collection of his essays originally written between 1959 and 2012, has now been published: Carl R. Holladay, John T. Fitzgerald, James W. Thompson, and Gregory E. Sterling, eds., *Light from the Gentiles: Hellenistic Philosophy and Early Christianity: Collected Essays, 1959–2012, by Abraham J. Malherbe*, 2 vols., NovTSup 150 (Leiden: Brill, 2013).

8. Troels Engberg-Pedersen, ed., *Paul in His Hellenistic Context* (Minneapolis: Fortress, 1994); and *Paul Beyond the Judaism/Hellenism Divide* (Louisville: Westminster John Knox, 2001).

9. Engberg-Pedersen, *Paul Beyond the Judaism/Hellenism Divide*, 15; see also Troels Engberg-Pedersen, ed., *From Stoicism to Platonism: The Development of Philosophy, 100 BCE–100 CE* (Cambridge: Cambridge University Press, 2017), 15. Joseph Dodson and Andrew Pitts, eds., *Paul and the Greco-Roman Philosophical Tradition*, LNTS (London: T&T Clark, 2017), borrow Engberg-Pedersen's language of moving "beyond" the Judaism/Hellenism divide and encourage an approach of "dialogue" (xv).

10. Engberg-Pedersen, *Paul in His Hellenistic Context*, xvi; *Paul Beyond the Judaism/Hellenism Divide*, 4.

11. Engberg-Pedersen, *Paul in His Hellenistic Context*, xvi.

### *Recent Research*

If SBL's annual meeting program is any indication, interest in the NT and Greco-Roman philosophy waned somewhat in the early years of the 2000s. The Hellenistic Moral Philosophy and Early Christianity section held their last session in 2011, in which they hosted a book review panel on Engberg-Pedersen's *Cosmology and Self in the Apostle Paul* (2011). Moreover, SBL's closely related *Corpus Hellenisticum Novi Testamenti* section has in recent years rarely featured papers on Greco-Roman philosophy.

More recently, however, a resurgence of interest in the NT and Greco-Roman philosophy seems to be underway Engberg-Pedersen's contributions in this area maintain a steady flow.[12] Recent years have also seen a small explosion of new collections of essays,[13] as well as the appearance of a new volume series (Brill's Ancient Philosophy and Religion) dedicated to ancient philosophy.[14]

## Overview of the Volume

The following chapters offer an introduction to Greek and Roman philosophy, from the pre-Socratic philosophers in the Classical period (sixth/fifth c. BCE) to the emergence of Neoplatonism in the early stages of Late Antiquity (mid-third c. CE). Following a chapter introducing the main stages in the historical development of

---

12. See Engberg-Pedersen's monograph, *John and Philosophy: A New Reading of the Fourth Gospel* (Oxford: Oxford University Press, 2017), and a collection of essays in Troels Engberg-Pedersen, *Paul and Philosophy: Selected Essays*, WUNT 509 (Tübingen: Mohr Siebeck, 2023).

13. These collections of essays include: Joseph R. Dodson and David E. Briones, eds., *Paul and Seneca in Dialogue*, APhR 2 (Leiden: Brill, 2017); Dodson and Pitts, *Paul and the Greco-Roman Philosophical Tradition*; Joseph R. Dodson and David E. Briones, eds., *Paul and the Giants of Philosophy* (Downers Grove, IL: InterVarsity, 2019); Athanasios Despotis and Hermut Löhr, eds., *Religious and Philosophical Conversion in the Ancient Mediterranean* (Leiden: Brill, 2022). Monographs include: Nathan J. Barnes, *Reading 1 Corinthians with Philosophically Educated Women* (Eugene, OR: Pickwick, 2014); Kristin Divjanovic, *Paulus als Philosoph: Das Ethos des Apostels vor dem Hintergrund antiker Populärphilosophie* (Münster: Aschendorff, 2015); Kavin Rowe, *One True Life: The Stoics and Early Christians as Rival Traditions* (New Haven: Yale University Press, 2016); Runar Thorsteinsson, *Jesus as Philosopher: The Moral Sage in the Synoptic Gospels* (Oxford: Oxford University Press, 2018); Justin Allison, *Saving One Another: Philodemus and Paul on Moral Formation in Community*, APhR 3 (Leiden: Brill, 2020); Max J. Lee, *Moral Transformation in Greco-Roman Philosophy of Mind*, WUNT 2/515 (Tübingen: Mohr Siebeck, 2020); Simon Dürr, *Paul on the Human Vocation: Reason Language in Romans and Ancient Philosophical Tradition*, BZNW 226 (Berlin: De Gruyter, 2021); Annalisa Phillips Wilson, *Paul and the Jewish Law: A Stoic Ethical Perspective on His Inconsistency*, APhR (Leiden: Brill, 2022); Matthew Sharp, *Divination and Philosophy in the Letters of Paul*, Edinburgh Studies in Religion in Antiquity (Edinburgh: Edinburgh University Press, 2022); and Michael J. Gorman, *The Self, the Lord, and the Other According to Paul and Epictetus* (Eugene, OR: Cascade, 2023).

14. Plans are currently underway to revive the agenda of the defunct Hellenistic Moral Philosophy and Early Christianity section—now with broader interest than philosophical ethics—in a new SBL consultation titled Greco-Roman Philosophy and Early Christianity.

Greek philosophy (ch. 2), part 1 covers Classical philosophy, ranging from the early sixth century BCE to the transition into the Hellenistic era with the death of Alexander the Great (323 BCE). Chapters in part 1 cover the pre-Socratic philosophers (ch. 3), Socrates and the sophists (ch. 4), Plato and Aristotle (ch. 5), and Cynicism and other Socratic philosophies (ch. 6). Part 2 treats Hellenistic philosophy, extending from roughly the late fourth to the early first century BCE. This part includes an introduction to Hellenistic philosophy (ch. 7), followed by individual chapters on each of the major schools of this period: Stoicism (ch. 8), Epicureanism (ch. 9), and the Skeptical Academy (ch. 10). Part 3 treats post-Hellenistic philosophy, with chapters covering the transition between Hellenistic and post-Hellenistic philosophy (ch. 11), the emergence of Roman philosophy (ch. 12), school revivals and new doctrinal developments (ch. 13), philosophy as a popular and a social phenomenon (ch. 14), and the relationship between philosophy and rhetoric in the Second Sophistic (ch. 15). We conclude in part 4 with chapters on philosophy and early Christianity (ch. 16) and philosophy and the NT (ch. 17). The book's *terminus ad quem* (its "limit up to which") in the mid-third century CE precludes coverage of later Neoplatonist and Christian writers.

This sequence aims as much as possible to maintain a linear chronological progression. Consequently, chapters that cover the beginnings of schools do not treat their later stages of development. For the most part, later stages are discussed in the chapter on school revivals and developments (ch. 13). For instance, Stoicism in the era of Seneca and Epictetus (neo-Stoicism) is not covered in the chapter on Stoicism (ch. 8) but more briefly in chapter 12 (Part 3: Post-Hellenistic Philosophy) and likewise for the other schools. In chapter 13, we also give brief attention to the emergence of Neoplatonism, although this development occurs at the close of post-Hellenistic philosophy and the beginning of Late Ancient philosophy, our chronological terminus.

Chapters on individual philosophers (Plato and Aristotle) and on specific sects (Stoics and Epicureans) follow a roughly uniform structure. These chapters typically begin with a biographical section on the philosopher or school founder (e.g., Zeno for the Stoics), followed by an epitome of their philosophical system using the divisions adopted by that philosopher or sect (e.g., physics, logic, and ethics for Stoicism). These, and nearly all the other chapters, conclude with a succinct overview of the pertinent primary sources followed by key terms and a representative, rather than exhaustive, bibliography of secondary literature.

I have tried to reduce the number of citations and footnotes by omitting references where facts are basic or widely agreed on. Hence, for coverage of the doctrines of individual philosophers and sects, my general approach has been to omit primary source citations. Since these sections represent epitomes of basic doctrines—in the case of the schools, generally affirmed unanimously by representatives—such citations seemed superfluous. Where a particular primary source, on the other hand, provides extended or representative coverage of a specific doctrine, I often provide the name of that work (for instance, Plato's *Timaeus* or *Phaedo* for his views on the afterlife). Outside of these epitome sections, I cite chapter and verse more abundantly, particularly where facts are less amply attested or are disputed. In this regard, for biographical sections, I am extensively indebted to the biographies in Diogenes Laërtius's *Lives*. In these sections, I cite references copiously since the biographical data is less amply attested and is often a matter of report to Diogenes rather than established fact.

I have likewise reduced citations by generally including references only where scholarship is divided or a study offers novel insights. Hence, bibliographies at the close of chapters are not intended as comprehensive lists of sources accessed but as representative resources for further study.

Finally, it should be noted that although this book introduces Greek and Roman philosophy primarily with students of the NT and early Christianity in mind, I do not integrate relevant discussion of Christianity into the philosophy chapters. I have, however, sought to honor the intended interface by means of the book's framing. Having offered in the present introduction a brief history of modern interest in the interface of Greek philosophy and Christianity, I come full circle in the final two chapters with consideration of the NT and early Christian engagement with philosophy closer to our chronological terminus. With regard to the NT in particular, appendix 1 consists of an annotated bibliography of studies on Greco-Roman philosophy and the NT, especially from the last half century.

# 2

# The Greek Philosophical Tradition: An Overview

The present chapter discusses the origins of Greek philosophy, the stages of its history, and the available sources for its study.

## The Origins of Greek Philosophy

Simply speaking, the question of when Greek philosophy began can be answered from two different perspectives. From one point of view, Greek philosophy began when the first people who speculated in a particular way referred to their line of inquiry as "philosophy" (*philosophia*) and to themselves as "philosophers" (*philosophoi*). From another point of view, ancient writers recognized that such an account didn't push philosophy's history back far enough. In his account of the origins of philosophy,[1] Cicero (106–43 BCE) observes that Greek philosophy could indeed be traced back to before the name *philosophia* or *philosophos* was used. For even before the first *philosophoi*, there were the Seven Sages of the sixth and fifth centuries BCE; before that, there was Homer, a wise man, and still earlier, in the heroic age, there were Ulysses and Nestor, of whose intelligence Homer sang. Even Prometheus of primeval times could be considered a philosopher, though he didn't bear the name.

Agreeing with a common tradition, Cicero nevertheless affirms that as far as the name is concerned, the first "philosopher" (*philosophos/philosophus*) was the Classical figure Pythagoras. Cicero observes, however, that even Pythagoras wasn't the fountainhead from which *all* Greek philosophy sprang. There was also another figure, of an independent intellectual lineage, interested in a different line of philosophical inquiry: This was Socrates (469–399 BCE), the first philosopher to direct attention away from speculation about nature (physics) to the all-important question of how best to live (ethics).

Doxographer Diogenes Laërtius (180–240 CE) traces philosophy back still earlier—in fact, many thousands of years earlier. Diogenes begins his collection of *Lives of Eminent Philosophers* by saying that, according to some, philosophy had its beginning "among the barbarians."[2] According to this tradition, the wise men of the Persians (the Magi), the Babylonians (the Chaldeans), the Indians (the Gymnosophists), and the Celts and Gauls (the Druids) had been speculating about celestial phenomena, ethics, and metaphysical questions like the immortality of the soul for thousands of

1. Cicero, *Tusc.* 5.3.7–5.4.11.
2. Diogenes Laërtius, *Vit. phil.* 1.1 (LCL, Hicks).

years before Pythagoras and Socrates. According to the Egyptians, Hephaestus was already studying celestial phenomena nearly 50,000 years before Alexander the Great. But Diogenes isn't willing to cede such claims. Rather, he says that those who trace philosophy back to barbarians "forget that the achievements which they attribute . . . belong to *the Greeks, with whom not merely philosophy but the human race itself began*."[3]

TABLE 1. The philosophical sects and their founders[4]

| SECT | FOUNDER |
|---|---|
| Old Academy | Plato |
| Middle Academy | Arcesilaus |
| New Academy | Lacydes [Carneades] |
| Cyrenaic | Aristippus of Cyrene |
| Elian | Phaedo of Elis |
| Megarian | Euclides of Megara |
| Cynic | Antisthenes of Athens |
| Eretrian | Menedemus of Eretria |
| Dialectical | Clitomachus of Carthage |
| Peripatetic | Aristotle of Stagira |
| Stoic | Zeno of Citium |
| Epicurean | Epicurus |

Agreeing with the tradition that Pythagoras was the first Greek to call himself a philosopher,[5] Diogenes adds additional detail by supplying a genealogical scheme outlining the entire history of Greek philosophy, from its origins with Pythagoras through its continuous stages of doctrinal succession up to his own day. According to this account, philosophy actually had "a twofold origin."[6] Originating independently in Italy and Ionia, it had as its one source Pythagoras (in Italy), and as its other Anaximander (in Ionia). Both men had learned from teachers before them—Pythagoras from Pherecydes and Anaximander from Thales—yet it was the students who were the true authors of philosophy. From Pythagoras and Anaximander, Diogenes next traces a traditional succession of teachers and students in the respective Italian and Ionian lines, all the way up to the founders of the major philosophical schools that formed in the Classical and Hellenistic periods. Thus Diogenes identifies the following schools and founders (see table 1 above):

3. *Diogenes Laërtius, Vit. phil.* 1.3 (LCL, Hicks); my italics.
4. *Diogenes Laërtius, Vit. phil.* 1.19; cf. 4.59; Sextus Empiricus, *Pyr.* 1.220
5. *Diogenes Laërtius, Vit. phil.* 1.12.
6. *Diogenes Laërtius, Vit. phil.* 1.13.

Beginning in the Classical and Hellenistic periods, these schools came to be known as "sects," or literally, "choices" (*haireseis*). Sources don't agree as to which groups qualified as true *haireseis* and thus how many *haireseis* there were. Diogenes cites Hippobotus's work *On Philosophical Sects* as having identified nine sects (in slight disagreement with his own list): (1) Megarian, (2) Eretrian, (3) Cyrenaic, (4) Epicurean, (5) Annicerean, (6) Theodoraen, (7) Zenonian or Stoic, (8) Old Academic, and (9) Peripatetic. Diogenes observes that Hippobotus passes over the Cynic, Elian, Dialectical, and Pyrrhonist schools; though, as Diogenes points out, whether the Cynic and Pyrrhonist movements qualified as true "sects" was a matter of dispute.[7]

In tracing the philosophers' lineage, Diogenes relies on "successions" (*diadochai*) traditions preserved in more ancient studies on the history of philosophy, perhaps stemming originally from Theophrastus in the fourth century BCE, which was more fully elaborated in Sotion's *Successions* (*Diadochai*), written around 200 BCE. The succession model was a way of mapping out a history of the discipline by tracing the genealogical relationships between teachers and students and their respective traditions. From a historical standpoint, this model was somewhat contrived and oversimplified. For one, it ignored the fact that the word *philosophos* had not been applied to every earlier thinker whom later thinkers perceived to be philosophizing. It also ignored the fact that the words *philosophos* and *philosophia* did not acquire standard meanings until Plato and Aristotle in the fourth century BCE, a century or two after Pythagoras. The term *philosophos* seems to have originated as a pejorative label, first applied to Pythagoras by critics, with the connotation of "one who wants to be wise." Pythagoras, however, was willing to accept the title as being in some sense true.[8] For more than a century thereafter, the term carried varied connotations, sometimes positive, sometimes neutral, but often still negative.

The variability of the term *philosophos* at this stage was cognate to the question of what kinds of pursuits fell within the ambit of "philosophy," or *philosophia*. Many thinkers who pursued matters agreed *later* to fall within the scope of *philosophia* were more polymathic in their interests than the later *philosophoi* were. The earlier thinkers were indeed "pursuing wisdom" in their own ways, but not always in the same ways as the later "philosophers" were. Hence, even up to the time of Socrates—perhaps a century or more after Pythagoras—a variety of competing definitions of *philosophia* persisted,[9] still largely negative and encompassing a broad range of interests.[10]

It was Socrates's student Plato who succeeded in establishing the meaning of philosophy that became standard. While he did not invent a wholly new notion of the *philosophos*, he did opt for a more specific and exclusive definition. For Plato, philosophy was a pursuit concerned most fundamentally with the improvement of self and others. Plato strove, indirectly and directly, to establish this as the most legitimate definition of philosophy while straining out the negative baggage carried

7. Pyrrhonists: *Vit. phil.* 1.20; Cynics: *Vit. phil.* 6.103. One also notices no mention of a "Pythagorean" school in either list, on which see chapter 13.

8. Christopher Moore, *Calling Philosophers Names: On the Origin of a Discipline* (Princeton: Princeton University Press, 2020), 6–7.

9. Moore, *Calling Philosophers Names*, 257.

10. Moore, *Calling Philosophers Names*, 25, 28.

by the term's broader range of meanings.[11] Largely succeeding, Plato was able to vindicate his teacher, Socrates—an infamous Athenian who "wanted to be wise"—and to establish him as the paradigm of the philosopher in the very best sense: One who wants to improve himself and others.[12]

If Plato can be credited with establishing a standard definition of *philosophos*, it was Aristotle (384–322 BCE) who can be credited as the author of the "discipline" of *philosophia*.[13] Identifying himself as a *philosophos* more or less in Plato's sense, Aristotle retrospectively applied this title to those who shared interest in the kinds of questions he himself was asking: people whose opinions on these matters he could then compare with each other's and with his own.[14] The configuration of interests that fell within Aristotle's scope of concern became the defining criteria of a discipline—that of *philosophia*—which could now be traced backwards and associated with earlier thinkers who may or may not have considered themselves *philosophoi* per se.[15]

Aristotle's approach allowed him to identify as the first true *philosophos*, not Pythagoras—who all agreed was the first to call himself a *philosophos*; but rather, Thales—who did not identify as such but who shared the interests of the disciple that Aristotle had defined.[16]

Consequently—and contra Diogenes Laërtius—Aristotle held that the first philosopher, Thales, was active in Ionia before Pythagoras adopted the title of *philosophos* in Italy (see table 2 below).

TABLE 2. The first philosophers

| **IONIAN TRADITION** | **ITALIAN TRADITION** |
| --- | --- |
| [Thales] | [Pherecydes] |
| Anaximander | Pythagoras |

While ancient chroniclers like Diogenes Laërtius structured the history of philosophy according to the traditional succession of teachers and students, modern scholars tend to structure its history according to its major stages of development. On the one hand, periodizing philosophy risks the imposition of artificial boundaries between historical periods, potentially leaving the impression of greater discontinuity between stages than there really was. Certain ways of periodizing the history of ancient philosophy and the history of the school traditions, on the other hand, have become standard in modern scholarship. The main periods of philosophy are demarcated in part by factors such as critical figures, changing philosophical interests, the

11. Moore, *Calling Philosophers Names*, 257.

12. Plato works out contrasts between sophistry and philosophy in several dialogues, including *Sophist*, *Gorgias*, *Protagoras*, and several other eponymously titled works. See also chapters 4 and 15 here.

13. Moore, *Calling Philosophers Names*, 257.

14. Moore, *Calling Philosophers Names*, 258.

15. Moore, *Calling Philosophers Names*, 260–61.

16. Aristotle, *Metaph.* 983b.

founding of new schools, revivals of old schools, and doctrinal innovations within schools; and in part by certain significant changes in the world's political landscape.

The standard division of philosophical periods is as follows (see table 3 below):[17]

1. The *pre-Socratic* period (ca. sixth–fifth c. BCE) embraces Thales, Anaximander, Pythagoras, and other philosophers who predated or were contemporary with Socrates.
2. The *Classical* period (ca. fourth c. BCE) extends from Plato and the schools founded in the generation after Socrates to the conquests of Alexander the Great.
3. The *Hellenistic* period reaches from the late fourth century BCE with the founding of the Stoic school, the Epicurean school, and the New Academy, until the early first century BCE.
4. The *post-Hellenistic* period runs from the early first century BCE to the mid-third century CE.
5. *Late Ancient* philosophy begins around the middle of the third century CE with the emergence of Neoplatonism and runs through the end of antiquity around the year 500 CE.

TABLE 3. The periods of ancient philosophy

| PERIOD | DATE |
|---|---|
| Pre-Socratic/Classical | 600 BCE |
| Classical/Socratic | 500 BCE |
| Hellenistic | 400 BCE |
| | 300 BCE |
| | 200 BCE |
| Post-Hellenistic | 100 BCE |
| | 1 CE |
| | 100 CE |
| Late Ancient | 200 CE |
| | 300 CE |
| | 400 CE |

17. These partly overlap but are not identical with the periods of ancient history. See appendix 3 for a timeline of philosophers by philosophical period.

Ancient sources for the study of philosophy are abundant. Among the most significant philosophers, some wrote nothing (Pythagoras and Socrates) and others wrote too much for subsequent generations to read (Chrysippus and Epicurus). Sources are scarce for some periods (the pre-Socratic period and the Hellenistic period), while other periods are represented prolifically (the Classical period, the post-Hellenistic period, and the Late Ancient period). Many gaps are filled in by later writers who preserve the works of their predecessors in excerpts or paraphrases or who report views in summary. Such writers are in some cases sympathetic adherents, and in others neutral tradents (someone who preserves or hands on traditions) or polemically motivated opponents.

Our best and most extensive sources are literary. Philosophers presented their own views and the views to which they adhered through a variety of literary genres. There were philosophical *treatises*, such as Aristotle's work *On the Soul* or his *Metaphysics*. On the other hand, the fictive *dialogue* form dogmatized less straightforwardly by exploring philosophical questions through questions and answers. Dialogues were sometimes aporetic—that is, intending only to leave the listener in doubt (like Plato's Socratic dialogues); sometimes they were exploratory (like many of Plato's Platonic dialogues); and sometimes they were the means of refuting the views of other parties while promoting one's own views (Cicero's dialogues). Some authors reduced the main ideas of their systems into handbooks or epitomes. Alcinous's *Didaskalikos*, for instance, is a post-Hellenistic example of a handbook on Middle Platonism. *Discourses* representing something like classroom lectures are preserved in the cases of Musonius Rufus, Epictetus, and others. Some authors used *fictive letters* as a means of promoting the views of their school. The Cynic epistles are fictive as are, quite possibly, Seneca's *Moral Epistles*. *Sayings collections* (or *chreia* collections, which were short but useful anecdotes about characters) are associated especially with Cynic philosophers. Diogenes Laërtius's biographies of the Cynics incorporate sayings sources.

Among genres that report on the views of others are the following. *Polemical treatises* report the doctrines of schools or thinkers in order to refute them. Examples include Plutarch's treatises *On Stoic Self-Contradictions* and *That Epicurus Makes a Pleasant Life Impossible*, as well as Sextus Empiricus's *Against the Dogmatists*. Diogenes Laërtius left *biographies* of eighty-three different philosophers ranging from the pre-Socratics to the third century CE, in which are also included doctrinal summaries of the respective philosophers' views. *Doxographies* record the main doctrines of the schools in summary, usually from a neutral standpoint. Extant examples include those of Aetius (late first century CE), Sextus Empiricus (second c. CE), and Stobaeus (fifth c. CE) who preserves the doxography of Arius Didymus (first c. BCE). Diogenes Laërtius's biographies (probably third c. CE) also contain doxographical content. The doxographic tradition had a precursor genre in earlier surveys that arranged the views of philosophers by topic. Aristotle, for instance, surveyed views on the soul in his treatise *On the Soul* and views on nature and its first principles in *Physics*. The doxographies, moreover, seem to rely on earlier "successions" literature like the *Diadochoi* of Sotion (ca. 200 BCE). Cicero's philosophical *dialogues* (mid-first c. BCE) are invaluable as records of Stoic and

Epicurean views, though Cicero is largely critical and writes as a representative of the skeptical Academy.

Several modern collections have gathered together the fragments and testimonia of philosophers by period or philosophical school. Pre-Socratic evidence is gathered in Diels and Krantz (1954); Kirk, Raven, and Schofield (2nd ed., 1983); and Graham (2010); and the Hellenistic sources in Long and Sedley (1987) and Inwood and Gerson (1997). Sourcebooks are available also for individual schools, as will be referenced in the following chapters.

The literary evidence is augmented by a vast body of inscriptional evidence. Although much more fragmentary (and more difficult to access) than the literary evidence, inscriptions bring to light otherwise obscure or unknown philosophers who either didn't write or whose writings are not extant. This evidence also reveals something about the prevalence of the philosopher population, philosophers' roles in public life, and the manner of their social lives. Inscriptions in many cases report sayings or teachings of famous philosophers and occasionally even promulgate lengthy doctrinal messages.

## Key Terms and Concepts

- Classical era
- Doxographies
- Epitomes
- Hellenistic era
- Ionian tradition
- Italian tradition
- Late Ancient era
- Post-Hellenistic era
- Pre-Socratic era
- Sects (*haireseis*)
- Successions

## For Further Study

### *The Origins of Greek Philosophy*

Clark, Stephen R. L. *Ancient Mediterranean Philosophy: An Introduction*. Bloomsbury History of Philosophy. London: Bloomsbury Academic, 2013.

Iribarren, Leopoldo, and Hugo Koning, eds. *Hesiod and the Beginnings of Greek Philosophy*. Mnemosyne Supplements 455. Leiden: Brill, 2022.

Moore, Christopher. *Calling Philosophers Names: On the Origin of a Discipline*. Princeton: Princeton University Press, 2020.

Sassi, Maria Michela. *The Beginnings of Philosophy in Greece*. Princeton: Princeton University Press, 2018.

Seaford, Richard. *The Origins of Philosophy in Ancient Greece and India: A Historical Comparison*. Cambridge: Cambridge University Press, 2020.

### *The History of Greek Philosophy*

Annas, Julia. *Ancient Philosophy: A Very Short Introduction*. Oxford: Oxford University Press, 2000.

Blackson, Thomas A. *Ancient Greek Philosophy: From the Presocratics to the Hellenistic Philosophers*. Malden, MA: Wiley-Blackwell, 2011.

Perilli, Lorenzo, and Daniela P. Taormina, eds. *Ancient Philosophy: Textual Paths and Historical Explorations*. New York: Routledge, 2018.

Shields, Christopher. *Ancient Philosophy: A Contemporary Introduction*. 2nd ed. New York: Routledge, 2023.

# Part 1

# Classical Philosophy: Early Sixth to Late Fourth Century BCE

# 3

# The Pre-Socratics

As the first of all Greek philosophers,[1] Pythagoras and Anaximander represented the first in a loosely defined group of early philosophers known collectively as the "pre-Socratics." Modern scholarship includes under this heading the following: Thales (Anaximander's teacher), Democritus, Xenophanes, Empedocles, Heraclitus, Pythagoras, Anaxagoras, Anaximander, Anaximenes, and several others.

While the pre-Socratics did not invent philosophical systems on the scale of the Hellenistic and post-Hellenistic philosophers, they did introduce some of the major speculative issues that continued to be debated for centuries to come and offered answers that influenced later philosophers in foundational ways. Tradition connects the pre-Socratics in lines of succession from teacher to student (see table 4) reaching back to Socrates.

TABLE 4. Successions of the pre-Socratics[2]

| IONIAN TRADITION | ITALIAN TRADITION |
|---|---|
| [Thales] | [Pherecydes] |
| Anaximander | Pythagoras |
| Anaximenes | Telauges |
| Anaxagoras | Xenophanes |
| Archelaus | Parmenides |
| | Zeno of Elea |
| | Leucippus |
| | Democritus |

## What the Pre-Socratics Said

### *The Poets*

Among the many factors that made the first philosophers "philosophize," one of them was surely this: They were provoked. The chief agitators were the Greek

1. According to Diogenes Laërtius, *Vit. phil.* 1.13.
2. Diogenes Laërtius, *Vit. phil.* 1.13–14.

poets, whose poems enshrined in their myths the most common and deeply cherished beliefs of Greek people at the time but that seemed highly offensive to this new class of men when they stopped to think about it.

Although he was not the first to criticize the poets—nor the last—Xenophanes (mid-sixth c.–early fifth c. BCE) was the first philosopher to launch a serious attack against the two most eminent poets of the Archaic period—namely, Homer and Hesiod.[3] Xenophanes ridiculed the poets for their anthropomorphic depictions of the gods—gods who were, to be sure, more powerful than us humans, but who in all other respects looked and acted like us. In fact, as Xenophanes pointed out, the gods always seemed to appear in the image of the beholder. He noted, for instance, that the gods of the Thracians had blue eyes and red hair, and the gods of the Ethiopians dark skin and broad noses.[4] He even joked that if cattle and horses could talk about gods, their gods would look and act like cattle and horses.[5] Worse were the poets' depictions of the gods' character. Homer's gods committed all the vices that would be considered shameful even for human beings: "stealing, committing adultery, deceiving each other."[6] And who could condone Cronus for castrating his father and eating his children, acts most unconscionable even for the most savage humans, let alone gods?[7]

Not that Xenophanes disbelieved in the gods. He only disbelieved in the gods of popular myth. There were indeed many gods.[8] Most were lower-level deities. These were subordinate to the One god, the ultimate divine reality.[9] This supreme God was not at all like mortals in body or in thought.[10] This God was pure mind, the mightiest of all,[11] eternal and omnipresent, and the mover of all things.[12]

## *Physics*

### Causes

Criticism of the poets, however, went further than this moral and theological critique. The poets, and the general population who shared their worldview, located the "causes" of things in the free acts of the gods. The gods hurled down lightning, shook the earth, and flung stars across the sky. They struck people with illness, they put them to death. They were the direct causes of fortune and misfortune. In all this, they acted unpredictably, sending now fortune and now misfortune, perhaps in recompense for vows or offerings (or for neglect of these), but ultimately according to their whims.

---

3. The fragments of Xenophanes are collected in DK §21.

4. Clement of Alexandria, *Strom.* 7.22 [DK 21b 16].

5. Clement of Alexandria, *Strom.* 5.110 [DK 21b 15].

6. Sextus Empiricus, *Math.* 9.193 [DK 21b 11]. See also Diogenes Laërtius, *Vit. phil.* 9.18 [DK 21a 1]; cf. DK 21a 33, 35; DK 21c 1.

7. Sextus Empiricus, *Math.* 1.289 [DK 21b 12].

8. DK 21a 32.

9. DK 21a 28, 31.

10. Clement of Alexandria, *Strom.* 5.109 [DK 21b 23].

11. DK 21b 25; a 31.

12. DK 21a 33, 35.

Many philosophers demurred from such thinking. They suggested that careful examination of nature was bound to reveal that celestial and terrestrial phenomena like meteors and earthquakes, as well as human health (sickness or general afflictions of the body), could be explained by natural rather than supernatural causes. Nature operated with a kind of regularity that belied the supposition that things happen according to the capricious inclinations of gods. To philosophers of this mind, a more accurate knowledge of causes could potentially enable us to *predict* natural phenomena like eclipses and famines, to cure illnesses, and perhaps above all, to allay our fears of divine affliction. This interest in nature and causation was one of the foremost concerns of the pre-Socratic philosophers. For their interest in "nature," the pre-Socratics came to be considered, above all, "*natural* philosophers" (*physiologoi*).

## Cosmic Principles

It is evident from these views that the natural philosophers could not have considered their age's account of the origin of the universe to be very credible. On the one hand, Hesiod's cosmological account in his classic poem "Theogony" was—as a sort of reflection on natural origins—in its own way "philosophical."[13] That the account, however, narrated origins in terms of the generations of the gods—beginning from the preexistent Earth (Gaia), and proceeding to her offspring Heaven (Ouranos), followed by their intercourse and production of the generation of Cronus, Rhea, and the Titans, and on from Cronus to the generation of the Olympians, and so on—was, as far as most philosophers were concerned, more "myth" (*mythos*) than "argument" (*logos*), and more "theology" (*theologia*) than "physics" (*physiologia*).[14]

The philosophers wanted to identify the fundamental natural "principle" (*archē*) from which all things in the universe derived without taking recourse to myth. Thales of Miletus (fl. early sixth c. BCE) is credited as making the first guess that is usually considered *reflective* and *philosophical*: Everything, he said, is *water*.[15] There are two reasons why Thales's proposal was novel. First, his answer entailed a stance of *monism*: that is, all things in the universe are ultimately one thing. Second, it entailed *materialism*: that is, all things in the universe consist of matter and are subject to the same natural laws; there is no separate domain of ethereal spirits that interrupts the natural chain of causes and effects.[16]

---

13. Some philosophers later counted him among the philosophers for this reason. Cf. Aristotle, *Metaph.* 1.3.983b, 6–984a,2; *Cael.* 3.298b29–30. On Hesiod and the beginnings of Greek philosophy, see Leopoldo Iribarren and Hugo Koning, *Hesiod and the Beginnings of Greek Philosophy*, Mnemosyne Supplements 455 (Leiden: Brill, 2022).

14. Hesiod as a "theologian" (*theologos*) who argues "mythically" (*mythikōs*) in Aristotle, *Metaph.* 3.1000a; cf. 13.1091a.

15. This begs the question concerning the difference between what Hesiod was doing and "philosophy." For this debate among ancient philosophers, especially regarding the difference between *mythos* and *logos*, see Maria Michela Sassi, *The Beginnings of Philosophy in Greece* (Princeton: Princeton University Press, 2018), 18–20; Luc Brisson, *How Philosophers Saved Myths: Allegorical Interpretation and Classical Mythology*, trans. Catherine Tihanyi (Chicago: University of Chicago Press, 2004); and note 14 above.

16. The fragments of Thales are collected in DK §11.

Thales's idea that all things were water doesn't seem to have been widely accepted. While many philosophers did accept his materialist premise, they proffered alternative proposals as to the nature of the most basic principle. Anaximenes (fl. 546–525 BCE), for instance, declared that all things are *air*, which when rarefied becomes fire and when condensed becomes solid, reaching its most condensed form in earth and then rock.[17] In a twist on material monism, Anaxagoras (probably 500–428 BCE) held that "everything is in everything."[18] No individual thing exists as a discrete entity, but all things are portions of other things. For instance, black contains a predominance of black, but also portions of white.[19] Sperm contains flesh, hair, and everything else.[20] And so on for everything.[21]

While sharing the monistic assumptions of Thales and Anaximenes, Anaximander (died sometime after 427 BCE) proposed a subtler kind of substrate as first principle. He called this fundamental material *apeiron* or the "boundless." *Apeiron* lacks any definite qualities of the type we can observe, like wetness, dryness, or color. *Apeiron* was eternal and, as being by its nature "boundless," infinite in substance. *Apeiron* as a principle (*archē*), then, was subtler in substance and not quite "material" in the way that Thales's water or Anaximenes's air was. Anaximander's principle was less a "physical" than a "metaphysical" entity, for it transcended the physical (*meta*-physics = "after-physics").

Another monist, Heraclitus (fl. ca. 500 BCE) posited a metaphysical principle that he called the *logos*. According to Heraclitus, reality was one, but in its oneness, unity and diversity cohered in irreconcilable tension. It was the *Logos* that unified plurality and provided order and regularity in the universe. Although Heraclitus's *Logos* was a transcendent principle, it seems to have been more of an impersonal abstraction than a personal intelligence.[22]

Not all the pre-Socratics were monists. At the opposite end of the spectrum were metaphysical *pluralists* like Leucippus (second half of fifth c. BCE) and Democritus (b. 460–457 BCE).[23] For these philosophers, there was indeed only one kind of thing in the universe; but it was not, metaphysically speaking, one. Rather, there were an infinite number of them—particles so tiny, they were indivisible: that is, atoms (*atomon* = "that which is indivisible"). According to this view, all the objects we can see are variegated agglomerations of these fundamental particles, which come in various sizes, shapes, and weights. Only atoms exist in themselves. Every composite of atoms—and every quality of these composites—exists only by convention; i.e., as something derived from human perception. What is not atoms is only void, of which there is, likewise, an infinity.

---

17. The fragments of Anaximenes are collected in DK §13.
18. DK §59b 4b; b 6; b 11; b 12; a 41.
19. DK §59b 10.
20. DK §59b 10.
21. The fragments of Anaxagoras are collected in DK §59.
22. The fragments of Heraclitus are collected in DK §22.
23. The fragments of Leucippus and Democritus are collected, respectively, in DK §67; 68.

### Change

Other recurring topics among the pre-Socratics include stability and change and, relatedly, of unity and plurality. The fundamental question was how to define a thing's existence when all things seem to change. One might argue that when change occurs to a thing, that thing becomes what it was not before. Solutions to this problem varied. Parmenides's (fl. ca. 450 BCE) solution was simply that change is only an illusion. His student Zeno of Elea (fl. early fifth century BCE) offered proof in what became known as "Zeno's paradox." The paradox pointed to the example of motion. To get from point A to point B, Zeno observed, we must first traverse half that distance. However, before crossing this half-distance, we must first cross half of *that* distance. For every half-distance, another divides it. If distances can go on being halved infinitely, Zeno concluded, then it will be impossible to traverse all the distances and hence to arrive at our destination. One may *appear* to have reached it, but this must be an illusion, for reason has shown that this feat is impossible.[24]

Other philosophers contended that neither change nor stability alone described the fundamental state of reality, but rather that change and stability stood in irreconcilable tension. For instance, Empedocles (ca. 492–432 BCE) held that the four basic elements (earth, water, fire, air) themselves could not change, but that composites composed of these elements could. For Empedocles, what caused this tension—between the unchanging elements and their changing composites—were the opposing "forces" (*dynameis*) of Love (*Philotēs*) and Strife (*Neikos*) that alternated in their predominating effect. Elements combined into a homogeneous whole when Love prevailed, and they disintegrated when Strife prevailed.[25]

As noted, Heraclitus also emphasized tension between stability and change. His famous axiom "One does not step into the same river twice" did not suggest (as it is often taken to mean) that only change is real. Rather, it illustrates the doctrine of the unity of opposites: The river is *both* a different river *and* the same river at the same time. One might say that while the water changes, change (or running water) is part of what defines a river as such. The river example illustrates Heraclitus's more general view that the universe remains in flux even while remaining—due to the ordering principle of the *logos*—a unified "something."

Anaxagoras's theory of "mixture" (see above) allowed for still a different solution to the change problem: Since everything is in everything, nothing really changes at all.

## *Metaphysics*

### Theological Monism

Not all the pre-Socratics were exactly materialists. In distinction from material monism, several pre-Socratics posited what might be called "theological monism."

---

24. The fragments of Parmenides and Zeno of Elea are collected, respectively, in DK §28–29.

25. The fragments of Empedocles are collected in DK §31.

In this inflection, rather than one kind of *material,* there exists one *divine reality.* As noted, Xenophanes abandoned belief in the traditional gods for a monotheism that described God as pure mind. Somewhat differently, Pythagoras held that the universe was composed of and ordered by numbers, immaterial realities that *caused* material reality.[26] Like Xenophanes, Anaxagoras also held that behind everything was a single mind. Consistent with his theory of mixture, however, he described this mind as an all-powerful God who created and supplied everything with its respective faculties and ordered the mixture of preexisting infinite substance. Heraclitus's *logos* was a unified "one." It caused the orderliness of the universe and unified its multiplicity. The organizing activity of the *logos* built laws into the universe—a "natural" law.

#### The Soul

Many pre-Socratics speculated about the nature of the soul. For some, the soul consisted in part of the same kind of matter as other materials in the world; only some additional quality was added. Heraclitus thought of the soul as a fiery substance, but necessarily connected with the *Logos* for its life-source. Empedocles identified the soul as the blood permeating the heart, while at the same time apparently identifying it as a *daimōn* ("spirit," "daemon") that transmigrated from one body to another at death. Like Empedocles, Pythagoras believed the soul transmigrated from body to body after each cycle of life; though differently from Empedocles, he held that this soul was an immaterial entity.

### *Epistemology*

In challenging traditional beliefs, the pre-Socratics were at a fundamental level challenging the authority of those who had most firmly established these beliefs: the poets. The philosophers were also challenging the very notion of common sense—even the very reliability of the senses. They were prepared to justify these moves by critically reflecting on how we know what we know or whether we can know at all. That is to say, they reflectively dealt with the area of inquiry we call "epistemology."

Credit for instituting epistemology as a field of inquiry, at least in practice, can be given to Xenophanes. Xenophanes believed that knowledge was impossible to attain, since even if what we believe happens also to be true, we cannot *know* that what we believe is true. In this regard, Xenophanes was the first philosopher to advocate for epistemological skepticism.

Other philosophers emphasized that while the senses may seem reliable, reason often proves them wrong. From this standpoint, justification for belief cannot be rooted in *a posteriori* argument (i.e., based on sense perception). It can only be rooted in *a priori* argument (i.e., based on reason). This was the position of the Eleatic philosophers Parmenides and Zeno. As noted, Parmenides contended that despite what our senses might tell us, change is not real but illusory. Zeno's paradox

26. The fragments of Pythagoras are collected in DK §14.

about the impossibility of motion underscored precisely this epistemological claim. One must trust reason over the senses.

## *Religion*

The foregoing discussion suggests that many pre-Socratics, even while attacking traditional views of the gods, tended toward some version of monotheism or henotheism. They emphasized, moreover, that this divinity, mind, or *logos* was responsible for ordering and moving the universe, even though phenomena do have natural or predictable causes.

In fact, the pre-Socratic tradition retained many elements from traditional religion. Several pre-Socratics (Pythagoras, Parmenides, Empedocles) alleged they received their ideas by divine revelation. Parmenides poetically describes his passage to the paths of night and day (perhaps an allegory for understanding), at the entrance to which, young maidens beseeched justice to open the gates so that the truths of each path could be revealed to him. Other philosophers of religious bent believed that the poets, despite their mythical depictions of the gods, left embedded in their works vestiges of philosophical views held in more ancient times that could be recovered through allegorical interpretation. Some philosophers wrote in poetic form despite their almost univocal objections to the ideas of the poets. The poetic philosophers also happened to be those who claimed to be recipients of divine revelation (Parmenides and Empedocles).

With a sort of speculation that differed markedly from the "natural philosophy" aimed at discovering predictable causes, Pythagoras reportedly believed that he, now in a new body, had in a previous life been Patroclus, friend of Achilles (of Homer's *Iliad).* Legend had it that Pythagoras was the son of either Apollos or Hermes, and that he had a thigh of gold, worked miracles, and talked to animals and rocks. In later antiquity, this portrait solidified Pythagoras's reputation as a "divine man." Not to be outdone by Pythagoras, Empedocles alleged that he was not just a divine man but a god, a *daimōn* trapped in a mortal body, waiting to return to the celestial abode from which he was in exile.[27]

## *Ethics*

Tradition connects Pythagoras not only with doctrines about first causes, numbers, and the nature of the soul, but also with certain ethical practices. Traditional Pythagorean practices included a dietary element with restrictions on eating meat (because human souls could transmigrate into animals) and, for unknown reasons, beans. Pythagoras also seems to have been the first philosopher to institute community practices focused on self-examination and moral improvement.

Later philosophers, however, relate in quite categorical terms that ethical theory was not a major concern among the early (i.e., "natural") philosophers. It

27. DK §31b 115.

is said that ethics began to occupy attention in a serious way only when a certain man turned his gaze away from speculation about nature and, as Cicero poetically puts it, "brought philosophy down from heaven to earth."[28] This man was Socrates, to whom we turn in the next chapter.

## The Influence of the Pre-Socratics

The philosophical issues broached by the pre-Socratics continued to be debated for centuries to come. Naturally, later philosophers offered new ideas; yet on many points, the special influence of individual pre-Socratics is evident. For instance, we can clearly see the influence of Pythagoras on Plato's theory of numbers and of Pythagoras and Empedocles on Plato's doctrine of the immortality of the soul; the influence of Leucippus and Democritus on the atomic theory of Epicurus; of Anaxagoras's idea of material mixture and Heraclitus's idea of a fiery ordering *logos* on the Stoics; and of Xenophanes's, Democritus's, and Heraclitus's skepticism on the Skeptical Academics and Pyrrhonists.

## Notes on the Primary Sources

No complete treatises survive from pre-Socratic writers, and some pre-Socratics wrote nothing. Fragments and testimonia are preserved, however, in later writers. Ancient doxographers and biographers provide schematic coverage of pre-Socratic views, dividing philosophical discussion into common topics and summarizing the various views subsumed under each. Diogenes Laërtius's *Lives of Eminent Philosophers* treats pre-Socratics in books I, II, VIII, and IX. Aristotle provides more extensive coverage of pre-Socratic views than any other writer, offering a survey of their views on the soul in his work *On the Soul*. Cicero summarizes pre-Socratic views on the "prime substance" in *On the Nature of the Gods* (1.25–56) and *Tusculan Disputations* (1.18–22). Attesting directly to pre-Socratic views are the Derveni Papyri, a fourth-century BCE roll found at Derveni near Thessalonica. The contents of the roll, which date to around the end of the fifth century or beginning of the fourth century BCE, instantiate the pre-Socratic practice of allegorical interpretation of the poets.

The Loeb Classical Library contains the collected fragments of early Greek philosophers in the nine volumes translated by Laks et al. (2016). A collection of the pre-Socratic fragments is available in Diels and Krantz (1954), with Greek and German on facing pages. A sourcebook with commentary is available in Kirk, Raven, and Schofield (2nd ed., 1983). More recent is Graham's (2010) two-volume collection, featuring the Greek and English text of fourteen sixth- and fifth-century BCE philosophers (vol. 1) and a number of sophists (vol. 2), accompanied by commentary on each section and a short introduction to each philosopher or sophist. Another collection of texts with commentary is available in McKirahan (2011).

28. Cicero, *Tusc.* 5.4.10.

## Key Words and Concepts

- Atomists
- Eleatic philosophers
- Four elements, the
- *Logos*
- Materialist
- Monist
- Natural philosopher
- Pluralist
- Principle (*archē*)
- Zeno's paradox

## For Further Study

### *Primary Source Collections*

Diels, Hermann, and Walther Krantz, eds. and trans. *Die Fragmente der Vorsokratiker: Griechisch und Deutsch.* 7th ed. 3 vols. Berlin: Weidmann, 1954.

Graham, Daniel W., ed. *The Texts of Early Greek Philosophy: The Complete Fragments and Selected Testimonies of the Major Presocratics.* 2 vols. Cambridge: Cambridge University Press, 2010.

Kirk, G. S., J. E. Raven, and M. Schofield. *The Presocratic Philosophers: A Critical History with a Selection of Texts.* 2nd ed. Cambridge: Cambridge University Press, 1983.

Laks, André, and Glenn W. Most, eds. and trans. *Early Greek Philosophy.* 9 vols. Loeb Classical Library 524–32. Cambridge, MA: Harvard University Press, 2016.

McKirahan, Richard. *Philosophy Before Socrates: An Introduction with Texts and Commentary.* 2nd ed. Indianapolis: Hackett, 2011.

### *Secondary Literature*

Adamson, Peter. *Classical Philosophy: A History of Philosophy Without Any Gaps.* Vol. 1. Oxford: Oxford University Press, 2014.

Blackson, Thomas A. *Ancient Greek Philosophy: From the Presocratics to the Hellenistic Philosophers.* Malden, MA: Wiley-Blackwell, 2011.

Curd, Patricia, and Daniel Graham, eds. *Oxford Handbook of Presocratic Philosophy.* Oxford: Oxford University Press, 2008.

Long, A. A., ed. *Cambridge Companion to Early Greek Philosophy.* Cambridge: Cambridge University Press, 1999.

Mansfeld, J. *Studies in Early Greek Philosophy: A Collection of Papers and One Review.* Philosophia Antiqua 151. Leiden: Brill, 2018.

McKirihan, Richard D. *Philosophy Before Socrates: An Introduction with Texts and Commentary.* 2nd ed. Cambridge, MA: Hackett, 2011.

Vassallo, Christian. *Presocratics and Papyrological Tradition: A Philosophical Reappraisal of the Sources.* Studia Praesocratica 10. Berlin: De Gruyter, 2019.

# 4

# Socrates and the Sophists

The label "pre-Socratics" is less accurate as a chronological description of the timeline than it is testimony to the importance of the individual in reference to whom these philosophers are named—Socrates (469–399 BCE). While his life postdates many of the so-called pre-Socratics, he actually lived concurrently with several of them. It is with Socrates, nevertheless, that several important transitions in the history of philosophy occur. At this point, the center of philosophical activity moves from Italy and Ionia to the flourishing city of Athens, Greece. It is at this point also that the main line of philosophical interest begins to veer from natural philosophy to ethics.

At the same time as Socrates, a group of intellectuals that became collectively known as the "sophists" entered the scene in Athens. For various reasons, some of Socrates's contemporaries associated him with these individuals. Certainly, they were similar in two important ways: both made major contributions with lasting influence on the Greek intellectual tradition, and both provoked the ire of their contemporaries.

## Socrates

### *The Life of Socrates*

#### Socrates in Plato's Dialogues

What we know of Socrates is limited by the fact that he wrote nothing. Although he features centrally in many of the philosophical dialogues of his student Plato (ca. 429–347 BCE), the Socrates of Plato's dialogues must be carefully distinguished from the Socrates of history. Indeed, even if some of Plato's dialogues are based on real conversations, they are primarily literary fictions. Hence, Socrates appears in Plato's writing as a character and often as a mouthpiece for Plato's own views (see chapter 5). Since antiquity, many of Plato's readers have noted that the earlier dialogues likely depict Socrates more accurately than the later ones.[1] While the latter more readily advance positive dogmatic claims reflective of Plato's opinions, the earlier dialogues are primarily dialectical and aporetic (i.e., ending in "doubt") and, as will be discussed, at least reflect Socrates's usual style of teaching.

#### The Historical Socrates

With the help of Plato and other ancient sources, a basic profile of Socrates the philosopher can be sketched. Socrates was born in Athens around 470 BCE, the son

1. Aristotle, *Pol.* 1264b; *Metaph.* 1.987b; 13.1078b; cf. *Metaph.* 1.1078b.

of a sculptor and a citizen of the city. It is said that he was a student of Anaxagoras the philosopher and later of Archelaus the physicist (see table 5 below).[2] Reputedly, he was a skilled public speaker and taught the techniques of the sophists—and he was taken by many to be one.[3] He married twice and had three children.[4] By choice, he lived humbly,[5] eating and drinking only what was plain and necessary, limiting his desires, and even despising wealth as an evil.[6] Eventually, he developed a reputation as being the wisest of all men.

TABLE 5. Succession from Thales to Socrates[7]

| [Thales] |
|---|
| Anaximander |
| Anaximenes |
| Anaxagoras, Damon, and Archelaus |
| Socrates |

Socrates's manner of engaging the public, as well as his choice of friends, incited several bitter accusations against him. In 399 BCE, he was brought to suit by the prominent Athenian citizens Meletus, Anytus, and Lycon.[8] According to Plato, in his defense before the Athenian assembly, Socrates cited two sets of charges his accusers brought against him: (1) "Socrates is a criminal and a busybody, investigating things beneath the earth and in the heavens and making the weaker argument stronger and teaching others the same things"; and (2) "Socrates is a wrongdoer because he corrupts the youth and does not believe in the gods the state believes in, but in other new spiritual beings."[9]

It is reported by Diogenes Laërtius that Socrates's accusers envied him because of his reputation as the wisest of all men and because he made those who were reputedly wise look like fools.[10] It is possible, moreover, that the charges against him were pretexts for concerns of a more political nature, for several young men who had opposed democracy in Athens were among Socrates's consorts. In any case,

---

2. Diogenes Laërtius, *Vit. phil.* 2.19; cf. Plato, *Phaed.* 97b–98c on Anaxagoras.
3. Diogenes Laërtius, *Vit. phil.* 2.19–20. On Socrates and sophistry, see note 9 below.
4. Diogenes Laërtius, *Vit. phil.* 2.26.
5. Diogenes Laërtius, *Vit. phil.* 2.27.
6. Diogenes Laërtius, *Vit. phil.* 2.27, 31.
7. Diogenes Laërtius, *Vit. phil.* 2.19.
8. On his accusers, see Plato, *Apol.* 24b; Diogenes Laërtius, *Vit. phil.* 2.38–39. Accounts of Socrates's imprisonment, trial, and death can be found in Plato's *Apology*, Xenophon's *Apology*, Plato's *Crito* and *Phaedo*, and Diogenes Laërtius, *Vit. phil.* 2.38–42. Plato's *Apology* indicates that Plato himself was present (*Apol.* 34a; 38b); Diogenes Laërtius reports that Plato stood up to speak (*Vit. phil.* 2.41).
9. The first charge in Plato, *Apol.* 19b; the second in Plato, *Apol.* 24b (LCL, Fowler). Cf. Diogenes Laërtius, *Vit. phil.* 2.40.
10. Diogenes Laërtius, *Vit. phil.* 2.37–38.

although he was permitted to make a defense, he failed to obtain acquittal (by a relatively slim margin) and was sentenced to involuntary suicide.[11]

### Socrates as Wise Man

Socrates's career as a philosopher began in a most intriguing way.[12] A certain friend by the name of Chaerephon visited the oracle at Delphi and asked the oracle whether there was anyone wiser than Socrates. The oracle replied that there was not. When word of this reached Socrates, he wondered at it, thinking to himself that he was not wise at all. From this time, he began to investigate whether the pronouncement might indeed be true. He visited all those reputed to be wise and, alas, he found himself disappointed. While these celebrities believed themselves to be wise, he reached the conclusion that he was indeed wiser at least in one respect: He knew that he knew nothing. Yet he *wanted* to know; and as no one else seemed to have answers, he set out on his own search for truth.

#### *Socratic Method*

The style of philosophy that Socrates adopted flowed naturally from his conviction that all people, including himself, were ignorant. As he knew nothing, he refrained from making dogmatic assertions and sought only to search for answers, using a method of dialogue called *skepsis* ("inquiring") or *elenchus* ("examination").[13] The customary procedure was to initiate a conversation, usually in public, by putting forward a question for discussion, usually to someone reputed to be wise, which once investigated resulted only in *aporia* (i.e., "doubt" or "uncertainty"). Such encounters are a central feature of Plato's early dialogues and surely reflect Socrates's actual practice, as Aristotle later confirms.[14] For instance, in Plato's *Meno*, Socrates seeks a definition of "virtue" (*aretē*), and in his *Euthyphro* a definition of "piety" (*eusebeia*). While Socrates and his interlocutors discover situationally appropriate definitions of these concepts, they fail to find univocal or all-encompassing definitions. Thus, *aporia*.

Socrates's practice was "skeptical" only in a specialized sense of the word—it involved *skepsis*, or "inquiry." The practice was not intended to demonstrate the impossibility of obtaining true knowledge (as the later Skeptics wanted to do). Rather, the strategy was to eliminate false beliefs first in order to then open up a space for the truth, which one could then proceed to seek. In this regard, the idea that Socrates's profession of ignorance was a veil concealing what is sometimes called "Socratic Irony"—according to which, he knew the answers but was having a good laugh at his interlocutors' expense—is probably not true to his usual approach. Given that he persistently claimed that he knew nothing (the very reason that he

11. Apparently, he fell short by thirty votes: 281 voting for a guilty verdict and 220 for innocent.

12. Plato, *Apol.* 21a–22e.

13. Cf. Plato, *Apol.* 33b.

14. Indeed, Aristotle reports that this was characteristic of Socrates (*Metaph.* 13.1078b).

was considered wise), his appearance of ignorance seems to have been genuine, not feigned. Hence, he shared in his audience's *aporia.*

## *Philosophy as a Way of Life*

Cicero memorably summarizes Socrates's legacy by remarking that he "brought philosophy down from heaven to earth."[15] What Cicero meant is that Socrates shifted the lines of philosophical inquiry from natural philosophy, the pre-Socratics' primary interest, to ethics.[16] Indeed, at the end of Socrates's life, he claimed that, unlike those before him, he had taken no interest in investigating "the things beneath the earth and in the heavens" (although he apparently took interest in these things at one time).[17] He was concerned rather with the best form of life or how to "live well" (*bene vivere*).[18] To live well, he insisted, one needed first to discover what living well consisted in. Through his dialectical method, he hoped to discover the answer.[19]

While many of Socrates's contemporaries chafed at his inquisitiveness, he made no apologies for it. In his defense speech before the Athenian council, he describes himself as a gadfly sent by God to examine himself and others and to reproach his fellows frankly for their ignorance.[20] This he did in their own best interest and in the larger interest of the city, even neglecting his own affairs to do so.[21] For what mattered was not simply living but "living well."[22] Achieving this required intense self-examination. Only by examining oneself could one know *if* one was living well. What was at stake was nothing less than the welfare of one's soul and the true acquisition of wisdom, perfection, and goodness.[23] Thus Socrates memorably averred that "the unexamined life is not worth living."[24]

Not that "doctrine" (*logos*) wasn't important.[25] According to Socrates, the "art" (*technē*) of living, like any art (e.g., medicine, navigation, architecture), requires not only practical skill but also a theoretical "account" (*logos*) upon which that skill is based. Thus the art of living well required some understanding, for instance, of what virtue or justice or piety *is*, so as to determine how then to act virtuously or justly or piously. Even metaphysical doctrines could tend toward practical benefit. In Plato's *Phaedo*, Plato has Socrates assert that metaphysical questions like that of

15. Cicero, *Tusc.* 5.4.10.

16. Diogenes Laërtius, *Vit. phil.* 1.14; 2.16.

17. Plato, *Apol.* 19c–d. Yet in the *Phaedo*, Socrates explains that he had been enthralled with natural philosophy (96a–e) before later confessing his ignorance (96e–97b); cf. Diogenes Laërtius, *Vit. phil.* 2.45.

18. Cicero, *Acad.* 1.15.

19. Aristotle claims that Socrates introduced this method (*Metaph.* 1.987b), though Plato is officially credited as the one who introduced dialectics as the third subject of philosophy (Diogenes Laërtius, *Vit. phil.* 3.56).

20. Plato, *Apol.* 28e–29a; 31a; 31e.

21. Plato, *Apol.* 23b; 31b; 37a.

22. Plato, *Crit.* 48b.

23. Plato, *Apol.* 29e–30b; 36b–d.

24. Plato, *Apol.* 38a.

25. *Logos* is used here in a sense different than Heraclitus's usage (ch. 3).

the (im)mortality of the soul have practical value. In fact, Socrates says, the one who studies the question of the soul studies "nothing but dying and being dead"; for if one knows what happens after death, then one will know whether death is anything to be feared.[26] Whether Plato's *Phaedo* factually represents Socrates's views here, Plato makes clear how such speculation would be consistent with Socrates's fundamental concerns.

Nonetheless, for Socrates, the final emphasis lay on the side of practice, or *askēsis*. For any art, theoretical knowledge was not sufficient to produce mastery.[27] As with the art of medicine, the art has been perfected only if one also has proficiency in practicing it. A physician is no use if he possesses theoretical knowledge of illnesses and their causes but has no skill in healing them. Likewise, the philosopher who has attained profound theoretical knowledge but fails to put it into practice is not rightly called a philosopher, but a pseudo-philosopher.[28] For his "deeds" are not in accordance with his "words."[29]

### *Virtue Among Other Goods*

Socrates reflected that not all things we call "good" are created equal. Among all life's goods, virtue was the highest, if not the only, true good.[30] At his trial, Socrates protested that he had never sought political or economic gain, but only the welfare of the soul and the acquisition of wisdom, perfection, and goodness.[31] He pled that the soul should be prioritized above all else, not to be forsaken for money, honor, or anything else,[32] not even in exchange for one's life.[33] Socrates's priorities reflect in rudimentary form what after Plato's time became a traditional threefold classification of "goods": external goods (money, honor), bodily goods (health, life), and goods of the soul (virtue).

### *The God and the Gods*

One allegation that instigated Socrates's trial was that he didn't believe "in the gods the state believes in, but in other new spiritual beings (*daimonia kaina*)."[34] At his trial, Socrates did not deny believing in these "spirits" (*daimonia*).[35] As to

---

26. Plato, *Phaed.* 64a; cf. 67e.
27. Plato, *Gorg.* 465a.
28. Plato, *Phaed.* 64b; 69d; *Rep.* 485d. Later in, for example, Epictetus, *Diatr.* 3.21.22–23; 3.24.38–41, 81; 3.26.23; Dio, *Or.* 13.11; Musonius Rufus, *Diatr.* 17.14–16; Lucian, *Fug.* 15.
29. Xenophon, *Mem.* 4.4.10.
30. Diogenes Laërtius, *Vit. phil.* 2.31; Plato, *Phaed.* 64d–e.
31. Plato, *Apol.* 29e–30b; 36b–d.
32. Plato, *Apol.* 29e–30b; cf. *Phaed.* 78a.
33. Plato, *Apol.* 28b.
34. Plato, *Apol.* 24b.
35. Belief in *daimonia* (or *daimones*) was not exactly new. The pre-Socratic Empedocles believed that his own soul was in fact a *daimōn*, awaiting its release and return to the heavenly abode (DK §31b 115). Centuries earlier, Hesiod (*Theog.* 783–806) had already written about certain *daimones* who had been expelled from Mount Olympus because they had sworn false oaths.

whether these *daimonia* were "gods," he responded that they must at the least be children of gods and that children of gods can only be gods themselves.[36] Hence, he did believe in gods.

Socrates not only claims that he believed in such divinities, he also claims that from time to time, "something divine and spiritual" (*theion ti kai daimonion*) actually *came* to him. It was a kind of "voice," one that he had heard from his childhood. The voice acted only to warn him, to restrain him from doing what he was thinking of doing, never to urge him forward.[37]

More frequently, Socrates refers to "the God" (*ho theos*).[38] The God, like the *daimonia*, speaks to him. He says that the God told him "through oracles and dreams" to examine those who think they are wise but are not.[39] His inquisitiveness, scrutiny, and frankness toward others, in other words, were obligations to which he was bound by a divine calling. It was a "station" charged upon him.[40] He acted at the God's behest, doing business of the highest import.[41] He would not disobey, heeding people rather than the God, and he would not cease scrutinizing them, not even to save his life.[42] He was not a public nuisance. He was a gift.[43]

### *Politics*

Socrates never held political office. This was to his good fortune, for he attests that he wouldn't have lived long had he done so.[44] At his defense, he assured his fellow citizens that he had always chosen justice over his own safety. In proof, he adduced two earlier events: first when he opposed public orders during the time of the democracy, and again when he opposed the Thirty Tyrants of the oligarchy.[45] It is not clear whether Socrates actively or vocally opposed Athens' democratic regime. Some of his associates, however, did; and this may have influenced his fate. The fact that the democratic assembly voted in favor of his condemnation may explain why Plato, his most illustrious student, presented democracy in his *Republic* as the worst of all forms of government. Socrates was one among many philosophers to come whose philosophical convictions conflicted with the interests of the state and incurred backlash from fellow citizens or rulers. His reputed steadfastness in the face of likely death was held up as a paradigm for later philosophers threatened by punishment from the authorities due to their Socratic-like criticism.[46]

---

36. Plato, *Apol.* 27c–e.
37. Plato, *Apol.* 31d; cf. 41a–b.
38. Plato, *Apol.* 22a; 23b; 29d; 31a.
39. Plato, *Apol.* 33c.
40. Plato, *Apol.* 28e–29a; cf. 21e; 22a; 30a.
41. Plato, *Apol.* 21e; 30a.
42. Plato, *Apol.* 29b–d.
43. Plato, *Apol.* 31a.
44. Plato, *Apol.* 32b; 31d.
45. Plato, *Apol.* 28b; 32c–d.
46. See Epictetus, *Diatr.* 1.29.16–18; Seneca, *Ep.* 24.3–5; cf. Seneca, *Ep.* 13–14; Lucian, *Peregr.* 18; 37.

### *Death*

Unsurprisingly, Socrates reflected much on death at his trial. He believed in principle that choosing right over wrong was more important than the potentially fatal repercussions of this commitment.[47] As noted, he had often acted in the interest of justice even when his choice jeopardized his safety or his life. In his final speech, he considered that the council might acquit him if he promised to cease philosophizing. Instead, he resolved this: "I shall never give up philosophy or stop exhorting you and pointing out the truth to any one of you whom I may meet."[48]

In any case, he believed he had received divine confirmation that this choice was the right one. That "prophetic spirit" (*hē . . . mantikē hē tou daimoniou*) that had so often come to him and restrained him from acting now remained silent. It did not oppose him in his resolve to meet death by refusing the council's demands. If the spirit previously opposed him in paltry matters, then how much more would it have acted now when he faced what was reputedly the worst of all evils—namely, death?[49] This silence, he inferred, could only mean one thing: Death is not an evil but is "doubtless a good thing."[50]

Of course, Socrates was not entirely certain what would happen when he died.[51] The possibilities, however, seemed to him promising: Death is either nothingness or it is migration to a better place. If it is unconsciousness, then "like a sleep in which the sleeper does not even dream," death will be "a wonderful gain." If it is migration of the soul to a better place where all the dead will be—our friends, Homer, Hesiod, the demigods—and we will pass our time examining one another as we do here, then "what greater blessing could there be?"[52] On these grounds, Socrates concluded that the wise have no reason to fear death.[53] His contempt of death would become paradigmatic in depictions of the "wise man" among the later philosophical schools.

## The Sophists

### *Who They Were*

The term "sophist," or *sophistēs*, had a varied semantic history, but it developed a specialized meaning during the period of Socrates and his follower Plato. Usage predates Classical times (480–323 BCE). In the days of Homer (eighth century BCE), *sophistēs* meant simply "a wise person," referring usually either to some kind of teacher or to one who was wise in a craft. During the early Classical period (first half of the fifth century BCE), *sophistēs* was used in reference to those who

47. Plato, *Apol.* 28b.
48. Plato, *Apol.* 29c–d (LCL, Fowler); cf. 34e; 35c–d; 37e; 38a.
49. Plato, *Apol.* 40a–c; 41d.
50. Plato, *Apol.* 40b.
51. Plato, *Apol.* 37b.
52. Plato, *Apol.* 40c–41c (LCL, Fowler).
53. Plato, *Apol.* 29a–b.

collectively came to be known as the "Seven Sages," so called because they were considered wise as rulers and legislators. In the latter half of the fifth century BCE, the term developed special connotations in reference to a loosely knit and loosely defined class of individuals who were highly active in Athens' intellectual culture: *the* Sophists.

The Classical Sophists were nearly exact contemporaries of Socrates. They were educated Greek immigrants renowned for their encyclopedic knowledge in subjects as varied as linguistics, literary analysis, history, and geometry, and most especially for their eloquence in public speaking. They came to Athens to offer their knowledge and training in speech—for high fees. Their motives were, to a certain extent, opportunistic. Following the final victory of Athens over the Persians in the Greco-Persian wars (ca. 450 BCE), Athens entered a time of unprecedented economic and cultural prosperity. Art, literature, and philosophy were flourishing, and democracy had never been stronger. The political situation afforded nonaristocratic citizens opportunities for greater involvement in the democratic government, giving them incentive to better equip themselves for success by developing knowledge in statecraft and acquiring especially the skills necessary for debate and public address. Those who were ambitious—and could afford it—availed themselves of the sophists.

The sophists developed a mixed reputation in Athens. They were highly regarded for their skills and were deemed valuable to those who benefited from their services. Students, however, were sometimes disappointed by the quality of instruction, particularly in view of the fees. The general public, moreover, was troubled that the sophists seemed to direct their skills to unjust ends. The charge leveled at Socrates that he "made the weaker argument the stronger" was actually a charge commonly applied to the sophists; in fact, the allegation itself was a way of characterizing Socrates *as* a sophist.[54] The sense of this criticism was that in the sophists' training in public speaking, they taught their students how to effectively argue on either side of an issue (expedient for the students), but with the result that the trainee could make even falsehoods look like the truth (concerning for the general public).[55] In addition, citizens were outraged that the sophists impugned traditional beliefs in the gods and questioned commonly embraced values, by which they undermined justification for the particular laws of the city. It is likely that the challenges brought by some sophists against traditional beliefs were partly a feature of their rhetoric (making the weaker argument appear the stronger). On the other hand, some sophists seem to have been genuine skeptics, relativists, or nihilists.

Ancient tradition identifies Gorgias (ca. 485–ca. 380 BCE) as the "father" of Classical Sophistry. He founded the art in Thessaly before stopping in Athens on his itinerant circuit.[56] Gorgias engaged with philosophers, though he was primarily a rhetorician by identity. It is said he invented the "extempore speech" and

54. It first appears as a description of the sophists (including Socrates) in Aristophanes's comedy *Clouds*.

55. It is said that for this reason the Athenians shut them out of the law courts (Philostratus, *Vit. Soph.* 483).

56. Philostratus, *Vit. Soph.* 492.

advertised that he could speak on any topic on the spot.[57] In the eponymous dialogue *Gorgias*, Plato depicts him as one concerned only with persuasion rather than with real knowledge. Sextus Empiricus (second century CE) later reports that Gorgias argued, "firstly, that nothing exists; secondly, that even if anything exists it is inapprehensible by man; thirdly, that even if anything is apprehensible, yet of a surety it is inexpressible and incommunicable to one's neighbour."[58] Unless Gorgias's argument is a mere rhetorical stunt, he indeed presents himself here as a skeptic (premise 2), a relativist (premise 3), and even a nihilist (premise 1).

One of the most infamous of the sophists, Protagoras (ca. 490–420 BCE), was known for coining the axiom "Man is the measure of all things." The axiom implies a stance of relativism, concerning not only the conviction that knowledge is limited by our varying perceptions, but also concerning the nature of reality itself. Whereas pre-Socratic philosophers emphasized grounds for doubt by undermining certainty of the senses, Protagoras's claim went much further. It is not just that we have grounds for questioning the certainty of our perceptions; reality in itself only exists according to our perceptions. Protagoras applied this principle not only to sense perception but also to morality. What is "good" is what is good for me, just as for you, "good" is what is good for you. Both you and I are correct because reality is inherently relative.

### *Sophists and Philosophers*

The Classical Sophists can be appropriately juxtaposed with the first philosophers for several reasons. In the first place, many sophists were students of philosophers, influenced by philosophers, or associated with philosophers. Moreover, like the philosophers, the sophists challenged traditional beliefs, and religious beliefs especially. In a manner comparable to the philosophers, sophists reflected upon epistemological questions and sometimes embraced a kind of skepticism reminiscent of the philosophers.[59] Philosophical themes frequently featured as subjects of their display speeches.[60] Because of these resemblances between the philosophers and sophists, the public tended to associate the two. As noted, two of the charges leveled against Socrates were that he "made the weaker argument the stronger" and that he took fees for his teaching,[61] practices both connected with the sophists. While Socrates denied these charges, rejoining that his reputation in this regard derived from Aristophanes's depiction of him in his comedy (*Clouds*), even if not

57. Philostratus, *Vit. Soph.* 482–83.

58. Sextus Empiricus, *Math.* 7.65 (LCL, Bury).

59. The sophists' practice of arguing on both sides of an issue is also resonant with the later Skeptical philosophers' truism that "to every argument there is an equal and opposite argument" (see ch. 10).

60. Philostratus says that ancient sophistry was essentially "philosophic rhetoric" (*Vit. Soph.* 480).

61. "Makes the weaker argument" the stronger: Plato, *Apol.* 19b, denies teaching or knowing anything in 19c; 33b. Taking fees: Plato, *Apol.* 19d–e; 31b; 33b; denied in *Apol.* 19e: 31b; 33b.

totally founded Aristophanes's depiction of him must have been common public perception, or at least generative of public perception.

A clearer distinction emerged between the philosopher and the sophist only in the time of Plato (ca. 429–347 BCE), as "philosophy" and the "philosopher" became more narrowly defined. As noted in the first chapter, competing definitions of *philosophia* coexisted in the time of Socrates.[62] Plato later established what became the standard definition: philosophy was a pursuit concerned most fundamentally with improvement of self and others. By establishing this as the normative definition, Plato was able to vindicate Socrates and install him as the paradigm of the true philosopher.[63] As such, Socrates and the genuine philosopher could rightly divide truth in the manner of an incisive dialectician. This sort of philosopher focused on truth and virtue. The sophist, by contrast, offered slick imitations of the truth. The *sophistēs* was not "wise" (*sophos*), but an ignorant "imitator" (*mimētēs*) of the wise.[64]

This rather unflattering depiction of the sophist might not accurately characterize all acclaimed sophists. Plato's more exclusive definition of the "philosopher," nonetheless, succeeded in becoming the predominant definition used throughout antiquity. Who counted as a true philosopher remained a matter of heated debate,[65] but the fact that a philosopher was not the same thing as a sophist did not.[66] What slowly emerged was a segregation of domains: The sophists prioritized rhetoric, and philosophers prioritized how to live.[67] Even philosophers who were rhetorically trained (as a large percentage of them were) separated the two identities, from Plato on through the Second Sophistic in the third century CE (chapter 14).[68]

## Notes on the Primary Sources

### *Socrates*

Socrates himself wrote nothing. The most extensive testimony about his life and philosophy is preserved by his students Plato and Xenophon who, as his students, also portray him most sympathetically. Socrates features as a character in more than two dozen of Plato's philosophical dialogues, in which he usually plays

---

62. Moore, *Calling Philosophers Names*, 257.

63. Plato works out contrasts between sophistry and philosophy in several dialogues, including *Sophist*, *Gorgias*, *Protagoras*, and several other eponymously titled works.

64. Plato, *Soph.* 268b 10.

65. See note 28 above.

66. For the distinction between philosophers and sophists during the Second Sophistic, see ch. 15.

67. "Seeming" vs. "being": Plato, *Rep.* 2.362a; 601b. Note also the common pairs "words" vs. "things": Seneca, *Ep.* 52.14; cf. 45.5–6; 75.7; "words" vs. "actions": Musonius Rufus, *Diatr.* 5.26–37; 6.7–10; "speaking" vs. "living": Seneca, *Ep.* 88.42; "speech" vs. "life": Seneca, *Ep.* 20.2.

68. Note in advance Philostratus's discussion in his *Lives of the Sophists* (*Vit. Soph.* §479–92).

the central role. Plato's earlier dialogues accurately reflect Socrates's *elenchic* teaching style (above) and his belief that virtue is the only good worth pursuing. As a longtime student of Plato, Aristotle was aware of differences between Socrates the man and the character who became an instrument for Plato's own views.[69] Xenophon preserves remembrances of Socrates in his *Memorabilia*. Both Plato and Xenophon provide accounts of Socrates's defense speech prior to his execution (Plato's *Apology*; Xenophon's *Apology of Socrates*). Plato claims to have been an eyewitness;[70] and while his version of the speech is not likely a stenographic record, it surely preserves Socrates's main points and may indeed be only lightly reshaped.[71] Xenophon, on the other hand, received his account of the speech from Hermogenes (another member of the Socratic circle) and records only a portion of it.[72] In Aristophanes's comedy *Clouds*, Socrates is depicted, satirically, as a natural philosopher and sophist, a depiction that seems to have played an instrumental role in shaping his contemporary reputation and inciting the allegations that brought him to trial. Diogenes Laërtius includes a biography of Socrates in *Lives of Eminent Philosophers*.[73]

### *The Sophists*

The sophists composed both speeches and treatises, though none of their works have survived intact. Graham's (2010) two-volume collection of fragments and testimonia of "major pre-Socratics" includes those of Protagoras, Gorgias, and other sophists. Graham's work includes the original Greek text and English translation on facing pages, with commentary and a brief introduction before each text. Aristophanes's *Clouds* offers a satirical depiction of the sophists from the perspective of a contemporary. Sophists feature in many of Plato's dialogues, several of which are eponymously titled (*Protagoras*, *Critias*, *Gorgias*, etc.), and all of which are largely critical. Philostratus's *Lives of the Sophists* provides biographies of ten Classical Sophists, ranging from Gorgias (ca. 485–ca. 380 BCE) to Isocrates (436–338 BCE).

## Key Terms and Concepts

- *Aporia* (doubt)
- *Askēsis* (practice)
- *Elenchus* (examination)
- Extempore speaking
- Making the worse argument the better

69. See notes 1, 14, and 19 above.

70. Plato, *Apol.* 34a; 38b; Plato's presence is also attested in Diogenes Laërtius, *Vit. phil.* 41.

71. Most commentators believe that Plato's version is true to the substance of the speech. See Thomas C. Brickhouse and Nicholas Smith, *The Philosophy of Socrates* (Boulder, CO: Westview, 2000), 29.

72. Xenophon, *Apol.* 2; 14; et al.

73. Diogenes Laërtius, *Vit. phil.* 2.18–47.

- Relativism
- Seven Sages, the
- Socratic Irony
- Socratic Method

## For Further Study

### *Socrates*

Adamson, Peter. *Classical Philosophy: A History of Philosophy Without Any Gaps. Vol. 1.* Oxford: Oxford University Press, 2014.
Brickhouse, Thomas C., and Nicholas Smith. *The Philosophy of Socrates.* Boulder, CO: Westview, 2000.
Bussanich, John, and Nicholas D. Smith, eds. *The Bloomsbury Companion to Socrates.* London: Bloomsbury, 2013.
Marsico, Claudia. *Socrates and the Socratic Philosophies: Selected papers from Socratica IV.* International Socrates Studies 2. Baden-Baden: Academia Verlag, 2022.

### *The Sophists*

Billings, Joshua, and Christopher Moore, eds. *The Cambridge Companion to the Sophists.* Cambridge: Cambridge University Press, 2023.
Bowersock, G. W. *Greek Sophists in the Roman Empire.* Oxford: Clarendon, 1969.
Curnow, Trevor. "Were the Sophists Philosophers?" Pages 185–93 in *The Sophists: An Introduction.* Edited by Patricia O'Grady. London: Duckworth, 2008.
Dillon, John, and Tania Gergel, trans. *The Greek Sophists.* New York: Penguin, 2003.
Graham, Daniel W., ed. *The Texts of Early Greek Philosophy: The Complete Fragments and Selected Testimonies of the Major Presocratics.* Vol. 2. Cambridge; New York: Cambridge University Press, 2010.
O'Grady, Patricia, ed. *The Sophists: An Introduction.* London: Duckworth, 2008.
Stanton, G. R. "Sophists and Philosophers: Problems of Classification." *The American Journal of Philology* 94 (1973): 350–64.

# 5

# Plato and Aristotle

Athens succeeded in ending Socrates's life, but not his spirit of inquiring. As he had prophesied, others arose after his death to carry on his purposes—to examine others and seek the truth.[1] Among his students was Plato, who although deeply inspired by some of Socrates's convictions and methods, added far more substance in way of positive doctrinal claims. The impact of Plato in the history of philosophy was deep and long-lasting and would be matched perhaps by no one except one of his own students—namely, Aristotle.

## Plato

### *The Life of Plato*

Born of Athenian parents on the island of Aegina (b. 429 BCE), Aristocles "Plato" lived most of his life in Athens.[2] He commenced study of philosophy as a youth, learning first in the Academy, then in the garden at Colonus under a follower of Heraclitus. After hearing Socrates, he became a follower at age twenty and followed him until his teacher's death ten years later. Plato studied thereafter with a Heraclitean, a Parmenidean, and a Megarian. He studied also with a mathematician and then with a group of Pythagoreans in Italy before traveling to Egypt, where he learned divination. When he returned to Athens, he lived in the Academy, a gymnasium outside the city's walls, in a grove named after the hero Hecademus (whence "Academy"). There he established a school, which he headed until his death in 347 BCE.[3]

From his eclectic training, Plato created a synthesis that drew primarily from Heraclitus, the Pythagoreans, and Socrates.[4] Yet, unlike Socrates, who inquired (*skepsasthai*) intently after answers but insisted he knew nothing, Plato ventured positive theses, or dogmas, which he synthesized into a developing system that integrated metaphysics, epistemology, philosophy of mind, political philosophy, ethics, and other traditional areas of inquiry.[5] Ancient tradition credits him with

1. Plato, *Apol.* 39c.

2. *Platōn*, or "Broad," was his nickname, perhaps due to his stature (Diogenes Laërtius, *Vit. phil.* 3.4).

3. Diogenes Laërtius, *Vit. phil.* 3.5–8.

4. Diogenes Laërtius, *Vit. phil.* 3.8.

5. Cicero states that Plato was the first to formulate positive doctrines and synthesize them (*Acad.* 1.17).

inventing a threefold division of the parts of philosophy, which many accepted after him: the "physical" (*to physikon*), the "logical" (*to logikon*), and the "ethical" (*to ēthikon*).[6] He also formalized several taxonomies that became traditional in the ancient philosophical tradition, including the threefold definition of goods (intellectual, bodily, external), the four cardinal virtues (wisdom, courage, temperance, justice), and the four passions (pleasure, lust, grief, fear).

## *Physics (Metaphysics)*

### The Creator and the Created

Plato shared with the pre-Socratics an interest in natural philosophy, or *physics* (*to physikon*). His theory of physics, however, was integrally related to his theory of metaphysics. For, according to Plato, the physical "participates" fully in what transcends it.

Plato's fullest account of metaphysics appears in his dialogue *Timaeus*.[7] While *Timaeus* proffers positive doctrines (as opposed to simply apophatic assertions), it is not positivistic or dogmatic but rather presents what Plato calls a "probable" account,[8] while also mixing philosophical and mythical discourse. In summary, *Timaeus* proposes the following: There is one universe. Its maker or father, also called the "demiurge" (*dēmiourgos*), created it out of preexisting elements (air, fire, water, earth), using up their supply entirely. Furthermore, the universe is a living being. For in it was set a world soul (*psychē*), which was created prior to the material universe. This material universe is not an original creation, but an imitation (*eikōn*) modeled after the pattern of the eternal. The demiurge's creation is, on the whole, the best of all universes since it was, after all, based on the pattern of the eternal. Nonetheless, the demiurge was limited in his work by the nature of his materials, the preexisting elements. Consequently, the universe is a product of both reason (intelligent design) and necessity (the limitation of the available material)—orderly by design but less than perfect.

### The Forms and Their Copies

Plato's metaphysical perspective implies ontological dualism. The creator (the demiurge) and the created (the world), respectively, correspond ontologically with pattern and imitation. The pattern constitutes what Plato calls "forms" (*ideai* or *eidē*), of which the demiurge seems to be a mythic personification. The forms themselves are immaterial, immutable, and eternal realities. The created universe, on the other hand, is material, ever-changing, and dependent. Yet, as imitations of

6. Cicero says that Plato invented it (*Acad.* 1.19). Others, however, attribute it to his successor Xenocrates, saying that the division exists in Plato only "potentially" (Sextus Empiricus, *Math.* 7.16). Sextus says that the Peripatetics and the Stoics also adopted this division (*Math.* 7.17); Stoics in Diogenes Laërtius, *Vit. phil.* 7.39.

7. One finds extensive discussion also throughout his earlier dialogues *Phaedo*, *Republic*, and *Parmenides*.

8. Plato, *Tim.* 48c; 72d; cf. 68d.

the forms, the created copies nevertheless participate in their respective forms and are, indeed, caused by them.

Plato's theory of forms develops across his dialogues, so it is difficult to ascertain what kinds of forms he believed existed or how many forms there were. For instance, Plato is clear that forms existed of, say, the just, the beautiful, and the good. He also acknowledges forms of certain human artifacts.[9] In this regard, just as craftsmen who construct chairs and tables imitate the forms of chairs and tables, so also instantiations of justice in the sensible realm are but imperfect copies, or shadows, of the form of justice in which they participate.

#### Created Beings

The demiurge (or the forms) created several lower classes of beings. The highest of these were divinities, though of a lesser class than the demiurge himself. These lower divinities in turn created the bodies of human beings out of the elements, as well as the irrational part of the human soul out of the residue remaining from the world soul.

These created human bodies are subject to sensation and emotion, which are aroused in us by phenomena in the created physical world. God (the demiurge), however, added to the irrational part of the human soul—created by the lower divinities—a *rational* part. In fact, the human soul now consists of three parts: two of them irrational (the *thymikon* or "spirited," and the *epithymētikon* or "appetitive" part) and the third rational (the *logistikon* part). Different parts of the soul have different perceptive capabilities. The irrational soul is able to apprehend only what is subject to the senses, and thus only the material world. The realm of the forms is *in*sensible, or *not* apprehensible by the senses. Hence, the insensible can be apprehended only through the intellectual faculty of reason, which is seated in the rational part of the soul. Only the rational part of the soul is eternal. At death, the rational soul transmigrates into another body and then into another body and so on in perpetuity.

### *Logic*

The "logical" part (*to logistikon*) of Plato's philosophy concerned canons and methods for discovery of the truth. Key ideas here include Plato's notion of "recollection" and the critical role of "dialectic."

#### *A Priori* Knowledge and Recollection

Since the sensible world is an imitation of the unchanging, purely existing eternal, knowledge of *true* reality is tantamount to knowledge of the paradigmatic forms. Through the senses, one can know only the sensible world. The insensible world is known through reason. Still, the senses have an important part to play. In his *Phaedo*, Plato suggests that through the senses we can, for example, see in-

9. Couches, tables, and cabinets in Plato, *Rep.* 10.595a–598d; reference to the artisan who imitates the Forms in *Tim.* 28a.

stances of "equality" in the world—that is, a likeness of things to each other. Plato observes, however, that the things perceived as being equal by the senses actually share this likeness precisely because each of them strives to imitate equality in the absolute, or the *form of equality*. If therefore one possesses some notion of the equality to which sensible things strive to conform, one must already have acquired this knowledge of abstract equality *prior* to using our senses to notice specific instances of it. On these grounds, Plato comes to a striking conclusion: Knowledge is not acquired; it exists *a priori*.

Why then do we appear to learn? Contrary to appearances, Plato explains that "learning" is in fact nothing other than the recollection (*anamnēsis*) of things already learned in our pre-embodied states. As Plato tells us, transmigration of the soul from body to body is recurrent. It has happened before. At death, when the soul separates from the body, it encounters in its disembodied state the immaterial forms, and there learns the forms' full nature once again. While the soul forgets what it has learned when it enters (transmigrates) into another body, this prevenient knowledge can be recovered by beginning from the senses and then, as it were, climbing upward to the transcendent realm of the forms. While the senses, then, are not the final means by which we achieve knowledge, they are the means through which we come to recollect what we knew *a priori*—namely, the nature of the forms.

### Education and Dialectic

Education is an important means through which prior knowledge is recovered. Plato advised students to study mathematics (arithmetic followed by geometry) at a young age, since mathematics deals with abstraction and thereby trains our minds to rise above belief grounded in sense perception. Better still was the study of *dialectic*. Dialectic was a method of question and answer whereby one arrived through a series of easier questions at a correct conclusion without having been "taught" anything in the process. In one dialogue, for instance, Socrates successfully leads a slave boy to answer a geometry question.[10] The efficacy of this method, Plato suggested, would only be possible if the knowledge to which the participant comes through the process already exists in the mind *a priori*, being now merely recovered through the method. Although this dialectical method is similar to Socrates's method of question and answer (see chapter 3), Socrates's method began from a skeptical ("inquiring") stance and even ended in *aporia* (doubt), while in Plato's method, the teacher works with some general theory and then talks the listener through it, leading them to some intended conclusion.

### The Myth of the Cave

Plato illustrates the problem of forgetfulness in the body with his famous myth of the cave.[11] In this myth, we dwell in a dark cave. Chained in place, our eyes are fixed ahead onto a wall on which shadows of puppets are cast by a fire. These

10. Plato, *Meno* 81e–85b.
11. Plato, *Rep.* 514a–520a.

shadows correspond to the sensible world. Being shadows, they are obviously not real, but only imitations of what is real. It is the philosopher of strong mind who breaks free from these dim realities, exits the cave, and emerges into the light of the sun. The sun represents the form of the good, being both the cause (or nourishment) of the things that imitate it and the light through which we understand what is seen. In this way, the form of the good is what makes knowledge possible. In the meantime, the body distracts us from knowledge of the Good by drawing us to objects of sense perception. Only when the soul is separated from the body at death will it be able to attain wisdom and knowledge fully. For now, we must strive intellectually to separate the soul from the body as much as possible.

## *Ethics*

Socrates seemingly prioritized virtue over any kind of bodily (health, life) or external good (wealth, reputation).[12] Plato followed him in this. There was no good higher than virtue. Plato's theory of virtue was tightly integrated with his theory of forms and his dualism between body and soul, as we now discuss.

### The forms of Virtue

Plato's conception of the forms as absolute and unchanging realities entailed the fact that virtues, which participate in their forms, are not conventions of society or relative to the opinions of human subjects. Just as the form of the table exists independently of imperfect imitation tables, so justice, wisdom, courage, and piety exist absolutely as forms. By rooting morality in the unchanging forms, Plato's ethical theory countered both relativism (that virtues do not exist absolutely) and skepticism (that what is right or just cannot be known).

Preeminent among the forms was the form of the good, or simply *the* Good. The Good unites all other forms. Just as imitations in the sensible realm participate in their respective forms, so the other forms participate in the one form of the Good. As articulated in the cave myth, the Good is like the light of the sun, being both the means by which we perceive the other forms and that which nourishes and causes their existence. Philosophers are those who fix their gaze upon the Good and are guided, not by the senses, but by reason, the rational faculty through which alone the Good can be known.

### Body and Soul

What this conception of virtue suggests for Plato is that knowledge is nothing other than the soul ordered according to the form of the Good. Plato illustrates with another myth, that of the soul's chariot, presented in his dialogue *Phaedrus*.[13] In this myth, two winged horses draw a chariot guided by a charioteer. These three—the two horses and the charioteer—represent the three parts of the soul.

---

12. This distinction between intellectual, bodily, and external goods was established by Plato and became traditional in the later philosophical schools (Cicero, *Acad.* 1.19–22).

13. Plato, *Phaedr.* 246a–253d.

The charioteer is the rational part, who guides the chariot toward the Good on which he has set his vision. The two horses represent the irrational parts, the appetitive on the left and the spirited on the right. With their wings, the two horses bear the chariot aloft, up to the places of beauty, wisdom, and good where the gods dwell and the horses' wings are nourished. The spirited horse is of noble breed and by its nature follows reason's guidance willingly, thus having no need of the whip. The appetitive horse, on the other hand, is inferior in nature. So long as both horses obey reason, the three cooperate harmoniously, the chariot stays aloft, and it flies steadfastly towards its goal. When the horse of ignoble breed, however, rebels against the reason that guides it, disregarding the whip, it upsets its spirited mate and draws it off course. The chariot thereby veers from its course toward the Good, the horses' wings waste away, and the chariot begins to fall. This is an allegory for Plato's ethical theory. The soul rests in a disposition of good when reason (the charioteer) rules and the irrational parts (the horses) obey. Evil results when the ruled instead become the ruler.[14]

Although this tripartite psychology features in the *Phaedrus*, Plato's *Phaedo* describes a simpler psychology, involving simply body and soul. The *Phaedo*, nonetheless, complements the point of the *Phaedrus* myth. In the *Phaedo*, the body (identified in the *Phaedrus* with the appetitive part of the soul) draws the soul away from contemplation of wisdom and knowledge—the objects of rational thought—by succumbing to the pleasures received through the senses. In order to make moral improvements, therefore, we must separate soul from body as much as possible, even despising it, in order to weaken its influence and pull its gaze back toward wisdom and knowledge above.[15] Although we can make progress toward this goal while in the body, the body's influence can only be fully overcome and wisdom fully attained when the soul escapes its bodily prison at death.

### The Afterlife

In *Timaeus*, Plato poses that the Demiurge assigned each human soul to a star when that soul was created. A soul that has lived virtuously will return to its native star at death. The wicked soul, on the other hand, will transmigrate into some other body befitting its character in its previous life.

In *Phaedo*, Plato's account is different. Here he says that at death the good soul will depart to a better place; i.e., "that other land"[16] where one fully attains wisdom and dwells in the company of the gods. These are the souls of philosophers. The fates of other kinds of souls are different. Wicked souls are cast beneath the earth into Tartarus where, if they beseech those whom they have wronged, they abide only temporarily and return thereafter to another body. The more attached the soul is to the body during life, the more quickly transmigration to another body occurs.

---

14. In *Republic*, the parts of the soul and their functions find analogous counterparts in the three kinds of people in the ideal city: the guardians (rulers) and the artisans and warriors (the ruled).

15. Plato, *Phaed.* 63c–68b.

16. Plato, *Phaed.* 64a.

The worst souls abide in Tartarus forever. The souls that were good in life, but did not commit to philosophy, transmigrate into some social or gentle species such as bees, wasps, or ants, if not into another human body.

## Aristotle

### *The Life of Aristotle*

Born in Macedonia (384 BCE), Aristotle arrived in Athens at age seventeen to study in Plato's Academy. Here he remained for twenty years until Plato's death in 347 BCE. When leadership of the Academy passed to Plato's nephew Speusippus, Aristotle departed. Upon his return in 335 BCE, he established a rival school in the Lyceum, teaching in its promenade and notoriously pacing as he taught. Thus his circle came to be known as the "Peripatetics" ("walking around").

The breadth of Aristotle's philosophical interests exceeded that of any of his predecessors. He studied natural philosophy with alacrity, extending the pre-Socratic investigation of basic natural "principles" into the specialized study of plants, animals, marine biology, geographical features, meteorological phenomena, and more. Notably, he also speculated about forces outside of the physical universe, thus advancing, like Plato, from physics to metaphysics. He made significant advances in logic, particularly in the study of syllogisms and informal logic. He also carried forward the interests of Socrates and Plato in ethics, like them designating virtue as the highest of all goods that lead to happiness. It is a testament to his reputation as a philosopher that Philip of Macedon enlisted him for a time as the private tutor to his son Alexander, the future "Great." Aristotle died in 322 BCE, one year after Alexander.

As a philosopher, Aristotle showed some level of commitment to Plato. Yet, many of his doctrines are either explicit or implicit responses to him. Given both the size of his corpus and the breadth of his interests, Aristotle's philosophy is more difficult to summarize than his teacher's. It is said, however, that his followers (if not Aristotle himself) accepted the same threefold division of philosophy's departments that was implicit in Plato and explicitly recognized by Plato's successors: (meta)physics, logic, and ethics.[17]

### *Key Concepts*

It is challenging to find in Aristotle's works a fully integrated philosophical system. Several key concepts, however, underlie many of the topics he treats across his works and together unlock a certain coherence behind his wide-ranging thought.

Of first importance are his four causes: the material, the formal, the efficient, and the final. Any explanation for anything, Aristotle maintained, is essentially an explanation of these causes. Hence, for any philosophical explanation to be sufficient, it is necessary to address all four of them. For instance, one might ex-

17. See note 6 above.

plain a statue in the following way.[18] Bronze causes the statue's existence in that it constitutes the *material* out of which the statue is composed. The shape of the bronze in the *form* of a statue causes it to be a statue as opposed to something else. The sculptor causes the *effect* of a statue by imposing this form on the bronze matter. The *final* cause of the statue is that for which it was created: for instance, to honor the one it represents. Since explicating the four causes is essential to any philosophical explanation, Aristotle applies the four causes to various areas of inquiry throughout his works, including matters related to the soul, metaphysics, ethics, and politics.

Also foundational is Aristotle's distinction between potentiality and actuality. He employs this distinction to explicate various concepts like substance, existence, motion and rest, and causality. The distinction closely correlates with the above distinction between material and formal cause. In this regard, the *substance* of a thing—its "whatness"—is defined in terms of both its matter and its form: matter is *potentiality* (that which has the potential to become a certain thing), and form is its *actuality* (that into which the matter is actually molded).

Another central concept are his categories. Aristotle offers ten categories of existing things, here introducing his famous distinction between substance and *accidence*. Of the ten categories, the category of substance is the most fundamental. Substance is that *of which* something can be said or predicated. An accident is a feature that *exists in* a substance. For instance, in the sentence "Socrates is a human," the predicate "human" is *said of* Socrates. However, in the sentence "Socrates is bald," the predicate "bald" is not *said of* Socrates but *is in* Socrates. The difference is that humanness is an essential, ineliminable quality of what makes Socrates Socrates, whereas Socrates would still be Socrates whether or not he had hair. In short, humanness is an essential feature of Socrates's substance. Baldness is an accidental feature. The substance of Socrates, in other words, must be defined in terms not of accidental predicates but of essential ones. Aristotle asserts that his distinction of categories is what makes possible the application of more than one predicate-relation to a substance. Each of these predicates in turn represents another category. Socrates can now be not only human (the category of substance), but also five feet tall (the category of quantity), white (the category of quality), dressed (the category of *having*), and so on for other categories.

Of substances, Aristotle also said that some are primary and some are secondary. Secondary substances depend on primary substances for their existence. Horses, for instance, exist only if individual horses exist. The individual horse therefore is a primary substance and the *genus* of horses is a secondary substance. This distinction corresponds with what are often called "particulars" (primary substances) and "universals" (secondary substances). Applying this distinction to the question of essential predicates, a primary substance would be that which exists *in itself* and not *in* anything else. A secondary substance would be that which exists only *in* another substance.

---

18. Example from Christopher Shields, *Ancient Philosophy: A Contemporary Introduction*, 2nd ed. (New York: Routledge, 2023), 142.

## *Metaphysics*

### God

Like Plato, Aristotle surmised that something exists outside of the material universe. In his treatise *Metaphysics*, he identifies this something as God. This God has no body and therefore no soul. God is pure Intellect, an activity consisting of nothing but thinking, specifically thinking of Itself. Aristotle designates God also as the first or unmoved mover because through thinking, God moves the universe, beginning from the outer celestial sphere. Thus the mover is the efficient cause of the universe.

### The Soul

Aristotle lays out his theory of the soul in a work aptly titled *On the Soul*. According to Aristotle, all living things as substances have both "body" (*sōma*) and "soul" (*psychē*). In defining the relationship between body and soul, Aristotle applies both his theory of causes and his theory of potentiality-actuality. Indeed, an animal as such is "caused" by both the material cause of body and the formal cause of soul. The soul therefore is not material (for it is the body that is material) nor is it immaterial (for it is not separable from the particular body of which it is the formal cause). To use an analogy, the body is to wax as the soul is to a candle: the wax is the material cause, the candle the formal cause. Or to use a previous example, the body is to bronze as the soul is to the statue: bronze is the material cause, the statue is the formal cause. As the form of a body, a soul cannot exist outside of a body. Nor can a body (continue to) exist without a soul, its formal cause. Here the concept of potentiality and actuality again surfaces: The body is potentially a living thing, and the soul the actuality of its being alive.

While all living things have souls, not all souls are alike. Nutritive souls have only the capacity for growth (as in plants). Sensitive souls have the capacity not only for growth, but also sensation and thought (as in animals). Rational souls possess, in addition to these faculties, the faculty of reason (as in human beings). A human being as such therefore is defined by the faculty of reason, which when functioning constitutes "mind" (*nous*). Yet, since the *nous* is not at every moment operative, a human being must be defined as potentially a reasoning being, and actually so only when the *nous* is at work. Although as formal cause of a living being, a soul cannot exist apart from the body, the *nous* function can.

## *Logic*

Aristotle made major contributions to the study of logic, dividing this department into the branches of "demonstration" and "argumentation." Demonstration (*apodeixis*) involves scientific deduction from self-evident principles or premises universally accepted, resulting in a sure conclusion. Demonstration corresponds to what is usually called "formal logic." Aristotle discusses this kind of logic in his *Posterior Analytics*. In distinction from demonstration, argumentation (*dialectikē*) consists in logic based on probabilities or commonly accepted premises—or in any case, opinions that commend themselves "to all or to the majority of the wise."[19] In argumentation, one attempts not simply to demonstrate what everyone already agrees upon, but to persuade an audience to accept a conclusion predicated only on premises they are likely to accept.

Aristotle divides argumentation, in turn, into two subdivisions: dialectic and rhetoric.[20] As a kind of argumentation, *dialectic* is a form of inductive reasoning in which the subject works from commonly accepted premises to likely conclusions in search of general truths, especially truths of interest to philosophers. When an argument is not sound but fallacious, it is considered "contentious reasoning" and qualifies as sophistry.[21] Dialectic is the subject of several of Aristotle's treatises, including the *Topics* (on how to find arguments) and *On Sophistical Refutations* (dealing with fallacies). *Rhetoric* is an outgrowth of dialectic, since it also concerns persuasion from probable premises to an intended conclusion.[22] Whereas dialectic , however, is concerned with sound argumentation in search of general *truth*, rhetoric concerns the discovery of every possible argument with an end to *persuasion* (*to pithanon*) of an audience, particularly as regards concrete or practical situations. In this regard, rhetoric involves not only logical proofs (*logos*) like enthymemes (thus including dialectic), but also "inartificial" proofs such as appeal to laws, witnesses, or contracts, as well as proofs from the speaker's character (*ēthos*) and manner of delivery (*pathos*). The earliest extant treatise on the art of rhetoric, Aristotle's *On Rhetoric*, covers three of what became the traditional five parts of rhetorical theory: invention, arrangement, and style (the others are memory and delivery).[23]

## *Ethics*

### Virtue and the Happy Life

The fullest account of Aristotle's ethics can be found in his *Nichomachean Ethics*. The treatise begins: "Every art and every investigation, and likewise every practical pursuit or undertaking, seems to aim at some good: hence it has been well said that the Good is That at which all things aim."[24] In other words, every pursuit, art, or science has its own end, goal, or *telos*: For example, the *telos* of the science of medicine is health, the *telos* of the art of shipbuilding is a vessel, and so forth. Virtually everything done is done for the sake of something else; i.e., for some other end. That, however, for which all other things are done, and which is sought not for the sake of something else but for its own sake, will be the highest end. This Aristotle calls the good (*tagathon*), or indeed, the supreme good (*ariston*).[25] Moreover,

19. Aristotle, *Top.* 100b; distinction in 100a–b.
20. A division later accepted by the Stoics (see chapter 8).
21. Aristotle, *Top.* 100b; *Rhet.* 1.1.14.
22. Aristotle, *Rhet.* 1.1.14.
23. "Parts" (*partes*): Quintilian, *Inst.* 3.3.11; cf. Cicero, *Or.* 1.142; alternatively, "duties" (*officia*): Ps.-Cicero, *Rhet.* 2.1.1; or "functions" (*opera*): Quintilian, *Inst.* 3.3.11.
24. Aristotle, *Eth. nic.* 1.1.1.
25. Aristotle, *Eth. nic.* 1.2.1.

he identifies this goal, or good, as happiness or *eudaimonia*. Hence, the *happy* life constitutes "the *good* life" (*to eu zēn*).[26] For Aristotle, apart from the virtues—which alone are choices worthy in themselves—all other ends are merely instrumental toward the final goal of happiness.

According to Aristotle, the majority of people agree that happiness is indeed the highest good. Aristotle adds, however, that what exactly *constitutes* the happy life is debatable. He proposes that there are essentially three kinds of life, each corresponding with certain prioritized goods. Ordinary people, he says, look for happiness in "some obvious and visible good, such as pleasure or wealth or honour."[27] Hence, they seek either the life of enjoyment (which is pleasure seeking) or the life of politics (which seeks honor). Aristotle, however, observes that the goods of wealth, pleasure, and honor do not generate the complete happiness they seem to promise. In his view, the most complete happiness is achieved in a third sort of life—the one chosen by philosophers—namely, the life of contemplation.

In his classification of goods, Aristotle shares with Plato not only the threefold distinction between external goods (honor, wealth), goods of the body (pleasure), and goods of the soul (the virtues),[28] but also Plato and Socrates's view that the highest goods are those of the soul: i.e., the virtues.[29] If, in sum, the goods of the soul are nothing other than virtue, then it is life "in conformity with virtue" in which happiness consists.

Putting all this together, life in conformity with virtue is the very sum and substance of the Life of Contemplation, which is in consequence the best kind of life. Aristotle's preferred term for "virtue" (*aretē*), however, encompasses more than just ethics in the modern sense. Rather, it represents "excellence" (*aretē*) more broadly. The idea is this: Each living thing has some end for which it strives and that defines its excellence. For instance, it is the excellence of a plant to grow and of an animal to both grow and sense. But it is the excellence of a human being to exercise reason (*nous*), for this activity is unique to humans (and God). In other words, human excellence (virtue) consists in contemplation, in which humanity imitates God.

Aristotle distinguishes *two* types of virtue. Contemplation represents theoretical virtue, the excellence of theorizing. This is the highest form of rational activity possible; indeed, it is an *activity* and not just a *disposition* of the mind. In distinction from theoretical virtue is ethical virtue, which includes practical virtues such as generosity and temperance.[30]

---

26. Aristotle, *Eth. nic.* 1.4.2.

27. Aristotle, *Eth. nic.* 1.4.3.

28. Aristotle, *Eth. nic.* 1.8.2.

29. Aristotle, *Eth. nic.* 1.8.3. This view was espoused by a majority of the Greco-Roman philosophical schools throughout antiquity; see, however, the discussion on the Cyrenaics (ch. 6) and Epicureans (ch. 9).

30. See the distinction between "intellectual" and "ethical" virtues in Aristotle, *Eth. nic.* 1.13.20.

Aristotle maintains that while practicing the goods of the soul is sufficient for happiness, bodily and external goods can nevertheless *add* to happiness—an idea some later philosophers will contest.[31] While this point may seem to make happiness dependent on the vicissitudes of fortune—as fortune can take away "goods" just as readily as it can give them—Aristotle insists that one is able to reach the threshold of happiness without these goods, since the virtues are higher in the scale of value, are more permanent, and can occupy a person more continually than other goods.[32] Finally, once one reaches the goal of happiness, one will remain happy for the remainder of life, since one "will be always or at least most often employed in doing and contemplating the things that are in conformity with virtue."[33]

### The Ethical Mean

For Aristotle, virtue lies at a particular point on a gradient of action. Specifically, the sort of activity that qualifies as excellent is that which aims at a mean (*mesotēs*) between the extremes of excess (*hyperbolē*) and deficiency (*elleipsis*).[34] Virtue is located at the mean, vice at the extremes. For instance, temperance is the mean between the excesses of too much and too little; courage is the mean between the excesses of temerity and foolhardiness. We discern the mean through practical wisdom, or *phronēsis*. A virtue in itself, *phronēsis* gives us the ability to adjudicate how best to act—or to discern wherein the mean lies—under specific circumstances.

### Knowledge and Ethical Weakness

As virtue is a kind of rational excellence, vice is a product of ignorance. For Aristotle, there are then essentially four kinds of person. (1) The virtuous person, possessing secure knowledge, does right without ever wavering. (2) The vicious person does wrong without even deliberating. Between are the temperate person and the intemperate person. (3) The temperate person does the right thing but after being tempted by contrary cognitive impressions as to what is right. (4) The intemperate person is tempted by contrary impressions but ultimately does what is wrong. These two intermediate persons are subject to what Aristotle calls *akrasia*, or "weakness." Those in a state of *akrasia* both know and do not know what is right. They are torn between contrary cognitive impressions.

Fortunately, *akrasia* can be overcome, though perhaps not immediately. Virtues are strengthened by habit (ethos); gradually, habits form character (not *ethos* but *ēthos*); and out of character comes action. Aristotle's theory of *progressive* moral improvement stands in stark contrast with the doctrine of instantaneous transformation associated with one of the chief schools to emerge in the generation following him—namely, the Stoic school, which we will discuss in chapter 7.

---

31. Aristotle, *Eth. nic.* 1.10.9, 15.
32. Aristotle, *Eth. nic.* 1.10.10.
33. Aristotle, *Eth. nic.* 1.10.11.
34. This applies only to virtues of character, not intellectual virtue.

## Notes on the Primary Sources

### *Plato*

Plato left no philosophical treatises. Rather, his works belong almost exclusively to the genre of philosophical dialogue. More than three dozen authentic dialogues are extant, in addition to a few likely pseudonymous ones. Scholars usually separate the dialogues into Socratic and Platonic dialogues. The early Socratic dialogues instantiate the historical Socrates's real style of dialogue, and as such are genuinely skeptical ("inquiring") and aporetic. Examples of Socratic dialogues include *Euthyphro*, *Crito*, *Alcibiades*, and *Charmides*, among others. The later Platonic dialogues are more dogmatic; they drift away from the standard Socratic encounter; and even when Socrates is the central character, Plato essentially uses him as a mouthpiece to advance his own positive assertions. Examples of Platonic dialogues include *Timaeus*, *Critias*, *Sophist*, *Statesman*, and *Laws*. Chronologically, the dialogues also develop in the form of presentation. Whereas the earlier dialogues feature conversations punctuated by more succinct questions and answers and frequent interruptions of participants, the later dialogues tend to be much longer and more technical and feature protracted discourses with scant interruption. There seems to have been a period of transition between the early and late dialogues, sometimes called the middle period. It was during this time that Plato wrote his lengthy *Republic* as well as *Protagoras*, *Phaedrus*, *Phaedo*, *Parmenides*, and *Meno*.

In addition to Plato's many dialogues is his *Apology*, which presents as the defense speech given by Socrates at his trial. The content is probably true to the actual speech, even if the speech is not a verbatim record (see ch. 4). Apart from Plato's own works are various testimonia about him, some of which can be found in Book 6 of Diogenes Laërtius's *Lives of Eminent Philosophers*. In Book 3, Diogenes includes Plato's own biography.

### *Aristotle*

Diogenes Laërtius's biography of Aristotle in *Lives of Eminent Philosophers* 5.1–35 lists over one hundred and fifty works of Aristotle. Of these, perhaps only one-fifth are extant, though other works survive that Diogenes omits. Aristotle and ancient testimony distinguish between his esoteric and exoteric works.[35] The extant works do not seem to fit Cicero's characterization of Aristotle as consummately eloquent,[36] a fact that suggests the extant works may constitute something like lecture notes, thus representing Aristotle's esoteric rather than his exoteric works, intended for his students rather than for publication. Hence it may be, ironically, the exoteric works that are now lost (at least mostly). In any case, both the extant works and Diogenes's list illustrate how broadly Aristotle ranged in his study. He wrote philosophical treatises about justice, politics, ethics, the poets, the soul, and

35. Aristotle, *Pol.* 1278b 33; *Eth. Eud.* 1217b 24, 1218b 34–35.

36. Cicero, *Acad.* 2.38.119; cf. *Top.* 1.3; *Or.* 1.2.49.

rhetoric, and about a host of "natural" topics including plants and animals, not to mention the Nile River. Among his more significant treatises are *Nicomachean Ethics*, *Politics*, *Categories*, *Topica*, *Rhetoric*, *Metaphysics*, and *On the Soul.*

## Key Terms and Concepts

### *Plato*

- Cardinal virtues, the four
- Cave myth, the
- Demiurge, the
- Forms
- Good, the
- Goods, three types
- Irrational soul, spirited and appetitive parts
- Parts of philosophy, the three
- Passions, the four
- Rational soul
- Recollection (*anamnēsis*)
- Sensible vs. insensible objects of perception
- Socratic vs. Platonic dialogues
- Soul's chariot myth, the
- Transmigration (*metempsychōsis*) of the soul

### *Aristotle*

- Accidence
- Actuality
- Categories
- Dialectic
- Esoteric vs. exoteric works
- Ethos vs. ēthos
- First (or unmoved) mover
- Four causes
- Happiness (*eudaimonia*)
- Potentiality
- Practical wisdom (*phronēsis*)
- Primary vs. secondary substance
- Rhetoric
- Substance
- Supreme good
- Virtue, theoretical and practical
- Weakness (*akrasia*)

## For Further Study

### *Plato*

Annas, Julia. *Plato: A Very Short Introduction.* Oxford: Oxford University Press, 2003.

Benson, Hugh, ed. *A Companion to Plato.* Oxford: Blackwell, 2006.

Ebrey, David, and Richard Kraut, eds. *The Cambridge Companion to Plato.* 2nd ed. Cambridge Companions to Philosophy. Cambridge: Cambridge University Press, 2022.

Mason, Andrew S. *Plato.* Ancient Philosophies. Durham: Acumen, 2010.

Peterson, Sandra. *Socrates and Philosophy in the Dialogues of Plato.* Cambridge: Cambridge University Press, 2011.

Press, Gerald A., and Mateo Duque, eds. *The Bloomsbury Handbook of Plato.* 2nd ed. Bloomsbury Handbooks. London: Bloomsbury, 2023.

Waterfield, Robin. *Plato of Athens: A Life in Philosophy.* Oxford: Oxford University Press, 2023.

### *Aristotle*

Adamson, Peter. *Classical Philosophy: A History of Philosophy without Any Gaps.* Vol. 1. Oxford: Oxford University Press, 2014.

Blackson, Thomas A. *Ancient Greek Philosophy: From the Presocratics to the Hellenistic Philosophers.* Malden, MA: Wiley-Blackwell, 2011.

Meyer, Susan Sauvé. *Aristotle: How to Flourish; An Ancient Guide to Living Well.* Ancient Wisdom for Modern Readers. Princeton, NJ: Princeton University Press, 2023.

Natali, Carlo. *Aristotle: His Life and School.* Princeton, NJ: Princeton University Press, 2013.

# 6

# Cynicism and Other Socratic Philosophies

Socrates inspired not just one, but many of his students to found philosophical sects after his passing. Early tradition identifies a certain set of his students as "the Socratics" (*hoi Socratikoi*). Apart from Plato, four of these individuals founded new philosophical sects (or in one case, a movement). The most successful and long-lasting was the Cynic movement, which, although founded by Antisthenes, found its most infamous representative in his disciple Diogenes of Sinope, "the Dog." While both descended from Socrates, Plato and Antisthenes represented separate branches of the Socratic legacy, out of which other schools sprang in the Hellenistic period including the New Academy in the line of Plato and the Stoic school in the line of the Cynics (see fig. 1).[1]

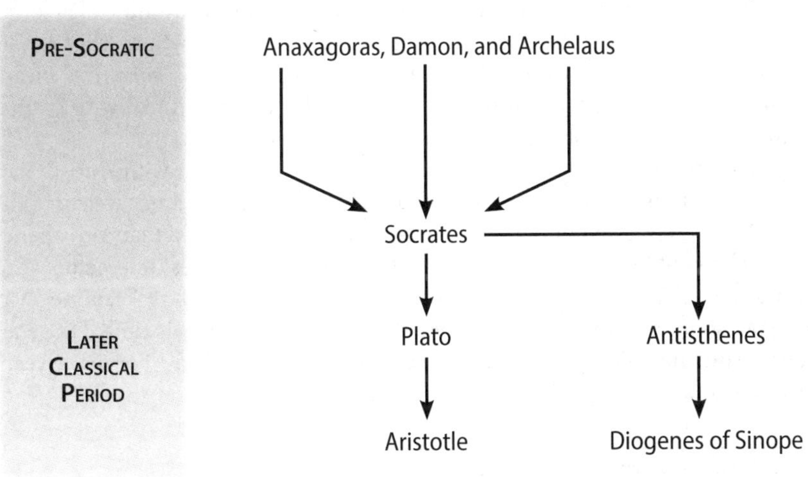


Figure 1. Traditional succession in the line of Socrates.[2]

1. Diogenes Laërtius, *Vit. phil.* 1.13–15.
2. Diogenes Laërtius, *Vit. phil.* 1.13–15; 2.19.

## Cynicism

### *Origins*

Antisthenes (mid-fifth–mid-fourth century BCE) was born a citizen of Athens, the son of an Athenian father and a Thracian mother. Well educated, he studied with the eminent sophist Gorgias and became an accomplished orator. He later encountered Socrates and was so taken with him that he would hike five miles to Athens every day to hear him speak and advised his own students to join him.[3] Antisthenes admired Socrates especially for his example of steadfastness against hardship and for his stoic disregard of feelings. Imitating these qualities fully, Antisthenes adopted a way of life that came to be known as the Cynic (*kynikos*) life.[4]

Although Antisthenes was the true founder of Cynicism,[5] his student Diogenes of Sinope (b. ca. 412/403–d. ca. 324/321 BCE) became antiquity's most paradigmatic representative of the Cynic way of life. Diogenes advocated for opposition to established social institutions and radicalized Antisthenes's ideas about endurance of hardship by underscoring the importance of moral training (*askēsis*) through voluntary suffering.

Tradition attributes Diogenes's defiance of social convention to an encounter he had with the oracle at Delphi. According to the story, the oracle had given him permission to alter the "political currency" (*to politikon nomisma*); but Diogenes, not understanding what this meant, instead adulterated the *coinage* in his home state of Sinope. When his deed was discovered, he was forced into exile—or as another version of the story goes, he took himself into exile voluntarily.[6] It was only later that he realized the oracle's true meaning: Altering the "currency" meant rejecting social convention and returning to the dictates of nature, living in total freedom from the precepts and customs devised by society.[7]

Having come in his exile to Athens, Diogenes there fell in with Antisthenes and beseeched him to be his teacher. Although Antisthenes did not welcome students, Diogenes wearied him with his persistence. A story is told that Antisthenes once reached out his staff to strike him, but "the pupil [Diogenes] offered his head with the words, 'Strike, for you will find no wood hard enough to keep me away from you, so long as I think you've something to say.' " From this time, Diogenes became Antisthenes's student and followed his simple way of life.[8] For many years, he lived in a tub in the public portico in Athens.[9]

3. Diogenes Laërtius, *Vit. phil.* 6.2.

4. Diogenes Laërtius, *Vit. phil.* 6.2.

5. Diogenes Laërtius, *Vit. phil.* 1.19; 6.2; and a majority of scholars at present, according to Marie-Odile Goulet-Cazé, *Cynicism and Christianity in Antiquity* (Grand Rapids: Eerdmans, 2019), 8–9. Philodemus, however, claims that the Stoics overemphasized the role of Antisthenes in order to connect their lineage back to Socrates (*On the Stoics* 3 [= *P.Herc.* 339, col. 13.1–9]).

6. Diogenes Laërtius, *Vit. phil.* 6.20–21.

7. Diogenes Laërtius, *Vit. phil.* 6.71.

8. Diogenes Laërtius, *Vit. phil.* 6.21 (LCL, Hicks).

9. Diogenes Laërtius, *Vit. phil.* 6.23.

Tradition offers conflicting explanations for the origins of the name "Cynic" (*kynikos*)/"Cynicism" (*kynismos*). Related to the word "dog" (*kyōn*), the name was said by some to have derived from the gymnasium where Antisthenes taught—namely, the Cynosarges (*Kynosarges*), meaning "white hound." Antisthenes himself was called a "hound" (*Haplokyōn*).[10] Diogenes, on the other hand, acquired the moniker "Diogenes the *dog*" (*kyōn*), which ample evidence attests had an integral connection with Diogenes's canine habits and way of life.[11]

## *Defining Cynicism*

Since antiquity, many have debated whether Cynicism is rightly considered a philosophical "school" or sect (*hairesis*).[12] The Cynics never devised a complex philosophical system, much less any extensive or unique doctrinal content. There were no Cynic heads of school (*scholarchoi*) and hence no successors (*diadochoi*). Many ancients therefore considered Cynicism a way of life (*entasis biou*) rather than a philosophical sect (*hairesis*) per se. Indeed, the Cynics themselves emphasized the priority of practice or training over written rules.[13] They boasted that this approach allowed the Cynic philosopher to bypass extensive technical study and thus to cut a "short path" to happiness.[14]

Cynicism's disengagement from dogma, however, freed Cynics to pursue the Cynic way of life while also adopting the dogmas of other schools, if they so chose.[15] While ancient sources often associate Cynicism with Stoic doctrines,[16] the latter were not intrinsic to Cynicism as a philosophy since, again, Cynicism was not intrinsically connected with dogma. Sources that present Cynicism in Stoic terms are rather "Stoicizing" Cynicism by joining Stoic doctrinal content with the Cynic way of life.[17]

Having then no established orthodoxy, Cynicism is perhaps more appropriately defined in terms of a cluster of common commitments or behaviors, many of which can be distilled into summary slogans.[18] (1) The idea of "altering the currency" was foundational to the Cynic way of life. Diogenes believed that social customs, civic laws, and even common religious beliefs were inventions of society—mere conventions—and that the only legitimate basis for belief and lifestyle was

10. Diogenes Laërtius, *Vit. phil.* 6.13.

11. E.g., Diogenes Laërtius, *Vit. phil.* 6.46; see also 6.60; Diogenes, *Epistle 28*, 1; Lucian, *Vit. auct.* 7; Dio Chrysostom, *Or.* 8.36.

12. Diogenes Laërtius, *Vit. phil.* 6.103; Augustine, *Civ.* 19.1.3; relying on Varro; cf. Diogenes Laërtius, *Vit. phil.* 1.19–20.

13. Diogenes Laërtius, *Vit. phil.* 6.48.

14. Diogenes, *Epistle 30*, 1–2; Lucian, *Vit. auct.* 11; Crates, *Epistle 16*, 2–3.

15. Augustine, *Civ.* 19.1.3; relying on Varro.

16. Diogenes Laërtius, *Vit. phil.* 6.103–4.

17. See for instance Epictetus's portrait of the ideal Cynic, in *Diatr.* 3.22.

18. Goulet-Cazé, *Cynicism and Christianity*, 85–86; summarizing the basics of Cynicism, 35–53. Downing focuses on "family resemblances" among Cynics in themes, attitudes, and commitments: F. Gerald Downing, *Cynics and Christian Origins* (Edinburgh: T&T Clark, 1992), 26–56, esp. 54.

nature itself. To "alter the currency" meant pushing against everything humanity had institutionalized and establishing new "currency," even if it required behaving in ways society deemed indecent. In this regard, the Cynics warned against the corrupting influence of the crowd and preached the importance of segregating oneself from it. (2) Cynic philosophers detached personal identity from the ordinary markers of kinship and political status, viewing themselves as citizens of the world. (3) The Cynics agreed with other philosophers that the ultimate goal of philosophy was happiness, yet they insisted that happiness is only guaranteed if one is able to withstand whatever assails it. In this regard, they considered pleasure to be a bad thing; for anything on which happiness depends that can also be taken away—as pleasure can be—is unreliable and therefore not worthy of being desired. (4) Cynics believed that one's changing fortunes were not determined by providence or intrinsic to a larger plan that is for the ultimate good of the universe. Rather, our experiences are a brute fact of the universe with which we must simply come to grips. (5) Practice, or training, was of the highest importance. The philosophical life is like an athletic contest. One wears out the body with physical training in order to make it stronger, more durable, and more capable of outperforming opponents. In the same way, philosophers put themselves through a rigorous regimen of self-inflicted hardship so that when struck by misfortunes outside their control, they can withstand these involuntary hardships. If through voluntary training they can build the toughness to remain unperturbed also in involuntary circumstances, then they are capable of sustaining happiness in any circumstances whatsoever. They have become self-sufficient (*autarkēs*). (6) Cynics held that nothing is good but virtue alone—and in particular, the virtues of self-mastery, impassivity, and firmness of soul, which training produces through subjection to hardship. (7) From the Cynic perspective, most people are so entrenched in the ways of society that they can only be freed from the bonds of convention through the philosopher's sharp tongue. The philosopher was like a physician, who sometimes had to resort to the scalpel to remedy malignant ailments. The Cynics' tongue was their scalpel. They imposed no limits on their free speech (*parrhēsia*) in service of correction. (8) The Cynics went about homeless, believing that their needs were no greater than what nature provided. They did, however, beg alms, believing these to be due payment for their guidance and correction of fellow humanity. (9) The Cynics' dress was suited to their ascetic lifestyle. Antisthenes established the standard equipment of a coarse cloak (folded over when cold), a staff, and a wallet as his only possessions.[19] So defining was their dress that opponents often accused Cynics of equating their dress and the standard beard with being a philosopher.[20]

The Greek demigod Heracles (or Roman Hercules) played a paradigmatic role for the Cynics. From their perspective, Heracles was, if not the founder of the

19. Diogenes Laërtius, *Vit. phil.* 6.13; cf. Diogenes, *Epistle 7*, 17–21; *Epistle 30*, 3, 25–34. Diogenes of Sinope carried a cup and a bowl (Diogenes Laërtius, *Vit. phil.* 6.37; Diogenes, *Epistle 30*, 3; cf. Diogenes, *Epistle 34*, 3; Lucian, *Vit. auct.* 7) before discarding them when he realized they were unnecessary (Diogenes Laërtius, *Vit. phil.* 6.37).

20. Epictetus, *Diatr.* 3.22.10; cf. *Diatr.* 4.8.12, 15–16, 20; Lucian, *Dem.* 13; *Fug.* 13; Apuleius, *Flor.* 7.9–10.

Cynic way of life, certainly the most exemplary representative of it—a man crudely dressed in a lion's skin (his Cynic cloak), always bearing a club (his Cynic staff), known for enduring hardship, for his labors on behalf of humanity, and for being ridiculed by others as most wretched.[21] This could have described Diogenes himself.

### *Chreia Collections*

Since Cynicism was not a dogmatic school, no doctrinal treatises on Cynicism exist. The Cynics' emphasis on action, however, engendered a veritable new literary genre generally referred to as the *chreia* collection.[22] A *chreia* is a brief anecdote recording something that a specifically named person either said or did and that was preserved because it was considered useful (*chreia* means "useful"). The *chreia* collection thus gave definition to Cynicism not by outlining dogmatic precepts (which it did not have), but appropriately by presenting Cynics like Antisthenes and Diogenes as lived embodiments of a philosophy defined by action.[23] Many *chreia*, particularly those featuring Diogenes, became stock illustrations of philosophical ideals or exemplary behavior, especially among later Stoic writers.[24]

In the collections, *chreias* were strung together one after another, often without transition or thematic connection. Verbal *chreia* (preserving what a person said) could be reported directly or indirectly. For instance (direct speech): Antisthenes used to say "I'd rather be mad than feel pleasure" or "Virtue is the same for women as for men."[25] Or (indirect speech): "When Diogenes begged a coat of [Antisthenes], [Antisthenes] bade him fold his cloak around him double," "He would prove that nobility belongs to none other than the virtuous," or "He held virtue to be sufficient in itself to ensure happiness."[26] Some *chreia* specified a setting: "When [Antisthenes] was asked why he was so bitter in reproving his pupils he replied, 'Physicians are just the same with their patients.' "[27]

The role of Diogenes as the most paradigmatic Cynic is evinced by the quantity of *chreias* preserved about him. These present him as an embodiment of the core convictions of the Cynic way. It is said he learned how to adapt to circumstances by observing a mouse.[28] He accustomed himself to hardship by rolling in hot sand in summer and on the frozen earth in winter.[29] When someone asked him what he had gained from philosophy, he replied, "This at least, if nothing else—to be prepared for every fortune."[30] He was once found begging alms from a statue, and

---

21. Dio Chrysostom, *Or.* 8.26–35; Lucian, *Vit. auct.* 8; Diogenes, *Epistle 26*.

22. Goulet-Cazé, *Cynicism and Christianity*, 38–43.

23. Chreias of Antisthenes in Diogenes Laërtius, *Vit. phil.* 6.3–19; *chreias* of Diogenes of Sinope in Diogenes Laërtius, *Vit. phil.* 6.21–79.

24. Chreias about Diogenes used as exempla in, e.g., Epictetus, *Diatr.* 1.24.6–10; 4.1.152; Seneca, *Ira* 38.1–2; *Ben.* 5.4.3–4.

25. Diogenes Laërtius, *Vit. phil.* 6.3, 12 (LCL, Hicks).

26. Diogenes Laërtius, *Vit. phil.* 6.6, 10, 11 (LCL, Hicks).

27. Diogenes Laërtius, *Vit. phil.* 6.4 (LCL, Hicks).

28. Diogenes Laërtius, *Vit. phil.* 6.22.

29. Diogenes Laërtius, *Vit. phil.* 6.24.

30. Diogenes Laërtius, *Vit. phil.* 6.63 (LCL, Hicks).

when asked why he did so, he replied, "To get practice in being refused."[31] When asked where he came from, he said, "I am a citizen of the world."[32] Observing a child drinking out of his hands, he cast away the cup from his wallet (a bag used for traveling), saying, "A child has beaten me in plainness of living."[33]

The Cynic ideal of self-mastery is epitomized in a particularly impactful and characteristically humorous *chreia* about Diogenes. It is said that he was once captured by pirates on a voyage to Aegina and put up for sale. When the auctioneer asked him in what he was skilled, he replied, "In ruling men." He then pointed to a Corinthian man with a purple-bordered robe and said, "Sell me to this man; he needs a master," in this way alluding to mastery over his inner desires.[34] Cynic *parrhēsia*, or frank speech, is put on splendid display in another example. Once when Alexander the Great came to Corinth, he paid a visit to Diogenes and found him sunning himself. When Alexander offered to grant Diogenes anything he wished, Diogenes responded: "Stand out of my light."[35] Another *chreia* offers a consummate example of Cynic shamelessness, or as the Cynic might have put it, acting "according to nature." At a feast, people threw all the bones to Diogenes as if he were a dog. He responded by urinating on them, just like a dog.[36]

## Other Socratic Philosophies

Plato and Antisthenes were among the chief (*koryphaiotatoi*) and certainly the most influential successors of Socrates.[37] But these were not the only students of Socrates to found new philosophical movements. Among the ten individuals traditionally labeled as "Socratics" (*Socratikoi*),[38] five founded philosophical sects or movements: Plato founded the Academy, Antisthenes the Cynic movement, Euclides of Megara (ca. 450–380 BCE) the Megarian sect, Aristippus of Cyrene (late fifth–early fourth c. BCE) the Cyrenaic sect, and Phaedo of Elis (fifth–fourth c. BCE) the Eleatic sect.

The chief interests of the Megarian school were metaphysics and ethics—the former by the influence of Parmenides, the latter by the influence of Socrates.[39] A branch of the Megarian school known as the Dialectical school later influenced the Stoics' study of logic. The Megarian school, however, never emerged as a major philosophical force and died out within a century. The Cyrenaic school drew from Socrates an interest in ethics, though it advocated quite a different lifestyle from the kind Socrates might have approved. The school's founder, Aristippus, identified pleasure as the chief ethical end, underscoring especially the priority of present pleasure over future possibilities. Cyrenaicism died out during the Hellenistic

31. Diogenes Laërtius, *Vit. phil.* 6.49 (LCL, Hicks).
32. Diogenes Laërtius, *Vit. phil.* 6.63 (LCL, Hicks).
33. Diogenes Laërtius, *Vit. phil.* 6.37 (LCL, Hicks).
34. Diogenes Laërtius, *Vit. phil.* 6.74 (LCL, Hicks).
35. Diogenes Laërtius, *Vit. phil.* 6.38 (LCL, Hicks).
36. Diogenes Laërtius, *Vit. phil.* 6.46.
37. Diogenes Laërtius (*Vit. phil.* 2.47) includes Xenophon with Plato and Antisthenes.
38. Diogenes Laërtius, *Vit. phil.* 2.47.
39. Diogenes Laërtius, *Vit. phil.* 1.18.

period. Of Phaedo's philosophy, little is known. Its legacy continued in the Eretrian school, though its tenets remain obscure, and this school also expired early in the Hellenistic period.

## Notes on the Primary Sources

### *Cynicism*

Sources written by Cynics as Cynics are scarce, due naturally to Cynicism's emphasis on way of life over doctrine. Tradition attributes a number of writings to Diogenes of Sinope, though their authenticity has been disputed since antiquity.[40] Fragments are preserved of the Cynic poet Cercidas of Megalopolis (fl. 225 BCE) and of the one-time Cynic Bion of Borysthenes (ca. 335–ca. 245 BCE), as well as extracts from the Cynic Oenomaus of Gadara (fl. 120 CE). Book 6 of Diogenes Laërtius's *Lives of Eminent Philosophers* includes biographies of Antisthenes, Diogenes of Sinope, and several other Cynics from the fourth and third centuries BCE. These biographies are essentially *chreia* collections, in which many *chreias* are surely apocryphal. The biographies and doxographic material in Diogenes's discussion of Cynicism is among the material that tends to align Cynicism with Stoicism by attaching doctrinal content to it (cf. *Vit. phil.* 6.104; 7.121). Otherwise, most sources for ancient Cynicism derive from the post-Hellenistic era and represent the Cynicism of this latter period (which we will discuss in chapter 12).

### *Other Socratic Philosophies*

Diogenes Laërtius includes brief biographies of the founders of each of the Socratic schools: Aristippus, the founder of the Cyrenaic school (*Vit. phil.* 2.65–104); Euclides, the founder of the Megarian school (*Vit. phil.* 2.106–12); and Phaedo, the founder of the Eleatic school (*Vit. phil.* 2.105).

## Key Terms and Concepts

- Altering the currency
- *Askēsis* (practice)
- Chreia collection
- Citizen of the world
- Heracles/Hercules
- Living according to nature
- *Parrhēsia* (frank speech)
- Philosopher's dress, the
- Self-sufficiency (*autarkeia*)
- Shamelessness
- Way of life vs. sect (*hairesis*)

40. Diogenes Laërtius, *Vit. phil.* 6.80; cf. 6.23, 31, 73.

## For Further Study

### *Cynicism*

Adamson, Peter. *Philosophy in the Hellenistic and Roman Worlds: A History of Philosophy Without Any Gaps*. Vol. 2. Oxford: Oxford University Press, 2015.

Branham, R. Bracht, and Marie-Odile Goulet-Cazé, eds. *The Cynics: The Cynic Movement in Antiquity and Its Legacy*. Berkeley: University of California Press, 1996.

Desmond, W. *Cynics*. Stocksfield, UK: Acumen, 2008.

Goulet-Cazé, Marie-Odile. *Le cynisme, une philosophie antique*. Textes et traditions 29. Paris: Librairie Philosophique J. Vrin, 2017.

Shields, Christopher. *Ancient Philosophy: A Contemporary Introduction*. 2nd ed. Routledge Contemporary Introductions to Philosophy. New York: Routledge, 2023.

### *Other Socratic Philosophies*

Adamson, Peter. *Classical Philosophy: A History of Philosophy Without Any Gaps*. Vol. 1. Oxford: Oxford University Press, 2014.

Blackson, Thomas A. *Ancient Greek Philosophy: From the Presocratics to the Hellenistic Philosophers*. Malden, MA: Wiley-Blackwell, 2011.

Perilli, Lorenzo, and Daniela P. Taormina, eds. *Ancient Philosophy: A Textual and Historical Introduction*. New York: Routledge, 2017.

Shields, Christopher. *Ancient Philosophy: A Contemporary Introduction*. 2nd ed. Routledge Contemporary Introductions to Philosophy. New York: Routledge, 2023.

# Part 2

# Hellenistic Philosophy: Late Fourth to Early First Century BCE

# 7

# Introduction to Hellenistic Philosophy

Somewhat coincidentally, the stages of ancient philosophy correspond roughly with the chronological periods delineated in the modern study of Classical history. According to traditional periodization, the latter stages of Classical history began during the time of the Greco-Persian wars (first half of the fifth century BCE) and ended with the conquests of Alexander of Macedon over the Greeks (336–323 BCE). The Hellenistic era then spanned from the time of Alexander to the fall of the last of the Greek dynasties to the Romans at the Battle of Actium in 31 BCE.

TABLE 6. Ancient history and ancient philosophy

| ANCIENT HISTORY | | ANCIENT PHILOSOPHY | |
|---|---|---|---|
| Classical Era | ca. 480–323 BCE | Classical | ca. 550–300 BCE |
| Hellenistic Era | 323–31 BCE | Hellenistic | ca. 300–80 BCE |
| Roman Era | 31 BCE–476 CE | | |
| Early Roman Empire | 31 BCE–ca. 250 CE | Post-Hellenistic | ca. 80 BCE–ca. 250 CE |
| Late Antiquity | ca. 250–476 CE | Late Ancient | ca. 250–500 CE |

Major changes occurred in the history of Greek philosophy at the turn from the Classical era to the Hellenistic era and from the Hellenistic era to the Roman era. Thus the Hellenistic era of *history* (323–31 BCE) can be said to share roughly the same boundaries as the era of Hellenistic *philosophy*. New philosophical schools formed at the beginning of this period and achieved predominance over the Classical-era schools. Chief among the new schools were the Stoic school, the Epicurean school, and the New Academy. Of lesser note was the Pyrrhonist school. As this period ended, several philosophical movements that had previously dwindled or that had virtually disappeared after the Classical era experienced revivals. It was at this point also that Latin philosophy was born. In the time between, the nature of the philosophical quest shifted in several ways as schools became more sharply defined, doctrines more systematic, and philosophers' interests more practical.

TABLE 7. The primary Hellenistic schools

| SCHOOL | FOUNDER |
|---|---|
| The Stoics | Zeno of Citium |
| The Epicureans | Epicurus |
| The New Academy | Carneades [or Lacydes] |
| The Pyrrhonists | Pyrrho of Elis |

The present chapter succinctly introduces some of the main features that characterize the concerns and practices of these schools, as well as the general philosophical climate of this period. Individual treatment of the schools and the recurrence of these themes in respect to each of them will be reserved for chapters 8–10.

## Philosophy as a Way of Life

Even several generations after his death, it was Socrates who set the agenda for Hellenistic philosophy. For Socrates, as for his student Plato, the quest for wisdom was above all about discovering how to not simply live but to live well.[1] Since the quest was about *living* a certain way, philosophy was something to which one had to wholly devote oneself. The final goal was a transformation of the soul. This required a full program of "therapy" complete with "spiritual exercises" geared toward moral improvement. With the right kind of instruction, one could reach the highest level of human fulfillment, the final end toward which nature intends for us to live. In this way, one could become a true wise man.

While these concerns put ultimate stress on the side of practical application, it by no means precluded interest in theory (a theory of ethics, the study of logic, or speculation about nature). To know how best to live, we also need a well-considered, holistic account of why that way is best, how we know it is best, and how this sort of life relates to the nature of the universe. On these issues, philosophers of the Hellenistic period were sharply divided.

### *The Art of Living*

Several sources from the Hellenistic period define philosophy as the art of living.[2] This definition entails two related points. On the one hand, it presents philosophy as something that fundamentally concerns *how* one lives ("living"). On the other hand, it presents way of life as something undergirded by a particular theo-

1. Plato, *Crit.* 48b.

2. *Technē peri ton bion* (Sextus Empiricus, *Math.* 11.170//*SVF* 3.598) or *technē tou biou* (Epictetus, *Diatr.* 1.15.2). In Latin, *ars vitae* or *ars vivendi* (Cicero, *Fin.* 1.42, 72; 3.4; 4.19; 5.16, 18).

retical account of the best kind of life (the "art").[3] Here the word *art* (*technē, ars*) refers broadly to something like a craft, a specific domain of activity constituted by a set of unique skills and a clearly circumscribed body of knowledge. The "art" consists properly not in the doing but in the theoretical knowledge that undergirds the doing. In its concern with both practice and theory, the art of philosophy was analogous to any other art. Take the art of navigation. One could learn the *theory* of navigation without ever having steered a vessel. Yet a passenger will feel greater assurance in a captain who has at some time safely guided a vessel to its destination than the one who has never done so but understands how to in theory. In philosophy, as in navigation, theory is important but practice is paramount.

### Therapy for the Soul

Recalling Socrates's interest in the health of the soul, the Hellenistic philosophers commonly described philosophy as kind of "therapy for the soul" and the philosopher himself as a physician.[4] If vices could be considered diseases of the soul, then philosophy was the medicine to cure them. Like the body, the soul becomes healthier with exercise; and like treatments of the body, treatment of the soul requires a rigorous regimen of therapy. Thus the Hellenistic philosophers emphasized the necessity of repetitious doctrinal instruction, and of bringing doctrines frequently to mind lest one forget them or react inappropriately when life springs circumstances upon one. The philosophers recommended preparation for hypothetical situations by mentally rehearsing appropriate reactions in advance. In short, living out doctrines in real life took consistent and sustained practice.

### Spiritual Exercises

Practice was a special emphasis of the Stoics.[5] The term "practice," or *askēsis* (whence the English word *ascetic*), became almost a technical term for living out one's philosophy. As a mode of *askēsis*, the Stoics devised certain kinds of rehearsals or "spiritual exercises." These practices represented, one might say, "practice in preparation for practice."[6]

### Lives and Exempla

Out of the Hellenistic philosophers' keen practical interest grew a prevalence of certain literary forms and literary genres. Appeal to ancient and contemporary exemplars who embodied the principles of philosophy—people who could

3. Philosophers commonly distinguished between "deeds" and "words," or *erga* (works) and *logos* (theory): Musonius Rufus, *Diatr.* 1; 5; cf. *Diatr.* 5 (*praxis* vs. *logos*); Dio Chrysostom, *Or.* 18.17; Seneca, *Ep.* 20.2 (*facere* vs. *legere*); 34.4 (*facta* vs. *dicta*).

4. This language is especially common in Epicurean sources. Cf. Epicurus, *Ep. Men.* 122//Diogenes Laërtius, *Vit. phil.* 10.122; and ch. 9 of the present book.

5. Clement of Alexandria, *Strom.* 7.16//*SVF* 3.490; Musonius Rufus, fr. 6//Stobaeus, *Anth.* 3.29.78; and Diogenes Laërtius, *Vit. phil.* 6.70.

6. Lee (*Moral Transformation*, 356) explains that "spiritual exercise" is a traditional translation of the phrase *askēseis tēs psychēs*. Lee summarizes exercises common among the Neostoics on pp. 360–2.

be considered *paradeigmata* or *exempla*—became exceedingly common in the discourse of moral philosophy. Biographies (*bioi*) of philosophers complemented doctrinal treatises by focusing on their exemplary lives. By their nature, *chreia* collections (see chapter 6) were geared less toward teaching doctrine than toward illustrating a life.

### *Philosophy and the Good Life*

For the Hellenistic philosophers, philosophy promised to do what nothing else could: Make a person supremely happy.[7] As Aristotle observed, happiness is the end toward which all people aim, yet he noted that most people look for happiness in things that cannot guarantee it.[8] Indeed, if happiness depended on wealth, power, reputation, or good health, then happiness would be vulnerable to the vicissitudes of circumstance.[9] Even if happiness could be gained this way (and that is questionable), then it could also be lost.

The philosophers reflected that if happiness depends on something altogether different, something entirely within our control, then everyone could not only achieve it but achieve it now—and perhaps even for as long as one lived. In fact, they contended that happiness is, indeed, within our control and that we as human beings inherently have the potential to reach it.[10] Put in a different way, that of which happiness consists—whatever that "good" thing might be—is the kind of thing we as humans can reach based on the faculties *naturally available* to us. One need not resort to prayer.[11] Religion, in any case, cannot avail us.[12] Only philosophy can promise the good life. And we need not wait until death. Philosophy can bring it now.

Among themselves, philosophers nevertheless debated what exactly that good was that if attained might make us supremely happy. The schools that traced their lineage back to Socrates generally identified this good with virtue.[13] In virtue is happiness; virtue is possible to attain by the inward resources available to us; and because virtue is something achieved from within, its acquisition never depends on circumstances, as the acquisition of external things does. One has only to turn to philosophy, which alone not only shows the way[14] but indeed guarantees happiness.[15]

Even philosophers who located the highest good elsewhere than virtue (for instance, the Epicureans located the good in pleasure) agreed that human beings have

---

7. Lucretius, *Rer. nat.* 1.146–8; 2.14–62; Cicero, *Tusc.* 5.1.1–2; 5.2.5.

8. Aristotle, *Eth. nic.* 1.4.1–1.5.6.

9. Seneca, *Ep.* 41.7–9.

10. Cicero, *Tusc.* 5.28.82.

11. Cicero, *Tusc.* 1.5.2; Seneca, *Ep.* 41.1.

12. See note 7 above.

13. Diogenes Laërtius (*Vit. phil.* 1.13–14) places the Socratic tradition in the Ionian lineage and the Epicurean tradition within the Italian. While the Epicureans dissented from the view that virtue was the highest end, locating it instead in "pleasure," they nevertheless believed that pleasure did not depend on externals but on a disposition of the mind "free from disturbance" (ch. 9).

14. Musonius Rufus, *Diatr.* 8; Cicero, *Tusc.* 5.1.1–2.

15. Cicero, *Tusc.* 5.2.5.

in themselves some faculty sufficient to bring us to the final goal of happiness. For all the philosophers, this innate faculty was the faculty of reason (*logos*, *nous*, *ratio*).

### *The Wise Man*

Socrates's reputation as the "wisest man" alive kindled a vision of a paradigmatic type of person referred to by the Hellenistic philosophers as "the wise man," or *ho sophos*.[16] The wise man was the one who, having achieved wisdom, embodied human perfection and remained in a perpetual state of supreme happiness.[17] As an embodiment of perfection, the wise man became for the philosophers a paradigm against which all people should measure themselves as human beings and to whose pattern all should aim to conform. Because the standard was perfection, wise man status was, the philosophers admitted, difficult to achieve and some questioned whether the concept did not represent an idealistic theory rather than an achievable reality. Some nevertheless maintained that although few achieved this status, it was at least possible to do so.

All the schools of the Hellenistic era articulated some vision of the wise man, although the vision differed for each of them. The key question was what constituted "wisdom." What is it that, once accomplished, qualifies one as "wise"? This question required reflection and a well-considered answer. If philosophy is ultimately about how one lives, then one first needs to articulate an "account," or theory, of what the best way to live is and why this way is best. In short, one needs doctrine (*logos*).

## Philosophical Systems

### *Theory*

Although like Socrates the Hellenistic philosophers made their highest priority "living well," they recognized that *acting* correctly had to be rooted in some account (*logos*) of how to act. Just as with any craft, knowledge of the craft is prerequisite to performing that craft well.[18] Articulating such an account is important for several reasons. First, devising an account of the good life ensures that one might act correctly not merely by accident but for *well-considered* reasons and for the *right* reasons. Second, an account of the good life provides a paradigm according to which one might *consistently* act rightly. Third, an account laid out in detail describes what the *best* kind of living looks like. For instance, a shoemaker ought to know not simply how to make a shoe but rather the *art* that teaches the shoemaker how to make the best shoe possible. In the same way, the philosopher was obliged to work out not just how to live but how to live *well*. Theory is necessary to delineate such a life.

16. The Delian oracle pronounced him the wisest man (Plato, *Apol.* 21a–22e), though Socrates himself denied that he was wise in most respects (*Apol.* 38c).

17. *SVF* 3.582–88; cf. Diogenes Laërtius, *Vit. phil.* 10.118.

18. In the *Gorgias*, Socrates emphasizes that an art (*technē*) must be rooted in a rational account (*logos*) (*Gorg.* 465a), though by itself the account is not sufficient for mastery of a *technē*; one also needs training, or *askēsis* (*Gorg.* 507c).

## *The Telos or "End"*

Whatever constitutes the happy life, here we find the *telos* of existence, that "good" for which we should most strive—not as a means to some higher good, but for its own sake. This *telos* was the final good, the highest *end* of goods.

The Hellenistic schools disagreed on how to define this end. Late in the Hellenistic period, the Roman philosopher Varro summarized no fewer than 288 accounts of the highest good.[19] Throughout the Hellenistic period, the most widely accepted answers were those associated with orthodox Stoicism and Epicureanism, as well as Academic Skepticism. For the Stoics, the end was living "according to nature," which was synonymous with living "according to virtue."[20] For the Epicureans, the end was "pleasure," defined as "freedom from pain" both physical and mental.[21] For the Academics, the end was "suspension of judgment."[22] Of lesser influence, the Pyrrhonists argued that "suspension of judgment" was instrumental for reaching the final end, which was actually "freedom from disturbance."

An account of the end belongs to the department of philosophy commonly referred to as "ethics" (*to ēthikon*).[23] For each school listed above, the ethical part of philosophy was constituent of a larger system that formed an integral whole. In this regard, ethics itself was believed to be rooted deeply in the nature of the universe, or "physics" (*to physikon*).

## *The Parts of Philosophy*

Plato was among the first philosophers to devise a philosophical "system" that offered a holistic theory about life and existence, one that integrated speculation about the universe, how we know what we know (or whether we can know it), and how we ought to live.[24] History in fact credits Plato as the author of what became a traditional threefold division of philosophical inquiry into the departments of physics, logic, and ethics. This became the standard division of philosophy's departments in Plato's Academy, as well as among the Peripatetics and Stoics. The

19. Referenced in Augustine, *Civ.* 19.1; cf. Cicero, *Tusc.* 5.30.84–85.

20. This was articulated in several different ways by the early Stoics; cf. *SVF* 3.16; Stobaeus, *Anth.* 2.75,11–76,8; Diogenes Laërtius, *Vit. phil.* 7.87–9.

21. The end as pleasure (Diogenes Laërtius, *Vit. phil.* 10.128 // *Ep. Men.*); defined as the "absence of pain" (Diogenes Laërtius, *Vit. phil.* 10.191–2 // *Ep. Men.*; *Vit. phil.* 10.139 // *Kur. Dox.* 3).

22. Cicero, *Fin.* 3.31. In describing the position of the Skeptic Arcesilaus, Sextus Empiricus (LS, §681) adds that suspension of judgment has as its end freedom from mental disturbance, but this may only be an aside of Sextus, thus representing only the Pyrrhonist position; see A. A. Long and David Sedley, *The Hellenistic Philosophers*, 2 vols. (Cambridge: Cambridge University Press, 1987), 446.

23. Diogenes Laërtius, *Vit. phil.* 7.39; 10.29–30; Sextus Empiricus, *Math.* 7.17; etc.

24. Chapter 4, n5 above. Cicero states that Plato invented this division (*Acad.* 1.19). Others, however, attribute it to his successor, Xenocrates, saying that the division exists in Plato only "potentially" (Sextus Empiricus, *Math./Contra Log.* 7.16). Sextus says that the Peripatetics and the Stoics also adopted this division (7.17).

Epicureans accepted the departments of physics and ethics but replaced logic with a department that they called "canonic" (*to kanonikon*).[25]

As systematic thinkers, the Hellenistic schools ushered in the dogmatic era of philosophy. Their philosophical systems far exceeded Plato's in complexity, technicality, and fixity of dogma. Moreover, their heightened dogmatic tendencies not only established clear doctrinal boundaries between schools, but they also tightened the criteria of sectarian identity. The result was a culture of staunch philosophical allegiance to school founders as canonical authorities. This level of commitment gave rise to intense inter-school polemics and often bitter contention.

## Philosophical Allegiance

That the schools of the Hellenistic era were known as sects (*haireseis*) conveys a lot about the commitments of philosophers at this stage. The Greek term *haireseis*, meaning literally "choices," implied definite boundaries between schools and generally a decision of exclusive commitment to one's sect of choice. Since the dogmatic parameters that defined these sects stemmed specifically from the school's original founders, sectarian choice was essentially a matter of philosophical allegiance to the teachings of the founder, an allegiance that has been likened to "a virtually religious commitment."[26] Thus the Epicureans inherited their name from Epicurus, just as the Stoics, first known as Zenonians, did from Zeno.[27] Pyrrho's pupils were known as Pyrrhoneans (*Pyrrōneioi*). Later, Antiochus wanted his Old Academy to be called the Antiochians (*Antiochii*).[28] Commitment was most fervent among the Epicureans, who often depicted Epicurus as a sort of "god,"[29] on the grounds that his philosophy "saved" humanity from fear of the gods and showed the way to highest bliss.[30]

The loyalties of the dogmatic schools elicited a vehement response from those who could not countenance such unconditional devotion. This negative response issued primarily from the skeptical philosophers associated with the New Academy, emerging around the same time as the Stoic and Epicurean schools. Unlike the Dogmatic philosophers, the Skeptics defined themselves not in terms of commitment to a particular founder but by their very refusal to so commit themselves. Fittingly, they were named after their predilection for investigating, hence Skeptics (*skepsasthai*). The Skeptics relentlessly ridiculed the dogmatic philosophers for

25. Diogenes Laërtius, *Vit. phil.* 10.29.

26. For the dynamic of philosophical allegiance in the Hellenistic and Roman eras, see David N. Sedley, "Philosophical Allegiance in the Greco-Roman World," in *Philosophia Togata*, eds. Mirian Griffin and J. Barnes (Oxford: Clarendon, 1989), 97–119. Whether this commitment can be considered fully "religious" has been disputed: Gregory H. Snyder, " 'Not Subjects of a Despot': Stoics," in *Teachers and Texts in the Ancient World: Philosophers, Jews and Christians* (London: Routledge, 2000), 14–44.

27. "Zenonians" in Diogenes Laërtius, *Vit. phil.* 1.19; 7.5; "Pyrrhonians" in 9.69–70.

28. Cicero, *Acad.* 2.22.71.

29. Cicero, *Tusc.* 1.21.48; *Nat. d.* 1.16.43; Lucretius, *Rer. nat.* 3.1–30; 5.8–10.

30. Epicurus a "savior" (*sōtēr*) in Philodemus, *Lib.*, fr. 40; cf. 43.

submitting to the authority of just one man and thus relinquishing their sense of individual discretion. Enslaving themselves to their masters, they restricted their freedom to honestly explore the truth on each individual matter,[31] whereas Skeptics were always free to judge what doctrines seemed most probable.[32] Polemical disagreement in the Hellenistic period, therefore, proceeded both between the dogmatic schools and between the dogmatic schools and the Skeptics. These inter-school polemics gave rise to a veritable genre of philosophical literature defined by the standard title formula "Against the *X* [Stoics, Epicureans, etc.]."[33]

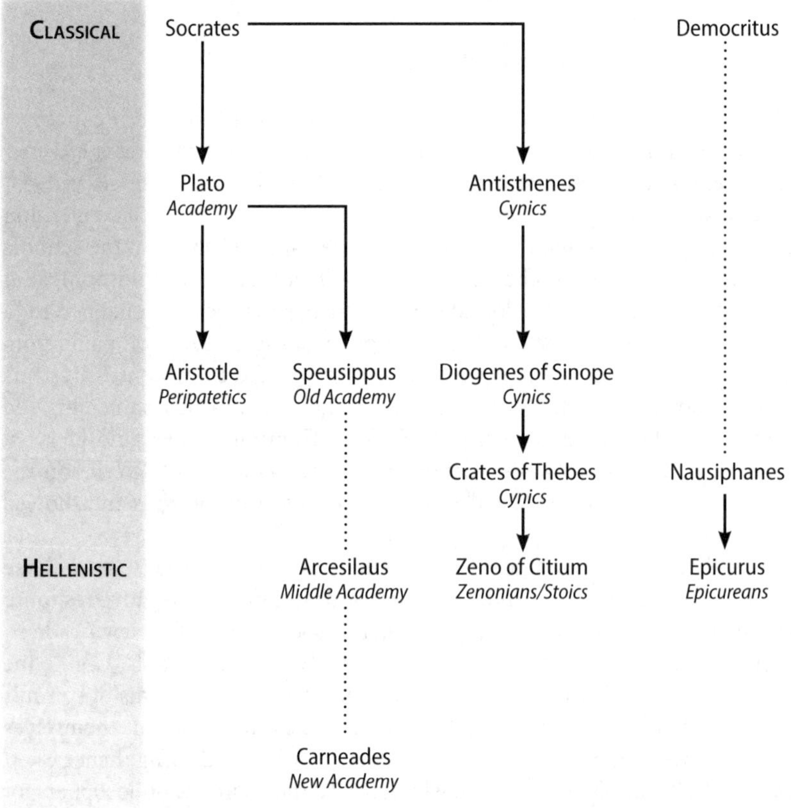


Figure 2. Successions of the Hellenistic schools.[34]

31. E.g., Cicero, *Nat. d.* 1.5.10; 1.24.66–67; 1.26.72; *Acad.* 2.3.8–9.

32. E.g., Cicero, *Tusc.* 4.4.7; 5.29.82; *Acad.* 2.3.8.

33. E.g., Plutarch, *On Stoic Self-Contradictions*; *Against the Stoics on Common Conceptions*; *That Epicurus Makes a Pleasant Life Impossible*; *Reply to Colotes in Defense of Other Philosophers*; Galen, *Against Lycus*; Sextus Empiricus, *Against Dogmatists*; Alexander Lycopolis, *Against the Doctrines of the Manichees*; Augustine, *Against the Academics*. Disputes in the form of dialogues in Cicero (*Academica*, *On the Nature of the Gods*, etc.) often rely on traditional arguments dating back to the third and second centuries BCE.

34. Diogenes Laërtius, *Vit. phil.* 1.13–15; cf. Sextus Empiricus, *Pyrr.* 1.220.

## Notes on the Primary Sources

Surviving philosophical literature from the Hellenistic period is scant, though not for lack of production. Diogenes Laërtius relays that Epicurus's writings filled three hundred scrolls and that Chrysippus more than doubled this in attempt to rival him.[35] In general, only fragments of the Hellenistic philosophers remain. These are preserved in the writings of later authors, some of whom were advocates or at least sympathetic, others of whom were critical or hostile. The fragments representing the main schools have been collected by topic in Long and Sedley (1987) and by either topic or source in Inwood and Gerson (1997). Long and Sedley's collection consists of two volumes, with the English translation in volume 1 and the original Greek and Latin text in volume 2.

Though written in Latin (and by a Roman) near the end of the Hellenistic period, Cicero's philosophical dialogues provide the best available summations of the views of the main Hellenistic schools. Among his more exhaustive dialogues are *On Ends of Goods and Evils*, *On the Nature of the Gods*, *Academica*, and *Tusculan Disputations*. The first two cover the respective views of the Academic, Stoic, and Epicurean schools on the topics indicated. Several of Cicero's other treatises also summarize the views of the Hellenistic schools, including *On the Stoic Paradoxes*, *On Duties*, *On Divination*, and *On Fate*. Cicero's treatises, however, should be consulted with caution since his express purpose is to adapt Greek philosophy into a Roman framework, not simply for informative purposes but for the practical benefit of the Roman people and direct application to the state (which we will discuss in chapter 11). For further sources on specific Hellenistic schools, see the chapters that follow.

## Key Terms and Concepts

- Art of living, the
- *Askēsis* (practice)
- Dogmatists vs. Skeptics
- End, the (*telos*)
- Exempla
- Good life, the
- Hellenistic philosophy
- Philosophical allegiance
- Philosophical systems
- Spiritual exercises
- Therapy for the soul
- Wise man, the (*ho sophos*)

35. Diogenes Laërtius, *Vit. phil.* 10.26.

## For Further Study

### *Primary Sources*

Inwood, Brad, and L. P. Gerson, trans. *Hellenistic Philosophy: Introductory Readings*. 2nd ed. Indianapolis, IN: Hackett, 1997.
Long, A. A., and David N. Sedley. *The Hellenistic Philosophers*. 2 vols. Cambridge: Cambridge University Press, 1987.

### *Secondary Sources*

Adamson, Peter. *Philosophy in the Hellenistic and Roman Worlds: A History of Philosophy Without Any Gaps*, vol. 2. Oxford: Oxford University Press, 2015.
Arenson, Kelly, ed. *The Routledge Handbook of Hellenistic Philosophy*. Routledge Handbooks. London: Routledge, 2020.
Blackson, Thomas A. *Ancient Greek Philosophy: From the Presocratics to the Hellenistic Philosophers*. Malden, MA: Wiley-Blackwell, 2011.
Long, A. A. *From Epicurus to Epictetus: Studies in Hellenistic and Roman Philosophy*. Oxford: Oxford University Press, 2006.
Machek, David. *The Life Worth Living in Ancient Greek and Roman Philosophy*. Cambridge; New York: Cambridge University Press, 2023.
Sellars, John. *Hellenistic Philosophy*. Oxford: Oxford University Press, 2018.
Sharples, R. W. *Stoics, Epicureans and Skeptics*. London: Routledge, 1996.

# 8

# The Stoics

From the pre-Socratics until Plotinus in the third century CE, the most impactful philosophical school by far was that of the Stoics. Founded by Zeno of Citium around 300 BCE, the Stoic school traces its lineage back to Socrates through the Cynics. Despite direct Cynic influence, however, Zeno's system was really a product of diverse doctrinal influences, supplemented by ample innovation. The philosophical system that Zeno and his immediate successors devised introduced a new level of complexity, integration, and consistency of philosophical speculation, surpassing the semi-systematic philosophy of Plato and the Old Academy.

## History of the Stoic School

A native of Cyprus, Zeno of Citium (335–263 BCE) arrived in Athens around 313. Unlike Aristotle, he had not come to study philosophy. Rather, he had set out on a voyage from Phoenicia to Piraeus with a cargo of purple cloth and was shipwrecked at Piraeus. Going from Piraeus to Athens, he found at a bookseller's shop a copy of Xenophon's *Memorabilia*. Being deeply impressed by Xenophon's portrait of Socrates, Zeno asked the bookseller where he could find a man like this. The bookseller pointed him to Crates, the Cynic who had followed the famous Diogenes. From that day on, Zeno became a pupil of Crates.[1]

Although he followed Crates for a time, Zeno's modesty prevented him from assimilating to the Cynics' shameless ways, and they soon separated. Zeno then attended the lectures of Stilpo the Megarian and the lectures of Xenocrates and Polemo the Academics.[2] After twenty years with his teachers, he began teaching in the painted colonnade in Athens known as the Portico or Stoa (*Stoa*). Those who attended took their name from the place, and became known as "those from the Stoa," or "the Stoics," after first being called Zenonians (*Zēnōnioi*).[3] And so Zeno's school became a philosophical sect.

Tradition traces Stoic descent from Zeno back through the Cynics Crates, Diogenes, and Antisthenes to the fountainhead of Socrates (see fig. 3).[4] Although the line to Socrates provided the Stoics with a respectable pedigree, when measured in terms of overall impact, the link with Socrates via the Cynics was a tenuous one.

1. This account in Diogenes Laërtius, *Vit. phil.* 7.2–3.
2. Diogenes Laërtius, *Vit. phil.* 7.2, 4.
3. Diogenes Laërtius, *Vit. phil.* 7.5.
4. Diogenes Laërtius, *Vit. phil.* 1.14–15; cf. 6.19; Cicero, *Or.* 3.62.

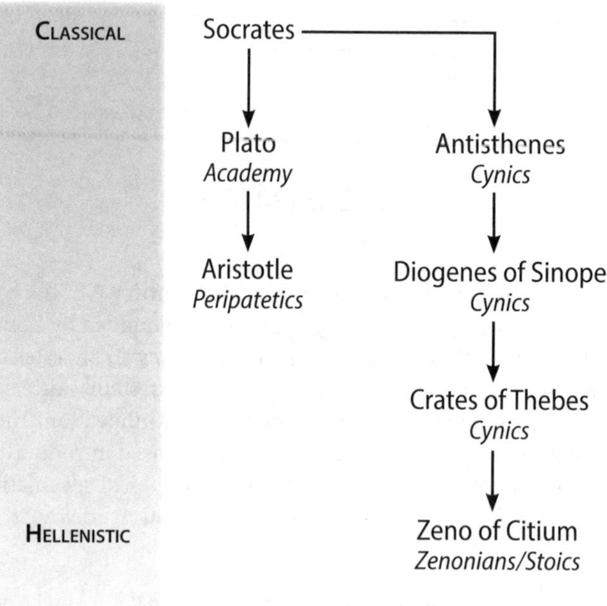


Figure 3. Succession from Socrates to the Stoics.[5]

The strength of this genealogy depends partly on how Cynicism is defined. If Cynicism was more a way of life than a doctrinal system (see chapter 5), then Stoicism can hardly be linked with Cynicism doctrinally. As noted, although later sources often associate them, such sources arguably Stoicize Cynicism by attributing to the Cynics what were technically doctrines of Stoicism.[6] When the doctrinal link is removed, the impact of Cynicism on Stoicism diminishes to the influence of the former's prescriptions for lifestyle and to a certain resonance with the doctrinally bare "life slogans" that grounded these prescriptions. On the one hand, Zeno and the Stoics never advocated for the all-consuming Cynic mission of "altering the coinage" (see chapter 6). On the other hand, evidence suggests that Cynicism did impact Zeno to some degree, presumably through Crates.[7] Above all, Zeno took from the Cynics his indifference toward external things such as possessions and power, his elevation of virtue as the only good, and his disapproval of the emotions.

To whatever degree Cynic indifference influenced Zeno's ethics, as a doctrinal system his philosophy inherited much from non-Cynic thinkers, including his Megarian (Stilpo) and Academic (Xenocrates, Polemo) teachers. He was notably

5. Diogenes Laërtius, *Vit. phil.* 1.13–15; 7.1–5.

6. Diogenes Laërtius summarizes these connections in *Vit. phil.* 6.104; 7.121. See also Epictetus's portrait of the ideal Cynic in *Diatr.* 3.22.

7. Zeno's views on the ideal city (in his *Republic*) reflect connections with Cynic views on several points. See Malcolm Schofield, *The Stoic Idea of the City* (Cambridge: Cambridge University Press, 1991), 11–13.

influenced in logic by the Megarians, and in his physics by the Old Academics.[8] One sees in his teaching the profound impact of Heraclitus, particularly in his doctrine of the *Logos*. Making substantial contributions of his own, Zeno integrated logic, physics, and ethics at a remarkable level of completeness and consistency. The "perfection" of the Stoic system became a common boast of the Stoics.

Upon Zeno's death in 261 BCE, headship of his school fell to Cleanthes of Assos (ca. 330–230 BCE), succeeded next by Chrysippus some thirty years later (beginning 230 BCE). His successors cemented Zeno's teaching as the authoritative foundation of Stoicism. Later thinkers sought solutions to doctrinal debates through exacting analysis of his writings. The most important thinker in the history of the school, Chrysippus synthesized and elaborated on Zeno's teachings, shaping them into a sharply defined orthodoxy. Subsequent heads of the school remained faithful to the received precepts, always looking back to Zeno as its ultimate source and their ultimate authority.[9]

Several doctrinal modifications introduced around the late second century BCE, however, inaugurated a new phase in the school's history known as Middle Stoicism.[10] While a consistent orthodoxy had emerged in the early phase, the heads of the middle period—most importantly, Panaetius (ca. 185–109 BCE) and Posidonius (ca. 135–51 BCE)—subtly revised some minutiae of Zeno's teaching based on Plato's views and controversially questioned some of Zeno's more defining doctrines.[11] However serious their revisions, the Middle Stoics considered themselves orthodox adherents of Zeno's teachings and they were invariably regarded as such in antiquity.[12] Stoicism prospered until well into the Roman era, after undergoing further developments that marked off a third, or Roman, stage of Stoicism. Concerning Roman Stoicism, more will be said in chapter 12.

## The Stoic System

As the third head of the school, Chrysippus integrated Zeno's teaching into an impressively complex system consisting of doctrines elaborated with extreme technical precision. The Stoics infamously boasted of their logical doctrinal "consistency" (*homologia*), insisting that every premise leads incontrovertibly to another, with each doctrine joined so tightly with every other that none of them could be

8. John Sellars, *Hellenistic Philosophy* (Oxford: Oxford University Press, 2018), 17.

9. Sedley, "Philosophical Allegiance," 98–99.

10. While this is a well-established way of periodizing Stoicism in modern scholarship, recent treatments have challenged these divisions. See Brad Inwood, *Later Stoicism 155 BC to AD 200: An Introduction and Collection of Sources in Translation*, Cambridge Sourcebooks in Post-Hellenistic Philosophy (Cambridge: Cambridge University Press, 2022), 2–3.

11. Panaetius questioned Zeno's doctrine of a final conflagration and cosmic regeneration (Cicero, *Nat. d.* 2.46.118), though even in the early phase, Diogenes of Babylon, one of the heads of school, had already doubted it and Boethus of Sidon rejected it (Philo, *Aetern.* [15] 76–77; Cicero, *Nat. d.* 2.46.118). Panaetius also questioned the legitimacy of divination and prophecy (Cicero, *Acad.* 2.107).

12. I. G. Kidd, *Posidonius, Volume 3: The Translation of the Fragments* (Cambridge: Cambridge University Press, 1999), 61–84, testimonia 90–102.

removed without the entire system collapsing.[13] The system was like the universe itself: a single body in which all the parts cooperated in harmony, each contributing to the integrity of the whole and none of them meaningful in isolation.[14]

The system followed the threefold division of parts said to have originated with Plato and accepted also by Aristotle: logic, physics, and ethics.[15] The Stoics, on the other hand, insisted that these parts were inseparable. Philosophy, they said, was like an animal: "Logic corresponding to the bones and sinews, Ethics to the fleshy parts, Physics to the soul."[16] Hence, some Stoic teachers taught all the parts together. Zeno and Chrysippus, however, began with logic, proceeded next to physics, and ended with ethics.[17]

### *Logic*

The "logical" department of the Stoic system concerned canons, or criteria, for the discovery of truth (hence embracing epistemology). Under this department belonged two main headings—namely, dialectic and rhetoric.[18]

Dialectic (*hē dialektikē*) was the science of "correctly discussing subjects by question and answer."[19] While dialectic included several subheadings, it was with the theory of presentations (*phantasiai*) that the Stoics made their most substantial contribution.

For the Stoics, a *phantasia* was a perception or presentation received by the senses—in other words, a sense impression received either palpably by the bodily senses or as a logical proposition imprinted on the mind. Naturally, when an impression occurs to someone, they must make some judgment about it; i.e., as to whether it is true or false as perceived and hence whether the impression should be assented to or rejected. When a person assents to an impression that is true, this constitutes knowledge (*epistēmē*). Some impressions occur to subjects as self-evidently true and hence are worthy of confident assent. Such impressions are known as cataleptic impressions (*katalēptikai phantasiai*), or cognitive impressions. Being firmly grasped (*katalēptikē*), cognitive impressions constitute secure knowledge, like a hand wrapped tightly around a tightly clenched fist. For instance, when we stand directly under the midday sun, it is self-evidently true that it is day. Our reasoning faculties have experienced a cognitive impression. The Stoics empha-

---

13. Plutarch, *Mor.* 1033a, b; Diogenes Laërtius, *Vit. phil.* 7.40; Sextus Empiricus, *Math.* 7.17–19; Cicero, *Fin.* 3.74; 4.53; 5.83; though opponents rejoined that it contained many contradictions (collected in Plutarch's *On Stoic Self-Contradictions*).

14. Seneca, *Ep.* 33.5; 89.1; Diogenes Laërtius, *Vit. phil.* 7.40; Sextus Empiricus, *Math.* 7.19.

15. Diogenes Laërtius, *Vit. phil.* 7.39.

16. Diogenes Laërtius, *Vit. phil.* 7.40 (LCL, Hicks); among other metaphors recounted here and in Sextus Empiricus, *Math.* 7.17–19.

17. Diogenes Laërtius, *Vit. phil.* 7.40. Hence, von Arnim's *Stoicorum Veterum Fragmenta* arranges the fragments in this sequence.

18. The logical part is covered in *SVF* 1.47–84 (Zeno); 2.1–298 (Chrysippus); LS §31–42; Diogenes Laërtius, *Vit. phil.* 7.43–83. Some Stoics add under this heading the study of words and definitions (Diogenes Laërtius, *Vit. phil.* 7.41).

19. Diogenes Laërtius, *Vit. phil.* 7.42.

sized that while discernment between true and false impressions can be challenging in some cases, a perfectly reasoning person is able to execute judgments with absolute certainty and thus to have firm *epistēmē*. The person who judges impressions correctly with perfect consistency—that is, who never errs in their use of the reasoning faculty—is considered to be a wise man (*sophos*). The wise man never assents to a false proposition, only true ones, and thus always assents according to knowledge (*epistēmē*), never according to opinion (*doxa*). A positivistic epistemology, the Stoic theory of cognitive impressions, was the primary basis for Skeptical opposition to Stoicism in the days of Chrysippus and the successors of the Hellenistic period (see chapter 10).

*Phantasiai* emanated not only from objects of sense perception but also from propositions. As the Stoics observed, when an idea or a verbal proposition occurs to our mental faculties, we must decide whether to assent to it as true or to reject it as false. Judging such impressions unerringly requires training. Chrysippus made substantial contributions to the study of logic by laying out several types of syllogisms designed for honing skills in evaluating propositional impressions. Although his emphasis on syllogisms was often ridiculed as trivial and pointless,[20] Stoics insisted that the study of syllogisms had wholly practical value. Through analyzing syllogisms, one became adept in unraveling the validity and invalidity of logical arguments, thus preventing assent to falsehoods or speciously reasoned conclusions, while also providing a method for defending the truths learned about good and evil.[21] In theory, the person perfectly adept in logic would assent only to cognitive impressions (constituting "knowledge") and would never err or opine (form opinions). Syllogistic reasoning, therefore, was no petty exercise; rather, it trained subjects in how to distinguish true from false—a veritable prerequisite for appropriate action. Consequently, aptitude in dialectic was truly a virtue (*aretē*). For if ignorance leads to error, then the art that removes ignorance must be a virtue.

In distinction from dialectic, rhetoric (*hē rhētorikē*) was the "science of speaking well on matters set forth by plain narrative."[22] As a science (*epistēmē*), Stoic rhetoric was not an art like Aristotle's rhetoric—consisting of theoretical principles that teach one how to be eloquent—but was a kind of knowledge whose end was demonstration of the truth. The Stoics argued that a *plain* style of speech (or rhetoric) was sufficient for any such purpose. For just as nature consists of an orderly arrangement of parts that work together in harmony, so speech ought to consist of well-ordered, logical discourse, the strength of which is its harmonious arrangement and logical consistency, not its artificial adornments. Rhetorical skill, then, had to do not with eloquence but with the right use of reason. In this regard, Stoic rhetoric, like dialectic, was a virtue: Dialectic was the science of distinguishing correctly between true and false and rhetoric the science of speaking the truth clearly—in both cases, through the correct use of the reasoning faculty. The virtue

20. Lucian, *Vit. auct.* 21–25; even the Stoics warn that logical exercises could become petty (Seneca, *Ep.* 117).

21. Epictetus, *Diatr.* 1.7; Cicero, *Fin.* 3.72; Diogenes Laërtius, *Vit. phil.* 7.47.

22. Diogenes Laërtius, *Vit. phil.* 7.40 (LCL, Hicks).

of rhetoric, like that of dialectic, was perfected only in the wise man, who alone knows how to reason well.

### *Physics*

Building on the study of logic (*to logikon*), physics (*to physikon*) came next in Zeno's sequence. Having strengthened the faculty of discernment between true and false perceptions, the student was now better positioned to inquire into the nature of the universe.

Properly speaking, physics consists of the study of the natural world (*physis* = nature). As a panentheistic system, however, Stoicism includes God as part of the physical universe. Thus Stoic physics also covers theology and, indeed, everything that exists.

Chrysippus elaborated a theory of physics with remarkable comprehensiveness and bewildering precision. Yet his theory can be summarized in a few main points.[23] The theory began with the dogma that the universe is constituted by two principles, matter (the elements) and causation (divine reason). Matter is passive (being "acted upon") and causation active ("acting upon"), the former as an enlivening, structuring, and intelligent power (*dynamis*). Through the creative action of the causative principle, undifferentiated matter becomes qualified into individuated elements and the elements are arranged into an orderly universe. In one sense, the mixture of elements constitutes the world (*kosmos*) and the creative agent constitutes "God" (*ho theos*). In another sense, the world and God are one and the same. For in the first place, nothing exists but what is bodily. Hence God, like the world, is corporeal and equally a part of the physical universe. Second, God and the world are so mixed as to be physically inseparable. The world, then, *is* God and God *is* the world. As body, God consists of a strongly constituted blend of air and fire, otherwise designated as breath or spirit (*pneuma*). This spirit pervades all things, uniting them (with itself) as one. As the causative principle of the universe, God is intelligent. Viewed from the perspective of his intelligence, God is reason (*logos*) or intelligence (*nous*). God, or reason, imposes structure on the universe and assigns natural purpose to each of its parts, which then carry out their purposes in harmonious cooperation. Now, because God both designed and governs the universe, God can be considered identical not only with the world, and with reason, but also with providence. This tightly ordered design, where each part of the universe carries out its God-given purpose both in itself and in harmony with all the other parts, builds into the universe an inescapable chain of causes and effects. Thus all occurrences in the universe are fated. Before the orderly universe came into existence, there was only reason by itself, in seed form. In the seed, or "seminal reason" (*spermatikos logos*), was contained all that would be, the entire universe—the heavenly bodies and the laws that govern their movements, animals and human beings and their natural stages of growth, the rises and falls of history—all to unfold according to the intelligent blueprint of this rational seed. By design,

23. The "physical" part is covered in *SVF* 1.85–177 (Zeno); 2.299–1216 (Chrysippus); LS §43–55; Diogenes Laërtius, *Vit. phil.* 7.132–60.

this universe is moving toward the telos of extinction. After passing through all its predetermined stages, the universe will end finally by conflagration. All the elements will be reduced again into the seed whence it came. "Zeus" (yet another name for God) will be alone with himself. Then, Zeus (God) will grow into the universe again. This cycle of cosmic rebirth and destruction will continue in perpetuity.

Humanity holds a special place within this cosmic order. Although reason pervades the universe, most living things do not possess the inherent capacity to use this reason, at least not completely. Reason infuses different orders of living things with different powers or faculties (*dynameis*). The available faculties accrue relative to varying levels of tension (*tonos*) with which fiery Spirit interacts with the affected material. Sticks and stones have cohesion (*hexis*), but no power of movement. Plants have the capacity to grow (*physis*), but not to sense (*psychē*). Animals have the capacity both to grow and to sense, but not to reason. Only humans—and God—have the capacity to reason (*logos*); for in humanity, the strength of pervading Spirit reaches the threshold necessary to make the reasoning faculty operative. Humans, therefore, share in divine reason itself. This faculty makes possible all that is necessary for attaining the good life.

## *Ethics*

The Stoic system tightly integrates all three parts of its philosophy: logic, physics, and ethics.[24] To begin with, reason is rooted in nature (= *logic* + *physics*). For since reason pervades nature, nature is, so to speak, intelligently designed. If all parts of a single body, each member of the universe follows the purposes of its design, then all the parts do so in perfect concord. Everything falls into its place. There are no flaws in this logically ordered universe.

Second, nature provides the paradigm for ethics (= physics + ethics). In this regard, the Stoics identified the ethical End as living "according to nature" (*kata physin*). Indeed, if nature is a harmoniously ordered system, then any person as a part of the universal body is obliged to act according to the role assigned to them. Any resistance to the natural order would reflect ignorance that one is part of something larger than oneself—even defiance of what is in the best interest of the whole. Put differently, if providence has determined things to be as they are, then resistance to this plan would reflect a miscalculation of what is in fact "good." Under the care of providence, the universe gives nothing "bad." Nature is without flaws. If, therefore, what I experience feels "bad" to me, it is because I have incorrectly evaluated the sense impression that I have received. It is not the universe that is flawed. It is my judgment about it.

### Good, Bad, and Indifferent

Realigning one's sense of evaluation requires a reorientation toward good (*to agathon*) and bad (*to kakon*). If this perfect universe never gives anything bad to its members, then we can only conclude that the bad things we *seem* to experience

24. The ethical part is covered in *SVF* 1.178–276 (Zeno); 3.2–768 (Chrysippus); LS §56–67; Diogenes Laërtius, *Vit. phil.* 7.84–131.

are not bad. In fact, the only thing bad is vice, and the only thing good is virtue. Additionally, our judgment to commit vice or virtue is entirely within our control. Consequently, there is nothing bad that is outside our control.

What then do we call the experiences of poverty or sickness, of wealth or health, or of good or bad repute? Since these things are neither virtues nor vices, the Stoics insisted, we must consider these things *adiaphora*, or "indifferent." In the category of indifferents, the Stoics put all bodily goods and evils (life, health, strength, and their opposites) and all external goods and evils (noble birth, power, high repute, and their opposites)—that is, *so-called* goods and evils. These things are not good or bad in themselves; they are indifferent.

### Self-Sufficiency

With this frame of mind, Stoics were now equipped to live conformably with nature and could always be happy, even when things did not seem to go their way. If their property were seized, if barbarians set fire to their city, or if they were driven into exile, they would have suffered only what is indifferent—for they themselves had committed no vice and would have suffered only what they could never fully control. They would merely have experienced the plan of the universe. If these occurrences are good for the universe, then they must resign themselves to this. Like a dog tied behind a moving cart, they can either follow willingly or be dragged.[25]

Living according to nature meant living not only according to the plan of the universe, but also according to one's nature as a human being. A human being is uniquely endowed with reason. It is the purpose of a human being to live according to the faculty that makes them uniquely human, a faculty no other creature has. Because humans are innately equipped with reason, moreover, they are equipped with the resources necessary to live as nature directs. They have the potential to be self-sufficient (*autarkēs*), requiring no aid, not even from the gods. They have only to conform to their own nature, and all that matters is within reach.

Integrating all three parts of Stoic philosophy, it could be said that living according to nature (physics)—or according to reason—amounted to correctly sorting sense impressions (logic) into the categories of good, bad, and indifferent (ethics). For instance, say one's hand is sliced off in battle. The subject receives a sense perception that says, "I have lost my hand." Reason now decides whether to evaluate this occurrence as something good, bad, or indifferent. Since hands belong to the body, and bodily states are neither good nor evil, and since the occurrence of losing one's hand is not something within one's control (at least not fully), and especially since the occurrence did not consist in the person's performing either virtue or vice, then the person must assess the loss of his hand as indifferent. To Stoic thinking, they will be wise for having so reasoned.

### The Passions

Misjudgments in the evaluation of what is good, bad, and indifferent constitute what the Stoics call "passions" (*pathē*) or "disturbances" (*perturbationes*). The pas-

25. This is a famous illustration of Zeno (LS §62a).

sions are actual shrinkings (fear, grief) and swellings (desire, pleasure) of the reasoning faculty, constituting literal changes in the shape of the soul. As movements of the soul—that is, of the reasoning faculty itself—the passions are not external forces that act upon the soul from without. They are the very judgments we make. Hence the passions are also entirely within our control to suppress. Only conform the mind to the true nature of things and reason will judge impressions rightly. The loss of my hand will not demand distress but resignation and indifference.

### The Wise Man

This ethical theory laid out a sure path to happiness, for it untethered happiness from the contingencies of external circumstance. Yet even the Stoics admitted that living consistently according to this pattern—that is, according to nature—was something few people had ever accomplished.[26] The true wise man (*sophos*) was perhaps as rare as the phoenix, of which there existed, every five hundred years, only one.[27] But the wise man had existed. Through perfect use of reason, he always avoided swerving into passion, consistently assessing his circumstances from the perspective of the larger design of the universe, never opining but assenting only to true sense impressions and rejecting the false.

### The Paradoxes

The Stoics were aware how strange this sort of wise man sounded from the standpoint of conventional wisdom (that losing hands, and other such things, are bad). They remained committed to their conviction, nevertheless, insisting that if one accepted their *re*definition of things good, bad, and indifferent, then the wise man's way of thinking made perfect sense. Because acceptance of this point required a total reappraisal of common values, however, the Stoics proceeded to articulate a definition of the wise man that utilized a deliberately subversive redefinition of terms. In statements known as the "paradoxes" (*paradoxa*, "incredible things"), they reapplied predicates conventionally used to describe a person's *social* qualities to refer now to the wise man's *virtuous* qualities.

The paradoxes conformed to variations of the formula "Only the wise man is *x*; only the wise man is *y*, etc.," coming often in a list involving a litany of predicates. For instance, "Only the wise man is rich, well born, and perfect"; "Only the wise man is free; only the wise man is king"; "Only the wise man is ruler, teacher, beautiful"; and so forth.[28] Again, these predicates were not social descriptions, but *character* descriptions. The wise man was "rich" because he was self-sufficient, having within himself everything needed for happiness. The wise man was "free" and "king," because everything that contributed to his happiness—virtue and nothing else—was within his power to control: namely, by choosing virtue and shunning vice.

---

26. While opponents ridiculed the Stoic idea of the wise man as an impossible ideal (Cicero, *Acad.* 2.145; *Tusc.* 2.51; Plutarch, *Mor.* 75b–76e; Sextus Empiricus, *Math.* 9.133–6// LS 54d; Lucian, *Herm.* 76–77), the Stoics insisted that wise men have existed (Seneca, *Const.* 7.1; cf. Seneca, *Ep.* 42.1; cf. Epictetus, *Diatr.* 2.19.20–28).

27. Seneca, *Ep.* 42.1.

28. Cf. *SVF* 3.364, 594, 619, 655; Cicero, *Fin.* 3.75.

From the Stoic concept of the wise man, the term *sophos*—originally meaning simply "a wise person"—emerged in the Hellenistic period as a technical term for the paradigmatic philosopher. The Stoic portrait of the wise man inspired counter portraits of the wise man in the other philosophical schools, as will be seen in the chapters that follow.

## Notes on the Primary Sources

Except for Cleanthes's *Hymn to Zeus*, no complete work of the Hellenistic Stoics has survived. Of Chrysippus's 705 writings, only a few papyri fragments remain. Records of Hellenistic Stoicism survive piecemeal. For the views of the early Stoics, we rely almost exclusively on later writers (including non-Stoics like Cicero and Philo of Alexandria, and Stoics like Seneca and Epictetus) who preserve their words or doctrines, some of whom are hostile witnesses (like Plutarch, Galen, and Sextus Empiricus). In *Stoicorum Veterum Fragmenta* (1903), Hans von Arnim collected in three volumes extensive fragments and testimonia attesting to the views of the early Stoics, including only the original Greek and Latin text without any accompanying translation. Volume 1 is dedicated to the views of Zeno and his disciples (including Cleanthes), and volumes 2–3 to Chrysippus; volume 3 includes the other successors of the early period. A fourth volume provides an index of Greek and Latin terms and names. The Stoic evidence is made most accessible in Long and Sedley's (1987) two-volume sourcebook on the Hellenistic philosophers. Long and Sedley's collection includes excerpts from the primary sources, collated by topic. Volume 1 includes the English translation, followed by commentary at the end of each section; volume 2 contains the original Greek and Latin texts. Sourcebooks are also available in Inwood and Gerson (1997) and Inwood (2022). Compendia of Stoic views can be found in the doxographies of Diogenes Laërtius (*Lives of Eminent Philosophers*, book 7) and Stobaeus (*Outlines of Pyrrhonism* and *Against the Professors*).

## Key Terms and Concepts

- Cognitive impression (*cataleptic* impression)
- Conflagration
- Indifferents (*adiaphora*)
- Living according to nature (*kata physin*)
- Paradoxes
- Reason (*logos*)
- Self-sufficiency (*autarkeia*)
- Sense impression (*phantasia*)
- Stoa
- Tension (*tonos*)
- Wise man, the (*ho sophos*)
- Zenonians

## For Further Study

### *Primary Sources*

Inwood, Brad. *Later Stoicism: 155 BC to AD 200; An Introduction and Collection of Sources in Translation*. Cambridge Sourcebooks in Post-Hellenistic Philosophy. Cambridge: Cambridge University Press, 2022.

Inwood, Brad, and L. P. Gerson, trans. *Hellenistic Philosophy: Introductory Readings*. 2nd ed. Indianapolis, IN: Hackett, 1997.

Long, A. A. and David N. Sedley. *The Hellenistic Philosophers*. 2 vols. Cambridge: Cambridge University Press, 1987.

von Arnim, Hans. *Stoicorum Veterum Fragmenta*. 4 vols. 1903. Reprint, Leipzig: Eubner, 1964.

### *Secondary Sources*

Arenson, Kelly, ed. *The Routledge Handbook of Hellenistic Philosophy*. Routledge Handbooks. London: Routledge, 2020.

Inwood, Brad, ed. *The Cambridge Companion to Stoicism*. Cambridge: Cambridge University Press, 2003.

Machek, David. *The Life Worth Living in Ancient Greek and Roman Philosophy*. Cambridge: Cambridge University Press, 2023.

Sellars, John. *The Art of Living: The Stoics on the Nature and Function of Philosophy*. Ashgate New Critical Thinking in Philosophy. Aldershot, UK: Ashgate, 2003.

Sellars, John. *The Pocket Stoic*. Chicago: University of Chicago Press, 2019.

# 9

# The Epicureans

Epicureanism was born at almost exactly the same time as Stoicism. The pair, however, could hardly have looked more different. The former's founder, Epicurus, is linked in the successions tradition not with the line of Socrates but with that of Democritus and the early Italian philosophers. Epicurus's doctrines so differed from Zeno's that they seemed virtually devised to oppose them. The schools of Epicurus and Zeno remained fierce rivals throughout the Hellenistic period and beyond.

## The History of the Epicurean School

A son of Athenian parents, Epicurus (341–270 BCE) lived his early life on the Aegean island of Samos. The question of when he first encountered philosophy is a matter of disagreement. According to his own testimony, he first encountered philosophy as a boy after reading the poet Hesiod.[1] He later purported that he learned philosophy from no one, being instead self-taught. Another account, however, relates that he developed interest in philosophy during his time as a schoolmaster after coming across the works of Democritus.[2] It was alleged that after he founded his own philosophical school, he put forward Democritus's "atomist" doctrines as if they were his own.[3] Sources also record that he was a student of Nausiphanes the Pyrrhonist skeptic, though Epicurus disparages Nausiphanes intensely in his philosophical writings and letters (see fig. 4).[4] It is also alleged that Epicurus heard Xenocrates the Old Academic; he himself states that he heard a certain Pamphilus, a student of Plato.[5]

At age eighteen, Epicurus arrived in Athens, where he lived for a time before moving to Colophon in Ionia.[6] At Colophon, he gathered disciples and then headed a school in Mitylene and Lampascus. Five years later, in the final years of the fourth century BCE, he moved the school to Athens.[7] In Athens, he purchased a garden

1. On Hesiod and philosophy, see chapter 3.
2. Diogenes Laërtius, *Vit. phil.* 10.2.
3. Diogenes Laërtius, *Vit. phil.* 10.13; 10.4; Cicero, *Nat. d.* 1.33.93.
4. That he was Nausiphanes's student (Diogenes Laërtius, *Vit. phil.* 1.15; 9.69); his alleged criticism of Nausiphanes (Diogenes Laërtius, *Vit. phil.* 10.7–8; cf. Cicero, *Nat. d.* 1.33.93).
5. Cicero, *Nat. d.* 1.26.72.
6. Diogenes Laërtius, *Vit. phil.* 10.1.
7. Diogenes Laërtius, *Vit. phil.* 10.15.

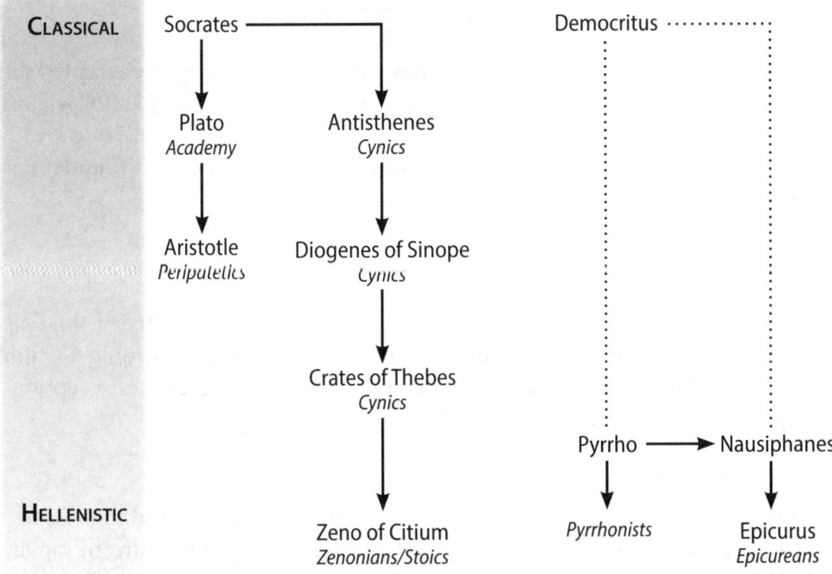


Figure 4. Successions of the Stoics and Epicurians.[8]

located near the site of the Academy where he and his circle of disciples withdrew to live in quiet simplicity according to the doctrines he had devised. His circle consisted of his close friends Hermarchus, Metrodorus, and Polyaenus, as well as a diverse assortment of students that included—somewhat exceptionally—women, prostitutes, slaves, and many members of the lower social orders.[9] Epicurus was a prolific writer, producing no fewer than three hundred scrolls—supposedly supplying Chrysippus his inspiration for his seven hundred.[10]

Epicurus died in Athens at age seventy-two, suffering direly from kidney stones and dysentery but finding serenity "at the remembrance of past conversations with friends."[11] His will designated Hermarchus as heir to his books and garden and as successor over his philosophical school. With the revenue bequeathed, Epicurus asked that his followers celebrate his birthday annually.[12] Students and teachers in his tradition always looked back to him as their preeminent authority. Their commitment was almost cult-like, owing to their belief that his teachings liberated them from fear of death and pointed out the path to unquenchable happiness, making him truly a savior (*sōtēr*) and something like a god.[13]

8. Diogenes Laërtius, *Vit. phil.* 1.14–15; 9.69; 10.7–8.
9. Diogenes Laërtius lists his disciples in *Vit. phil.* 10.22–23.
10. Diogenes Laërtius, *Vit. phil.* 10.36.
11. Diogenes Laërtius, *Vit. phil.* 10.22 = *Ep. Idom.*
12. Diogenes Laërtius, *Vit. phil.* 10.16–21.
13. "Savior" in Philodemus, *Lib.*//fr. 40; cf. 43. Like a "god" (*deus*) in Cicero, *Tusc.* 1.48; *Nat. d.* 1.43; Lucretius, *Rer. nat.* 3.1–30; 5.8–10; "divine sounding" (*thespesios*) in Lucian, *Alex.* 61.

## The Epicurean System

Like Zeno, Epicurus divided philosophy into three parts. Although he accepted the common divisions of physics and ethics, he rejected the study of logic (*to logikon*), putting in its place a division that he called "canonic" (*to kanonikon*).[14] It was with canonic that his system began, followed next by physics—and on these foundations, he based his ethics.

### *Canonic*

As the beginning of Epicurus's philosophy,[15] "canonic" concerned the epistemological standards (*kritēria*) by which truth is known. According to him, these standards of truth are (1) sense perceptions (*aisthēseis*), (2) preconceptions (*prolēpseis*), and (3) the feelings (*pathē*).

#### Sense Perception

Epicurus believed that sensations are the result of actual physical impressions (*phantasiai*) stamped on the mind by film-like images (*eidōla*) that stream rapidly from the objects we perceive while preserving the objects' original form. A person perceives a chair, for instance, because a chair's image has imprinted a physical impression on their mind. For Epicurus, every sense impression is "true." If an impression differs from the issuing object, it is not the sense impression that is false but one's judgment about it. The image itself actually *is* the way one's senses receive it. The difference between object and impression is attributable to the fact that images change as they are transmitted through space. Since images incessantly stream from all objects, these myriad images inevitably collide in space, occluding each other, tearing each other apart, and tangling into distorted masses or fantastic hybrids. For instance, if a cube-shaped object submerged in shallow water appears oblong, this is not an optical illusion but the true image of what appears before you stamped on your mind. Even visions, dreams, and figments of the imagination are true impressions. One dreams that one sees a deceased friend living and moving because the image of the friend has streamed from the corpse and mingled with the images of the living and moving as images traffic across space. Similarly, one envisages a centaur when one receives the conjoined images of a man and a horse that have collided while traveling through the air—a natural fiction to be sure, but no less true an impression. If one judges from such images that the dead yet live or that centaurs exist, then one has only drawn false conclusions from the true sense impressions stamped on the mind.

#### Preconceptions

The repeated experience of a particular sense impression creates a preconception, a generic concept stored in the mind that provides a prototype against which

14. Diogenes Laërtius, *Vit. phil.* 10.29.

15. Diogenes Laërtius, *Vit. phil.* 10.30. Diogenes Laërtius provides an epitome in *Vit. phil.* 10.31–34. See collected fragments and testimonia on Epicurean canonic (or epistemology) in LS §6–19.

further impressions of like kind can be self-evidently identified. Hence, for Epicurus, we know nothing *a priori* (contra Plato); we know only these conceptions that form over time from prior sense experiences. Preconceptions in turn establish a firm apprehension (*katalēpsis*) of concepts, in distinction from mere opinions (*doxa*). For instance, when one encounters a "man" time and again, one forms a preconception of the genus "man" and is now able to recognize particular "men" as such against this firmly established category.

Preconceptions are what account for humanity's universal belief in the existence of gods. Indeed, the gods also give off "images," which reach us over and over from their point of origin, thus imprinting a conception of them on our minds. Moreover, it is from these images that we know that the gods have anthropomorphic features. It is also from these images that we know that the gods are blessed, eternal, and untroubled.

#### The Feelings

Epicurus recognized as another canon of knowledge "the feelings." By feelings, he had in mind primarily the feelings of pleasure (*hēdonē*) and pain (*to algein*). He observed that all people seem naturally to avoid pain and to pursue pleasure. He therefore concluded that pleasure ought to be the starting point for all we choose and avoid.

### *Physics*

The foundation of Epicurus's physics derives almost wholly from the pre-Socratic atomist philosopher Democritus.[16] According to Epicurus (and Democritus), all that exists are infinite matter and infinite void. Matter consists entirely of atoms, tiny (literally "indivisible," *atoma*) primordial particles that teem in the empty void.[17]

#### Generative Atoms

Atoms come in various shapes and sizes, some smaller and some larger, some round and smooth, others barbed and twisted, and many such variations. These all fall downward through the void, carried by their own weight. Since they travel at a uniform speed, they never collide but by their occasional "swerving" (*declinatio*),[18] which happens at random. These collisions then alter the atomic trajectories, thus stimulating further collisions, like billiard balls shooting off each other helter-skelter. Because of their irregular shapes, the atoms become tangled and gradually accumulate. Over infinite time, and by infinite collisions of infinite atoms, worlds

---

16. Epicurus is said not to have credited him.

17. Epicurus offers an epitome of his physics in his *Letter to Herodotus* (= Diogenes Laërtius, *Vit. phil.* 10.35–83). See also Cicero, *On the Nature of the Gods*, book 2. See collected fragments and testimonia on Epicurean physics in LS §4–15.

18. While Epicurus's atomism is deeply indebted to Democritus, the "swerve" is his own innovation. *Declinatio* is the word given to this phenomenon in Latin texts (e.g., Cicero, *Fat.* 22).

arise across the infinite void as marvelous creations of these generative particles. In this way, atoms are the beginning and the cause of all things.

### The Corporeal Soul

Epicurus reasoned that nothing can exist apart from these atoms (and void) since only bodies (*sōmata*) can affect bodies. The immaterial can have no effect on the material. If then there exists a soul, this too must be bodily; that is to say, it too must be constituted by atoms. Sharing a common atomic nature, body and soul can now interact, "like affecting like."

The soul contains a unique mixture of atoms of three types in particular: one fire-like, one wind-like, and most importantly, a nameless third type responsible for gathering the soul into a unity. This third type, fine and smooth, moves quickly and easily and is responsible for human reason and judgment. Although the soul extends throughout the body, its command center, the rational part, resides in the chest.

Because the soul contains the reasoning faculty, the soul bears most of the responsibility for sensation. Yet, the soul would not have sensation were it not joined with the bodily frame. Therefore, the body on the one hand maintains sense perception even when some portion of the body is lost, for the soul remains. The soul on the other hand is so joined with the body that a loss of a portion of the body results in loss of some portion of the soul. When the body is sufficiently broken, the soul no longer remains but is dispersed. Just as the body loses sensation without the soul, so the soul loses sensation without the body.

In fact, due to its atomic nature, the soul dissipates completely, for while the atoms themselves are eternal, their combinations are not. As the soul disintegrates, its atoms disperse into the void in which countless crowds of atoms swarm. Death, then, is not only the separation of the soul from the body. It is the dissolution of the soul, the end of one's existence.

### Atoms and Sense Impressions

Atomic theory more fully elucidates Epicurus's theory of sense impressions. The images that stream from objects to our sense faculties are nothing other than films of *atoms*, which maintain the shapes of the objects from which they emanate, so long as their course and shapes are not altered by collisions with other flying films. These corporeal images—or atomic films—leave physical impressions on the corporeal soul. This is what makes all sense impressions "true": What is perceived is an atomically constituted (that is, a material) image imprinted on the sense faculties.

### Atoms and the Gods

All of this leads to some interesting conclusions about the gods. First, if the gods exist, then they also must be corporeal. Naturally, their atomic constitution will be of a finer sort, but they will nonetheless be material. Second, if atoms generate the universe and explain all of its recurring phenomena, then this precludes any causal contributions on the part of the gods. In fact, any such activity, which must be considered "labor," would be trouble to the gods and diminish their tranquility. This point leads, third, to the conclusion that the gods must be completely indifferent to human affairs. The immortal mother of Achilles would not lament that her son was not duly honored. Venus would not fret over whether Aeneas would fulfill his destiny. Juno would not malevolently contrive repeated devices to thwart the Trojans. These untroubled beings would never grow anxious about the well-being or conflicts of mortal favorites, or strive with one another over mundane matters, or indeed even notice human affairs at all.

In short, creation and causation can be sufficiently explained apart from the gods. Yet, eliminating the need for divine intervention was not, in Epicurus's view, the same as denying that the gods existed. In fact, as laid out above, we know from our preconceptions that they do exist. Epicurus concludes that while the gods do not busy themselves with mundane affairs, they do live, happy and untroubled, somewhere "between the worlds" (*intermundia/metakosmion*).

#### Natural Phenomena

By ruling out divine providence, Epicurus's notion of atomic causality brought back upon him the burden of discovering new explanations for celestial phenomena like comets, lightning, and rainbows, the risings and settings of the heavenly bodies, eclipses, and all the other phenomena that happen in nature. Epicurus remained convinced that such phenomena had natural explanations. He admitted, however, that he was none too concerned with locating the correct explanations or even with finding explanations that were particularly compelling. For him, it was sufficient if we could but set forth possibilities or even a range of possibilities—anything, so long as our explanation didn't appeal to providence, or as he called it, "myth."[19]

### Ethics

#### The Ethical End

With canonic and physics, Epicurus established a theoretical basis for his ethics.[20] The *kritērion* of the feelings establishes that pain is to be avoided and pleasure pursued. Moreover, this instinct is according to our nature, since it is instinctive to all creatures as soon as they are born. This observation furnishes the grounds for Epicurus's ethical *end*—that of pleasure (*hēdonē*). All other objects of pursuit are merely instrumental. Even virtue is not to be sought for its own sake but only as a means to pleasure, for practicing virtue engenders pleasure. Put differently, we practice virtue not because it is good for its own sake, but because it is expedient—indeed, pleasurable—to do so.

---

19. *Letter to Pythocles* // Diogenes Laërtius, *Vit. phil.* 10.104.

20. An epitome of Epicurus's ethics is preserved in his *Letter to Menoeceus* (= Diogenes Laërtius, *Vit. phil.* 10.122–35). An account is given also in Cicero, *On Ends*, book 1. See collected fragments and testimonia on Epicurean ethics in LS §20–25.

### Static and Dynamic Pleasure

It was, however, a particular kind of pleasure that Epicurus sought. He distinguished two types: static (*katastēmatikē*) and dynamic (*kata kinēsin*). Static pleasures pertain to pleasure as a state, like being not hungry. Dynamic pleasures pertain to pleasure in motion, like the pleasure of eating. Epicurus decided that the highest end consisted in the former—in the *state* of pleasure. Hence, Epicurus's kind of pleasure is not the kind that consists in titillation of the senses or in sensual indulgence. The very highest pleasure is achieved merely in the absence of pain (*algein*) or disturbance (*tarattesthai*). This pain-free pleasurable state is absolute, impossible to increase or decrease. Indeed, Epicurus contended, one cannot intensify an absence of pain.

But could one not *add* some positive delight to this absence of pain and thus achieve still a higher pleasure? Epicurus is prepared to answer: Dynamic pleasure does not add to the pleasure but only "varies" it.[21] One reaches supreme happiness when one has attained absence of pain only.

### Natural and Necessary Pleasures

If there is validity to the aspersions cast on Epicurus by his contemporaries—that he vomited twice a day due to overeating, that he consorted with prostitutes, and that he engaged in other such indulgences—such behavior was not, at any rate, consistent with his doctrines.[22] His understanding of pleasure as absence of pain rather entailed an austere kind of hedonism. He advised that one ought not pursue every pleasure, since an excess of pleasure often results in pain—the very thing one is trying to avoid.

Mindful of this, Epicurus said that one must carefully consider the nature of what one desires. Some desires are natural, some unnatural; some are necessary, others unnecessary; some are both natural and necessary; and others are neither natural nor necessary. Necessary pleasures include things like food, water, and protection from the elements. These things are always worthy choices, for their absence results in pain. Natural pleasures include things like better food, good wine, or enjoying a warm bath. Such things are acceptable objects of pursuit, so long as their acquisition, or the effort to obtain them, does not result in pain. For instance, if eating rich food (or too much of it) is likely to cause you indigestion, then you might want to content yourself with raw vegetables. Conversely, some pains actually lead to greater pleasure. For instance, if you neglect exercise because it makes you hot and tired, but you develop detrimental health conditions as a result, you come into pain on the back end—perhaps very intense, even fatal, pain. In some cases, ascetic practices might carry you to the ultimate End. Adopting a meager diet temporarily might reveal that your needs are slighter than you had realized, allowing you to reduce the level of effort needed to reach contentedness or pass the threshold of satiety necessary for happiness in the future. In short, attaining plea-

21. Diogenes Laërtius, *Vit. phil.* 10.144 = *Kur. Dox.* 18.

22. It was a former student who accused him of overeating (Diogenes Laërtius, *Vit. phil.* 10.6); on consorting with prostitutes, see Diogenes Laërtius, *Vit. phil.* 10.7.

sure requires balancing projected outcomes and then pursuing only those things that are most conducive to the goal.

### Bodily and Mental Pains

Epicurus noted that we experience not only bodily pleasures and pains, but also mental pleasures and pains. In his view, the mental kinds are more intense. Bodily pleasures are quickly forgotten, and bodily pains are either light or fleeting. By contrast, mental pleasures, like a good conversation with a close friend, last longer in the memory and are prepotent enough to trump concurrent sensations of pain. Conversely, while pains in the body are felt only at the moment of sensation and do not linger when the pain subsides, the thoughts of things past, present, and future can mount to afflict the mind more heavily. Hence, mental pleasure is more to be pursued and mental pain more to be avoided than bodily pleasures and pains.

### Freedom from Disturbance

Epicurus calls this freedom from mental pain *ataraxia*, or "freedom from disturbance." In his view, the weightiest impetus toward mental disturbance is belief in the gods of "superstition"—that is, the gods of tradition. These gods cause people immense mental pain, for people believe them to be fickle and vindictive, punishing both now on earth and in the underworld hereafter. Thus people live in constant insecurity and fearful expectation of divine punishment. Ignorant of the true causes of things, they tremble at the heavenly bodies, believing them to be endowed with intelligence and volition, and at celestial phenomena, which they fear are sent as warnings or instruments of imminent destruction. Epicurus emphasized that understanding how the universe really works banishes such fears. We need only believe that atoms cause everything, not the gods. Atoms bear no ill will. In any case, the soul, composed as it is of these atoms, will perish with the body. There can be no punishment, for we will not even exist. On these grounds, we can proclaim that "death is nothing to us." For "when we are, death is not, and when death has come, we are not."[23]

While Epicurus's views provoked charges of atheism,[24] he emphasized that he did not reject the existence of "the gods" per se, but only the gods "worshipped by the multitude."[25] Like many philosophers before him, he felt that the real gods had to be superior to the gods depicted in myths and civic cults.[26] In fact, the real gods are our greatest exemplars: models of perfect tranquility, untroubled by fear or labor, and in full possession of *ataraxia*. Moreover, their images, which are carried to our minds from their holy bodies, bring us peace. If we are to be untroubled, then, we should pursue "likeness to the gods."

Epicurus's concern for mental security compelled him to eschew involvement in politics and in the hard struggle for honors won by climbing the political ladder. He observed that the ambitious pursuit of political success causes subjects

---

23. *Epistle to Menoeceus* // Diogenes Laërtius, *Vit. phil.* 10.125.
24. Cicero, *Nat. d.* 1.30.85, 123.
25. *Letter to Menoeceus* // Diogenes Laërtius, *Vit. phil.* 10.124.
26. Cf. Cicero, *Nat. d.* 1.16.42–43.

considerable anxiety and that, even if one achieves the offices desired, it only ushers in pressures that induce mental distress. Epicurus himself, foregoing the stresses of city life, preferred a quiet life of withdrawal lived among a community of intimate friends—a way of life most conducive of *ataraxia*.

#### The Wise Man

For Epicurus, the kind of person who consistently pursues natural and (above all) necessary pleasures in such a way that they can live free of pain, or at least free of pains that don't promise greater pleasures, or of pains that can't be overcome by more potent mental pleasures—thus reaching a state of *ataraxia—this* kind of person is a true "wise man." Epicurus's presentation of the wise man was inspired by the Stoic prototype but deliberately formulated in opposition to its underlying substance.[27] The Stoic wise man, on the one hand, was the one who conformed his will to the perfect plan of providence, able to regard even his own physical condition as indifferent because he was able to discern his condition as part of a better plan for the universe. Epicurus's wise man, on the other hand, denied both providence and the indifference of pain, regarding pain rather as the greatest of all evils.

How then could Epicurus's wise man remain happy when pain is the greatest evil and it also falls outside our control? For the Stoic wise man, pain posed no obstacle to his happiness, for pain was no evil. But for Epicurus, pain was the worst evil of all. Two considerations explain how his wise man could yet achieve happiness. First, one has the ability to mitigate pain by pursuing only those desires that are necessary and natural—i.e., desires that will not lead subsequently to pain. Second, mental pleasures weigh more heavily than physical pain, making freedom from mental disturbance poignant enough to overwhelm bodily pain. In this way, the wise man could remain happy in all circumstances. In fact, he could be happy, Epicurus said, "even on the rack," though he will groan.[28]

In sum, Epicurus was convinced that neither honor nor power is able to engender happiness, nor dainties or rousing of the senses, and certainly not religion, which destroys rather than creates happiness. Only philosophy can engender happiness. And not just any philosophy, but his own philosophy. Due to his salutary doctrines, Epicurus's followers considered him a savior, indeed a god, who makes us also like gods if we but follow his precepts.[29]

## Philosophy as Therapy for the Soul

It is easy to see that Epicurus's philosophy was not simply theoretical but was supremely, if not primarily, practical. His philosophy was "therapy for the soul."

27. LS (*The Hellenistic Philosophers*, 1:138–39) observe that parallel descriptions of the wise man suggest that the Epicurean portrait was developed as a deliberate attempt to rival the Stoic one.

28. Diogenes Laërtius, *Vit. phil.* 10.118.

29. "Savior" in Philodemus, *Lib.*//fr. 40; cf. 43. Like a "god" (*deus*) in Cicero, *Tusc.* 1.48; *Nat. d.* 1.43; Lucretius, *Rer. nat.* 3.1–30; 5.8–10.

Like any therapy, it entailed a regimen of treatment. A post-Hellenist Epicurean named Philodemus distilled Epicurus's doctrines into a fourfold remedy, often called the *tetrapharmakon*: (1) God is no reason to fear, (2) death is no reason to worry, (3) pleasure is easy to get, and (4) pain is easy to endure.[30] Within Epicurean communities, members aided one another other by diagnosing one another's problems—problems of both thought and behavior—and prescribing appropriate remedies. For instance, a student troubled by the prospect of death would be reproached and reminded of Epicurus's doctrines that taught why death is not to be feared and how to banish such fears.

Epicurus advised committing his doctrines to memory, especially main headings and short formulas, so one could make ready use of them in moments of need. "Exercise yourself," he said, "in these and kindred precepts day and night, both by yourself and with him who is like unto you; then never, either in waking or in dream, will you be disturbed, but will live as a god among men."[31]

## Notes on the Primary Sources

Epicurus reportedly produced three hundred rolls (many of which are listed in Diogenes Laërtius, *Vit. phil.* 10.28–29), but no complete work of Epicurus has survived. There remain, however, three letters preserved by Diogenes Laërtius that provide epitomes, respectively, of Epicurus's physics (*Letter to Herodotus* = Diogenes Laërtius, *Vit. phil.* 10.35–83), his views on astronomy and meteorology (*Letter to Pythocles* = Diogenes Laërtius, *Vit. phil.* 10.83–116), and his ethics (*Epistle to Menoeceus* = Diogenes Laërtius, *Vit. phil.* 10.122–35). Diogenes Laërtius (*Vit. phil.* 10.139–54) also preserves Epicurus's principal doctrines (the *Kyriae Doxae*) in a collection of forty short articles, perhaps collected by a disciple of Epicurus. The so-called Vatican Sayings, preserved in a single Vatican manuscript, represent eighty-one sayings excerpted from Epicurus's thirty-seven-book, but no longer extant, work *On Nature*, which laid out his physics in full. The most complete account of Epicureanism is preserved in a work titled "On the Nature of the Gods," a Latin poem written by an Epicurean named Lucretius in the first half of the first century BCE representing what is believed to be a poetic rendering of Epicurus's *On Nature* itself. Additionally, large portions have been reconstructed of a 25,000-word inscription originally inscribed on a Lycian wall under the patronage of Diogenes of Oenoanda (probably second c. CE), displaying for the benefit of Diogenes's fellow citizens an account of Epicurus's philosophy and some of his sayings. A library of Epicurean texts was found at Herculaneum buried beneath layers of volcanic ash that rained on the city when Mount Vesuvius erupted in 79 CE. The papyri recovered from Herculaneum, in the eighteenth century, include partly legible portions of Epicurus's *On Nature*. Among other texts recovered were several works of Philodemus, a first-century BCE Epicurean who led a school in Herculaneum. Mostly preserved is his work *On Frank Criticism*, in which he discusses

30. Philodemus, *P. Herc.* 1000, col. V.

31. Diogenes Laërtius, *Vit. phil.* 10.135; translation based on LCL, Hicks.

pedagogical techniques for facilitating moral improvement based on the doctrines of Epicurus. Philodemus's treatises *On Anger*, *On Household Management*, and *On Piety* have also been recovered. Due to the stalwart commitment of Epicureans to the teachings of their founder, Lucretius, Philodemus, and other later sources likely provide reliable representation of the earliest Epicurean views. In addition, some nonphilosophical texts of the post-Hellenistic era commonly reflect Epicurean attitudes, such as Horace's *Epistles* and *Satires*.

Other Epicurean sources derive from authors who were not themselves Epicurean or who were hostile to Epicureanism. During the post-Hellenistic period, Cicero treats Epicurean views at length in his philosophical dialogues *On the Nature of the Gods* (book 2) and *On Ends* (book 1), respectively treating views on the gods and ethics. Polemical responses to Epicureanism are found in Roman-era treatises by Plutarch (*That Epicurus Makes a Pleasant Life Impossible* and *Against Colotes*) and Sextus Empiricus (portions of *Against the Dogmatists*).

Testimonia and fragments attesting to early Epicurean views have been collected and organized by topic in LS (1987), §4–25. Excerpts are also available in Inwood and Gerson (1997) and in Inwood (1994).

## Key Terms and Concepts

- *Ataraxia* (freedom from disturbance)
- Atoms
- Corporeal soul
- Images (*eidōla*)
- *Intermundia*, the
- Mental and bodily pain/pleasure
- Necessary and natural pains/pleasures
- Pleasure (*hēdonē*)
- Preconceptions (*prolēpseis*)
- Sensation (*aisthēsis*)
- Static and dynamic pleasure
- Swerve, the (*declinatio*)
- Therapy for the soul
- Tranquility of the gods, the
- Void

## For Further Study

### *Primary Sources*

Inwood, Brad, and L. P. Gerson, trans. *Hellenistic Philosophy: Introductory Readings*. 2nd ed. Indianapolis, IN: Hackett, 1997.

Inwood, Brad, and L. P. Gerson, trans. and eds. *The Epicurus Reader: Selected Writings and Testimonia*. Indianapolis, IN: Hackett, 1994.

Long, A. A., and David N. Sedley. *The Hellenistic Philosophers*. 2 vols. Cambridge: Cambridge University Press, 1987.

## *Secondary Sources*

Arenson, Kelly, ed. *The Routledge Handbook of Hellenistic Philosophy*. Routledge Handbooks. London: Routledge, 2020.

Nussbaum, Martha C. *The Therapy of Desire: Theory and Practice in Hellenistic Ethics*. Princeton, NJ: Princeton University Press, 1994.

O'Keefe, T. *Epicureanism*. Chesham, UK: Acumen, 2010.

Sellars, John. *The Pocket Epicurean*. Chicago: University of Chicago Press, 2021.

Sharples, R. W. *Stoics, Epicureans and Skeptics*. London: Routledge, 1996.

Warren, James, ed. *The Cambridge Companion to Epicureanism*. Cambridge: Cambridge University Press, 2009.

Wilson, C. *Epicureanism: A Very Short Introduction*. Oxford: Oxford University Press, 2015.

# 10

# The Skeptical Academy

Although the Academy was not exactly a new school in the Hellenistic era, Plato would nevertheless have been surprised to discover how it had changed from the school he had founded. After his death in 347 BCE, the Academy fell to the leadership of a line of successors who carefully safeguarded his teachings (including unwritten ones). At the beginning of the Hellenistic era, however, the school took a sharp turn of interest as its new heads shifted attention away from doctrinal Platonism and developed an overshadowing interest in epistemology. The new emphasis was primarily a reaction to the dogmatism of two newer schools that had recently come on the scene—namely, the Stoic and Epicurean schools. Against the dogmatists, the Academics argued that certainty of knowledge could not be achieved, a point that called into question the basic epistemologies on which the Stoic and Epicurean philosophical systems were based. The epistemological skepticism of the New Academy became the most defining feature of the school. Thus the Academics became known as Skeptics, or the Skeptical Academy.

## Dogmatism and Skepticism in the Academy

Whether the skepticism of the Academy in the Hellenistic period represented a complete departure from their Platonic heritage was a matter of some debate. Academics variably emphasized the skepticism of Socrates, and even of Plato, and thus variably emphasized their own continuity or discontinuity with the original Academy. Although some sources identify only one "Academy" across the school's history, with a continuous Socratic and Platonic heritage extending through the end of the Hellenistic period, the dominant ancient tradition identifies at least two, and sometimes as many as five, "Academies." What the Academy stood for was different at each stage.

After the death of Plato, the Academy fell to the headship of his nephew Speusippus (head 347–339 BCE), followed in turn by Xenocrates (head 339–314 BCE), Polemo (head 314/313–270/269 BCE), and Crates (third century BCE). Allegedly, these successors adhered to Plato's doctrines—including both written and unwritten ones—as they had received them. Xenocrates assembled these doctrines into a formal system organized according to the threefold division of physics, ethics, and logic.[1] The Academy of this period would later be referred to as the Old Academy.

1. Sextus Empiricus, *Math.* 7.16–19.

A middle period began when headship passed from Crates to Arcesilaus (head ca. 268 BCE).[2] Under Arcesilaus, the school took a more skeptical turn. Arcesilaus looked back with admiration to Socrates, who had insisted that he knew only that he knew nothing while being committed nevertheless to inquiring (*skeptesthai*) after the truth. Fittingly, Arcesilaus is said to have been the first of the Academics to advocate arguing on both sides of a question and to insist on suspension of judgment due to the possibility, in every case, of balancing opposing arguments.[3]

The precise views of Arcesilaus are difficult to extract from sources, and accounts conflict. He is depicted sometimes as a thoroughgoing skeptic who believed that nothing could be known.[4] He was, however, sometimes accused of promoting skepticism while being in truth doctrinaire,[5] even using his antagonism as a means of testing whether his interlocutors were prepared to receive Plato's doctrines.[6] Ultimately, Arcesilaus's skepticism seems to have been motivated less by a hard conviction that nothing whatsoever could be known than by specific concerns the dogmatism of some of his contemporaries. He was especially intent on undermining the epistemological positivism of the Stoics and urged others to keep an open mind rather than display blind allegiance to received teachings.

Head of the Academy from 155 to 137/136 BCE, Carneades (ca. 214/213–129/128 BCE) inaugurated what was later called the New Academy.[7] Like Arcesilaus, Carneades sought to defeat the dogmatism of the Stoics by demonstrating that truth cannot be known for certain. Carneades, however, exceeded Arcesilaus's skepticism by adopting a kind of "negative dogmatism," whereby he argued that nothing could be known whatsoever, not even the premise that we know nothing. Carneades's conviction that for every argument there is an equal and opposite argument induced him to argue strenuously against the existence of the gods—at least for the sake of argument—thus incurring charges that he was an atheist.[8] He also argued that the nature of virtue cannot be known. Thus, when in 155 BCE he traveled as an ambassador to Rome to protest a tax levied on Athens, he discoursed at length about justice in the hearing of the emperor and the censor but on the next day overturned his arguments and argued against justice, as if practicing a rhetorical exercise in which arguments are given pro and contra without resolution.[9]

Like Arcesilaus, Carneades's main intent was not to advance arguments as positive claims, but first and foremost to marshal proofs that dogmatism—particularly, the dogmatism of the Stoics—was unfounded. He challenged especially the Stoics' notion of *cataleptic*, or cognitive, impressions (see chapter 8). The Stoics had main-

---

2. Diogenes Laërtius, *Vit. phil.* 4.28.

3. Diogenes Laërtius, *Vit. phil.* 4.28.

4. LS §68a, f, k.

5. LS §68i; 69c.

6. LS §68i.

7. Sextus Empiricus marks Carneades as the transitional figure between the Middle and the New Academy (*Pyr.* 1.220), though Diogenes Laërtius credits Lacydes (head of the Academy ca. 242–216 BCE) as the founder of the new (*Vit. phil.* 4.59).

8. Cicero, *Nat. d.* 3.44.

9. LS §68m.

tained that it is possible always to adjudicate successfully between what is true and false in what occurs to the reasoning faculty, whether concerning sense impressions or propositional statements. They said that the wise man is capable of doing this infallibly, assenting only to true impressions, from every sense impression achieving secure knowledge (*epistemē*). Carneades countered that some impressions could be so deceptive that they would not occur as *cataleptic* even to the wise man. Say, if Socrates had a twin brother who matched him in color, size, shape, manner of conversation and dress, and indeed in every other way, then one's judgment as to whether this was Socrates or his brother would not be self-evident. Harder still, two eggs might look so nearly identical that no person, when asked to identify this one or the other, could discern the correct one with certainty, even if he could make an accurate guess.[10] In such cases, Carneades pointed out, the truth would not be *cataleptic* (self-evident), but non-*cataleptic* (non-evident). Consequently, either the wise man must suspend judgment, or he must assent without certainty; that is, he must "opine"—something the Stoic wise man is said never to do.

A half a century later, Philo of Larissa (head 110/109–88 BCE) determined to move the Academy from skepticism to a kind of probabilism. Rejecting suspension of judgment as the ideal resolution to inquiry, he argued that while the discerning philosopher could be mistaken (even the wise man cannot be certain), one should *aim* to land on the truth or at least on what appears "most *like* the truth." Hence, rather than suspending judgment after weighing arguments, it would behoove the philosopher to affirm the conclusion that seems most probable.

In 86 BCE, the Romans' invasion of Athens destroyed the physical site of the Academy. Two years later (84 BCE), an Academic named Antiochus returned to Athens and resumed teaching in the gymnasium known as the Ptolemy. Antiochus wholly abandoned skepticism and—contending that the Academy had forgotten the true doctrines of Plato—called for a return to dogmatic Platonism. Hence, Antiochus instituted, or rather reinstituted, the Old Academy; i.e., the Academy as it had been in the time of Plato and his early successors (see fig. 5).

This five-stage periodization finds testimony in ancient accounts. Schemas, however, vary according to authors' assessments of perceived continuities and discontinuities across the history of a school.[11] In the second century CE, Sextus Empiricus noted that some people said there were three Academies (those of Plato, Arcesilaus, and Carneades), others four (adding Philo), and others five (adding Philo and Antiochus).[12]

Cicero's *Academica* offers two alternative schemes. The *Academica* traces the history of the Academy from Plato down to Cicero's own times from two different perspectives. First, Varro—an advocate of Antiochus's dogmatism—presents the transition from Plato and the Old Academy in the early period up to the Skeptics of the later period as one of sharp discontinuity. While Varro admits that Socrates

---

10. Sextus Empiricus, *Math.* 7.408–10.

11. Modern scholars disagree as to which scheme (options below) is more historically accurate. Accepting Sextus Empiricus's scheme: Stefano Maso, *Cicero's Philosophy*, Trends in Classics 3 (Berlin: De Gruyter, 2022), 55; Cicero's scheme: LS, *Hellenistic Philosophers*, 1:448.

12. Sextus Empiricus, *Pyr.* 1.220.

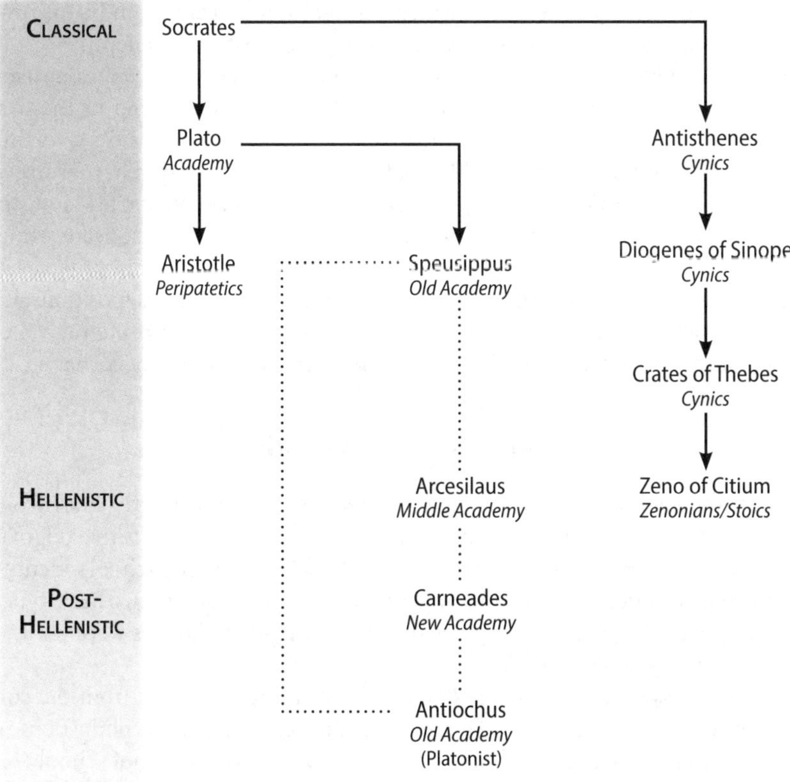


Figure 5. The Socratic tradition in the Classical and Hellenistic eras.

had emphasized his own ignorance and nothing more, Varro counters that Plato and the early Academics introduced positive dogmatic claims and devised a regular arrangement of subjects and a complete doctrinal system that integrated ethics, physics, and logic.[13] It was only with Arcesilaus that the school turned to skepticism and began idealizing the suspension of judgment.[14] Thus, according to Varro, the history of the Academy divided into *two*: the Old Academy, reaching from Plato to Crantor (d. 290 BCE) and the New Academy, spanning from Arcesilaus (head from 268 BCE) to Philo (head from 110/109–88 BCE). With Antiochus, the Old Academy was restored (reestablished 84 BCE).

Cicero himself takes up a counter position. Adopting the probabilism of Philo, Cicero sees the Academy as having always emphasized skepticism. From his perspective, even Plato argued both pro and contra, inquiring into all things without making decisive statements. In this way, Cicero highlights Plato's skepticism after the example of Socrates and as carried on in the period from Arcesilaus to Philo. Consequently, Cicero objects to Varro's distinction between an "Old" and a "New"

13. Cicero, *Acad.* 1.16–17, 19.
14. Cicero, *Acad.* 1.45.

Academy, seeing even Carneades's Academy as old, since it carried on Plato's own practices. In short, Cicero asserts that has always been just *one* Academy.[15]

This discrepancy over the school's traditional emphasis anticipates a divergence of trajectories that branched out from the school beginning in the first century BCE. Antiochus's interest in recovering dogmatic Platonism set forth a trajectory that would lead into Middle Platonism—a synthetic system that strove to harmonize Plato's diffuse teachings and, at the same time, to reconcile Platonism with other philosophical systems. On the other hand, one of the last heads of the Academy, Aenesidemus (ca. 80–10 BCE), leaned further into skepticism than even his Academic peers, advocating for the extreme, Pyrrhonist, skeptical position, and ultimately parting ways with the Academy. Middle Platonism and the revival of Pyrrhonism at the beginning of this period will be treated more fully in chapter 12.

## Skeptics Versus Dogmatists

The Skeptical methodology of the New Academy set them distinctly apart from the other schools. The New Academy refrained from advancing positive dogmas and hence was not defined by a particular doctrinal system. The school's identity was rooted in skepticism itself. Thus arose a recognized division of two basic types of philosophers: Skeptics and Dogmatists.[16] (Among other Skeptics were the Pyrrhonists, to be discussed in chapter 13.)

While the Skeptics, on the one hand, exulted in their freedom from the constraints of binding doctrine, the Dogmatic philosophers regarded philosophical systems as mutually exclusive choices (*haireseis*), with one's choice of school constituting a commitment to the founder who authored the system. This culture of philosophical allegiance (see chapter 7) created clear boundaries between opposing groups and sharp lines of identity. To the Academic Skeptics, these tendencies reflected an unfounded positivism and an irrational commitment to the authority of just one man.

## The Academy and the Highest End

With the Academy's turn toward skepticism, there surfaced another new perspective on the highest human good or end (see table 8). Socrates had declared virtue, wisdom, and the health of the soul worthy to be pursued above all else—more than health, wealth, power, fame, and all those bodily and external things that most people value. As noted in chapter 5, Plato introduced a formal distinction between goods of the body, external goods, and intellectual goods (i.e., the virtues), and like Socrates held up virtue as the highest of them all. After Plato, Speusippus and the Old Academy offered varying descriptions of the end that all tended to locate happiness in the possession of virtue and the excellences most proper to human

15. Cicero, *Acad.* 1.43–46 (see also *Nat. d.* 1.5.11); he finally concedes to Varro's distinction, though he disagrees with it (1.46).

16. Diogenes Laërtius, *Vit. phil.* 1.16; Sextus Empiricus, *Pyr.* 1.1–30.

beings—that is to say, in the combination of goods of the soul *and* the goods of the body.[17] Polemo, the last head of the Old Academy, is said to have defined the highest end as "living a virtuous life while enjoying those primary things that nature recommends to man."[18] In any case, this is the report given by Antiochus, who reestablished the Old Academy in the first century BCE. He himself also connected the highest end with virtue.

The New Academy held a different view. They argued that if reason is insufficient to secure us with certainty of knowledge, and if the nature of virtue cannot be known, then the highest end cannot be identified with the perfection of knowledge or the acquisition of virtue. One would not be able to attain this knowledge or even be aware of what kind of virtue at which to aim. Such as things are, our best recourse is to balance arguments on each question, weighing pro and contra. Then, seeing that it is impossible to decide between viewpoints, we should make no attempt to do so. According to Arcesilaus and the New Academy, this was the ethical end: the "suspension of judgment" (*epochē*).[19]

TABLE 8. "The End" according to the Classical and Hellenistic schools

| SCHOOL | "THE END" |
|---|---|
| Old Academy | Living according to virtue while enjoying the bodily goods that nature recommends |
| Stoics | Living in accordance with nature (= living virtuously) |
| Epicureans | Pleasure (= absence of pain) |
| Skeptical Academy | Suspension of judgment |

## The Academy and Traditional Religion

The thoroughgoing skepticism of the New Academy inevitably raised questions about their commitment to traditional religion. Cicero's dialogue *On the Nature of the Gods* showcases the kinds of arguments that proponents of the New Academy

17. See the various definitions and the primary sources in John Dillon, *Alcinous: The Handbook of Platonism; Introduction, Text and Commentary* (Oxford: Oxford University Press, 2003), xxxviii.

18. This according to Polemo and Antiochus, as reported by Cicero (*Acad.* 2.42.131; cf. *Tusc.* 5.10.30; 5.13.39; *Fin.* 4.6.14;); see also Augustine, *Civ.* 19.3.

19. Sextus Empiricus, *Pyr.* 1.232–4. According to Cicero, this was the position of "certain Academics" (*Fin.* 3.9.31).

used against not only divination practices, but also the notion of divine providence, and even the very existence of the gods. In theory, their primary intention was to undermine certainty, though uncertainty entailed final suspension of judgment as a matter of course. Ironically, Cicero's Academic spokesperson (Cotta) in *On the Nature of the Gods* was the incumbent high priest of the Roman commonwealth. Finding himself unable to justify civic religion philosophically, he justified its validity finally with one single argument: "Namely, that it has been handed down to us by our forefathers" and nothing more.[20]

## Notes on the Primary Sources

The writings of Academics from Arcesilaus to Antiochus survive only in fragments. Long and Sedley (1987) have collected and arranged the fragments by topic (§68–70), supplementing the text with commentary. For a similar resource, see Inwood and Gerson (1997). Cicero's philosophical dialogues are invaluable sources for Academic views. Of special note are *On the Nature of the Gods*, *On Ends of Goods and Evils*, and the *Academica*. Sextus Empiricus discusses the various stages in the history of the Academy in *Outlines of Pyrrhonism* (1.220), as well as the differences between the Academic Skeptics and the Pyrrhonist Skeptics (1.1–30). Diogenes Laërtius's *Lives of Eminent Philosophers* includes biographies of the heads of the Academy, covering Speusippus (4.1–5), Xenocrates (4.6–15), Polemo (4.16–20), Crates (4.21–23), and Crantor (4.24–27) of the Old Academy; and Arcesilaus (4.28–45), Lacydes (4.59–61), Carneades (4.62–66), and Clitomachus (4.67) of the New.

## Key Terms and Concepts

- Middle Academy
- New Academy
- Non-*cataleptic* impressions
- Old Academy
- Skeptics vs. Dogmatists
- Suspension of judgment (*epochē*)

## For Further Study

### *Primary Sources*

Inwood, Brad, and L. P. Gerson, trans. *Hellenistic Philosophy: Introductory Readings*. 2nd ed. Indianapolis, IN: Hackett, 1997.

20. Cicero, *Acad.* 3.9.

Long, A. A., and David N. Sedley. *The Hellenistic Philosophers*. 2 vols. Cambridge: Cambridge University Press, 1987.

### *Secondary Sources*

Arenson, Kelly, ed. *The Routledge Handbook of Hellenistic Philosophy*. Routledge Handbooks. London: Routledge, 2020.

Bett, R., ed. *The Cambridge Companion to Ancient Scepticism*. Cambridge: Cambridge University Press, 2010.

Sellars, John. *Hellenistic Philosophy*. Oxford: Oxford University Press, 2018.

Sharples, R. W. *Stoics, Epicureans and Skeptics*. London: Routledge, 1996.

Thorsrud, H. *Ancient Scepticism*. Chesham, UK: Acumen, 2008.

# Part 3

# Post-Hellenistic Philosophy: Early First Century BCE to Mid-Third Century CE

# 11

# The Transitional Period

As Roman power moved east over the course of the second and first centuries BCE, the Greek dynasties that had formed in the wake of Alexander the Great fell one by one. In the pivotal year of 31 BCE, the Ptolemaic dynasty met its demise at the Battle of Actium, marking the end not only of the last of the Greek dynasties, but also of the Hellenistic Age (323–31 BCE).

This political transition coincided with some historic changes in the development of Greek philosophy, thus inaugurating what can be regarded as a new era in its history—namely, the era of post-Hellenistic philosophy.[1] The Roman invasion of Athens in 86 BCE had disbanded the great Athenian schools, terminating the lines of succession that had ensured the pure transmission of the founders' teachings. Rome's blow to Athens at the same time sent these philosophies on an outward wave of expansion that rippled across the Mediterranean world. Local schools sprang up everywhere. Major philosophical hubs formed in Alexandria, Pergamum, and Rhodes in the eastern provinces, and in Herculaneum and Rome in Italy. The arrival of philosophy in Rome spawned a thriving Latin philosophical tradition beginning in the early first century BCE. Meanwhile, philosophical traditions whose visibility had waned during the Hellenistic era experienced revivals, including the Pythagorean, Platonic, Peripatetic, and Cynic traditions, as well as skepticism in the Pyrrhonist tradition. Although these revivals brought a sharper sense of identity to members of the respective schools, the period of transition between roughly 100 BCE and 100 CE—what is often called the "transitional period"—also saw increased interaction between rival schools and a tendency to assimilate one another's material. One of the most important consequences of this dynamic was a gradual decline in the predominance of Stoicism as it became assimilated into a newly constituted form of Platonism known as "Middle Platonism."

Thus began the era of post-Hellenistic philosophy. The present chapter introduces some of the main features of the transitional period. These features included new attempts at systematization through commentary writing among schools experiencing revivals, the development of uniquely "Roman" philosophy, the dynamics of inter-school interaction and its effects on innovation, the move from Stoicism to Platonism as the dominant tradition, and the emergence of a generic "moral

1. The label "post-Hellenistic" is not uniformly adopted but is the chosen term of G. R. Boys-Stones, *Platonist Philosophy 80 BC to AD 250: An Introduction and Collection of Sources in Translation*, Cambridge Sourcebooks in Post-Hellenistic Philosophy (Cambridge: Cambridge University Press, 2018), 1.

tradition." We will discuss specific revivals, new traditions, and adaptations to old traditions in post-Hellenistic philosophy in chapters 12 to 15.

## School Revivals and Commentary Writing

Pythagoras may have been the first Greek "philosopher," but there is little evidence that he devised anything like a detailed philosophical "system." While the Classical philosophers Plato and Aristotle sought to offer integrated accounts of wide-ranging philosophical issues, even they did not synthesize their ideas into tight systems elaborated in expansive detail, as Zeno and Epicurus would later do. Early on, the followers of Pythagoras and Plato had endeavored to elaborate their teachers' ideas more systematically. Such efforts at synthesis, however, became more deliberate during the post-Hellenistic period. These efforts emanated from the culture of allegiance that had emerged in the preceding era. Motivating this activity was a felt imperative to match the level of systematic sophistication already reflected in the Stoic and Epicurean traditions.

In the absence of living successors, adherents of Plato's and Aristotle's views in the post-Hellenistic period looked back to their teachers' writings as canonical authorities (Pythagoras, on the other hand, had written nothing). Behind these writings, they believed, lay unified and consistent systems that had only to be discovered and fully elaborated. This assumption necessitated the delineation of a well-defined and coherently organized canon of texts, scrupulous attention to the exact letter, and critical interpretation geared toward synthesis and harmonization. Put differently, the interpreters' goals required the undertakings of canon criticism, text criticism, and scientific exegesis.

These aims gave rise to a flourishing "philosophical commentary" tradition beginning in the first century BCE.[2] The commentary tradition strengthened the renewal of interest in Classical philosophers like Plato and Aristotle, sharpened doctrinal boundaries between the respective philosophical systems, and enhanced a sense of definite sectarian identity. Thus Platonism and Aristotelianism rose to new prominence during the transitional period, now in a more systematic form artificially devised by adherents of the originators' traditions.

## Roman Philosophy

The Roman road to philosophy was a long one. Although Rome had known of Greek philosophy during the Hellenistic era, it was not until the first century BCE that a vibrant tradition of Latin philosophy began to flower. Latin philosophy constituted more than mere passive transmission of Greek philosophy in translation. Rather, it represented an adaptation of Greek philosophy in the direction of Roman

2. On commentaries on Plato and Aristotle, see Myrto Hatzimichaeli, "The Texts of Plato and Aristotle in the First Century," in *Aristotle, Plato and Pythagoreanism in the First Century BC: New Directions for Philosophy*, ed. Malcolm Schofield (Cambridge: Cambridge University Press, 2013), 1–27.

lifestyles and political interests. Latin philosophy thus represented another stream of philosophical innovation during the transitional period, as we will discuss in chapter 11.

## Interaction and Innovation

Among its other features, the transitional period between 100 BCE and 100 CE was one of increased interaction between school traditions. The sources describe Stoics who sound like Peripatetics (Arius Didymus), Platonists who sound like Stoics (Antiochus), and Stoics who sound like Platonists (Posidonius). While inter-school interaction could involve a substantial exchange of material, contemporary scholarship has shown that in practice this interaction led not to philosophical "eclecticism" but rather a creative assimilation of foreign material into one's own doctrinal tradition. In fact, only one philosopher in antiquity is known to have described himself as an "Eclectic (*eklektikos*)": Potamon of Alexandria.[3]

The schools' manner of appropriation could sometimes be characterized as irenic (appropriating rival material with a conciliatory attitude toward it), and sometimes as more polemical (rejecting a competing philosophy or subversively reinterpreting it within a new framework).[4] Yet appropriation of foreign material did not, in the minds of adherents, compromise the overall structure of their respective traditions. Adherents remained firmly fixed in their commitments to their distinct sectarian identities.

## From Stoicism to Platonism

Despite the persistent presence of sharp doctrinal boundaries between schools, their exchange of material did lead to some innovation. More often, these innovations were tantamount to Stoic concession to the doctrines of Platonism than vice versa. Platonism was on the ascent, and as it revived, it absorbed elements of Stoicism. This allowed it to offer, in addition to what it already had, the best of Stoicism with an admixture of Aristotelianism and Pythagoreanism to boot. Since Plato's corpus, smoothed into a consistent system, ultimately provided the overarching framework, the resulting synthesis could still rightly be considered "Platonism." Due to the remarkable ability of Platonism to draw the language and doctrines of foreign philosophical systems selectively into itself, by the third century CE, Stoicism, Aristotelianism, and Pythagoreanism virtually ceased to exist as independent entities. Only Platonism remained.

---

3. See Engberg-Pedersen, *From Stoicism to Platonism*; also Christopher Gill, "The School in the Roman Imperial Period," in *The Cambridge Companion to Stoicism*, ed. Brad Inwood (Cambridge: Cambridge University Press, 2003), 33–53. The "Eclectic" was Potamon of Alexandria (*I.Eph.* III.789), from the early first century CE. Diogenes Laërtius, however, also mentions that Potamon had an "Eclectic school" (*Vit. phil.* 1.21).

4. This distinction is based on Engberg-Pedersen's language of "irenic" and "polemical"/ "subordinating appropriation" (*From Stoicism to Platonism*, 9–10).

## A Common Moral Tradition and Popular Philosophy

Though offset by a culture of sectarian allegiance, the phenomenon of mutual philosophical exchange began at some level to create a common moral tradition. As schools appropriated one another's material—sometimes to prove that foreign material could be fitted into their own systems with equal or better effectiveness, and sometimes in concession to their opponents on this or that minor point—a kind of general agreement emerged in the big picture. In this regard, some sources suggest that while, in theory, philosophers disagreed on "words," they nevertheless agreed in "substance."[5] Philosophers of this persuasion were generally among those who traced a common lineage of their traditions back to Socrates.[6]

In one form, this overlapping consensus constituted the essence of Middle Platonism (see chapter 13). In another, it manifested as popular philosophy (see chapter 13), a phenomenon often defined as a loose set of ethical principles associated most recognizably with the Stoic and Cynic traditions but that belonged to no particular philosophical system and found representation in a variety of public forms of discourse.[7]

The disappearance of the schools as distinct presences, however, was not to come until the second and third centuries CE. In the two centuries that preceded, many of the schools thrived as much as they ever had, as the next few chapters discuss.

## For Further Study

Boys-Stones, George R. *Platonist Philosophy 80 BC to AD 250: An Introduction and Collection of Sources in Translation*. Cambridge Sourcebooks in Post-Hellenistic Philosophy. Cambridge: Cambridge University Press, 2018.

Engberg-Pedersen, Troels, ed. *From Stoicism to Platonism: The Development of Philosophy, 100 BCE–100 CE*. Cambridge: Cambridge University Press, 2017.

Schofield, Malcolm, ed. *Aristotle, Plato and Pythagoreanism in the First Century BC: New Directions for Philosophy*. Cambridge: Cambridge University Press, 2013.

5. Cicero, *Tusc.* 5.11.32; *Acad.* 1.4.13–1.12.46; 5.41.120; *Nat. d.* 1.7.16; *Fin.* 3.12.41.

6. Cicero, *Off.* 1.1.2; *Acad.* 1.4.18. See fig. 5 in ch. 10.

7. Although Engberg-Pedersen in his "Setting the Scene" (in *Stoicism in Early Christianity*, ed. Tuomas Rasimus, Troels Engberg-Pedersen, and Ismo Dunderberg [Grand Rapids: Baker Academic, 2010], 1–14) emphasizes distinction over eclecticism during this period, he clarifies that a phenomenon did exist that could be called "popular philosophy," which he defines as "a more or less connected set of philosophical ideas in ethics that has no distinct profile as belonging to this or that other *haeresis*, but is rather shared by all or most of them" (23). Note, however, that other definitions of "popular philosophy" are current in scholarship (see ch. 14).

# 12

# Roman Philosophy

By the early first century BCE, Rome's growing power had extended its reach through Macedonia, Greece, and the furthest regions of Asia Minor in the east. With Rome occupying these Hellenized territories, the influence of Greek culture on the Romans was inevitable and before long, as one Roman poet intoned, "Conquered Greece took captive its savage conqueror."[1] Soon, the Romans were doing philosophy too—in Latin.

## The History of Roman Philosophy

As a fact of history, the Romans took up philosophy a half a millennium after the Greeks. Legend, however, tells a different story.[2] The story goes that philosophy came to the Romans through Pythagoras, the first man to call himself a philosopher (*philosophos*). Allegedly, Pythagoras's connection with the Romans was twofold. First, he was of Trojan lineage and thus a descendent of the very race that had lighted upon the shores of Italy centuries earlier and in time founded the city of Rome. Second, Pythagoras had come to Italy in the days of the first kings of Rome and at that time introduced philosophy to Rome's second king, Numa Pompilius.

In reality, it was centuries before Greek philosophy made an impact on the Romans. Its acceptance came in stages, for the Romans had long been distrustful of it. A first critical event occurred in the year 155 BCE when an embassy from Athens arrived in Rome to entreat for remission of a tax that Rome had levied on their city. The embassy consisted of delegates from three Greek philosophical schools—Peripatetic, Academic, and Stoic.[3] While in Rome, the philosophers attracted great crowds of listeners, dazzling them with their wisdom and eloquence and making a special impression on the city's youths. Reports of their brilliance spread rapidly across the city. While the Romans did not immediately embrace philosophy with open arms, many Roman nobles (*nobiles*) began importing Greek philosophers to serve as tutors for their children, thus adding Greek wisdom to Roman.

The next critical event was Sulla's siege of Athens in the Mithridatic Wars of 88 to 86 BCE. To their detriment, many philosophers had supported the losing side and in the siege were forced to flee. The devastation of the city caused the

---

1. Horace, *Ep.* 2.1.156–7.

2. This account is found in Cicero, *Tusc.* 4.1.2–3; 5.3.10. Though Cicero acknowledges that the Greeks had been doing philosophy far longer than the Romans: *Tusc.* 1.1.2–1.2.5.

3. Plutarch, *Cato Maj.* 22.2–3; Aulus Gellius, *Noct. Att.* 6.14.

philosophical schools to disband and send their philosophers abroad. The Academy was physically destroyed. Philo the Academic fled to Rome, where he established an Academic transplant.[4] Sulla is said to have seized a principal edition of the collected works of Aristotle and Aristotle's student Theophrastus, and to have taken it back with him to Rome in 84 BCE where the works were collated and edited.[5]

It was at this time that the Romans began to take interest in "doing philosophy." This activity at first consisted of leisurely philosophical conversation; but by the middle of the first century BCE, it had progressed to the production of the first Latin philosophical literature. Cicero deserves—or at least claims—pride of place as the first to produce Latin philosophical literature with care and elegance.[6] While acknowledging that Roman philosophers existed before him, he disparaged their attempts at philosophical literature as being "indifferent to definition, arrangement, precision and style."[7]

The very translation of philosophy into Latin required some originality for, as many Latin writers lamented, technical terms endemic to Greek philosophical discourse often lacked close Latin equivalents, which necessitated either the coining of new Latin terms or the development of new usages from old terms.[8] Latin writers, however, were not merely passively transmitting Greek philosophy through translation. They were also *doing* philosophy. More precisely, they were doing Roman philosophy. In short, the Roman philosophical tradition consisted not only of creatively devising philosophical discourse in the Latin language, but also in adapting Greek philosophy to fit a uniquely Roman culture and ideology.[9]

Even by this point, though, the general Roman attitude toward philosophy remained somewhat ambivalent. On the one hand, many Roman elites valued philosophy as vital to moral development and advocated for its study to begin early in a child's education.[10] Many Roman senators are known to have had Epicurean or Stoic leanings, though more often the latter. The emperor Augustus (ruled 27 BCE–14 CE) is even said to have written an "Exhortation to Philosophy"—surely in Latin, since he was not able to compose in Greek.[11] Roman philosophers such as Seneca (b. 4 BCE–1 CE/d. 65 CE) emphasized Plato's ideal of the philosopher-king and thus the necessity of moral grounding in philosophy for public servants and rulers.[12] Perhaps due precisely to this requirement, Roman rulers often resented the philosophers who held them to high moral standards and even subjected them

4. Cicero, *Brut.* 306; cf. *Acad.* 1.12.43–1.12.46; *Nat. d.* 1.7.17; *Tusc. Disp.* 2.11.26.

5. Plutarch, *Sull.* 26.

6. Cicero, *Tusc.* 1.3.6; 2.1.7.

7. Cicero, *Tusc.* 2.2.6–2.3.8, esp. 2.3.7 (LCL, King); cf. 1.3.6.

8. Cicero, *Acad.* 1.7.25; *Fin.* 3.4.15; 3.12.40; Lucretius, *Rer. nat.* 1.135–9; Seneca, *Ep.* 58.1.

9. See the focus of Gareth D. Williams and Katharina Volk, eds., *Roman Reflections: Studies in Latin Philosophy* (New York: Oxford University Press, 2016); see esp. vii.

10. E.g., Cicero, *Or.* 1.52–57; *Inv.* 1.1; Ps.-Cicero, *Rhet. Her.* 1.1.1; 4.55.69; Quintilian, *Inst.* 1.pr.9–20; 10.1.35–36, 81–84, 131.

11. Suetonius, *Aug.* 85; that he could not compose in Greek: *Aug.* 89.

12. Plato's ideal in *Rep.* 5.473d. Seneca's treatise *On Mercy* is an exhortation to Nero to rule based on the principles of Stoicism.

to severe public criticism. Between 66 and 95 CE, the emperors exiled a number of prominent Roman philosophers in resentment of their criticism or on suspicion of sedition. Such philosophers included the Stoics Thrasea Paetus, Cornutus, and Musonius Rufus, and the Cynic Demetrius during the reign of Nero (ruled 54–68 CE), all of the philosophers in Rome during the reign of Vespasian (ruled 69–79 CE), and the Stoic Epictetus and Cynics Demetrius (again) and Dio Chrysostom during the reign of Domitian (ruled 81–96 CE). These emperors even executed or forced some philosophers to commit suicide (the Stoics Seneca, Thrasea Paetus, and Lucan under Nero, Helvidius Priscus under Vespasian).

For a long time, loath to publicly identify as "philosophers" (*philosophi*) in name, Romans who participated in philosophical activity sometimes identified themselves instead with the circumlocution "devotees of philosophy" (*studiosi philosophiae*).[13] Their aversion to the name came from the strong sense of obligation to public service that was characteristic of Roman elites. Philosophy was a way of life, and to be a philosopher was to give oneself to it wholly.[14] They felt they could not turn their whole interest to philosophy without neglecting public duty.[15] The educated Roman was to be a statesman, not a philosopher.[16]

## The Nature of Roman Philosophy

The Roman commitment to civic duty, however, did not mean that philosophy couldn't shape the public servant's political theory or manner of political engagement. To the contrary, philosophy could be put to no better use. For Roman philosophers, philosophy articulated the theoretical basis for the ideas of a body politic and a natural law. It bolstered the Roman instinct toward the common good of the state, and it fostered the moral cultivation necessary for the statesman to govern wisely and justly.

---

13. Although Romans of Cicero's time were willing to talk about their "devotion to philosophy," the first occurrence of *philosophus* as a self-designation by a Roman does not occur in *literature* until Apuleius in the second century CE; so Harry Hine, "Philosophy and *philosophi*: From Cicero to Apuleius," in *Roman Reflections: Studies in Latin Philosophy*, eds. Gareth D. WIlliamd and Katharina Volk (New York: Oxford University Press, 2016) 13–29, esp. 14–21. The term did occur infrequently in epigraphy: Note application of *philosophus* to a Roman man in *CIL* VI 09785 (late first century CE); *CIL* VI 9784 (30–70 CE). For circumlocutions like *studiosi philosophiae* or *studia philosophiae*, moreover, see, e.g., Quintilian, *Inst.* 1.pr.14; 12.2.8; Cicero, *Off.* 2.5; *Tusc.* 1.1; 4.3.5; Seneca, *Ep.* 89.4, 6; *Vit. Beat,* 24.4; Tacitus, *Agr.* 4; cf. Lucretius, *Rer. nat.* 5.7–12, 1.635–44. Tuuli Ahlholm ("Philosophers in Stone: Philosophy and Self-representation in Epigraphy of the Roman Empire" [MPhil thesis, Oxford University, 2017], 38–45) observes that we find almost no examples of wealthy Romans in civil service who call themselves "philosophers."

14. Cicero, *Tusc.* 5.2.5; Seneca, *Ep.* 53.8; cf. *Ep.* 17.

15. Seneca, however, seems to directly counter this claim: "If, then, the time that you have stolen from public duties is bestowed upon studies, you will neither have deserted, nor refused, your office" (*Tranq.* 3.5 [LCL, Basore]). See ch. 14 nn42–43 on serving the public even in retirement.

16. Interestingly, a majority of individuals in the epigraphic record titled "philosophers" also have Roman citizenship, though these are primarily ethnically Greek magistrates in the eastern provinces. So Ahlholm, "Philosophers in Stone," 38–40.

With this frame of mind, many Romans developed a special affinity for Stoicism. In the first place, Stoicism provided an overarching framework that matched—and even helped legitimate—a Roman ideology of power. Rome's world hegemony was nothing but the realization of the gradual unfolding of fate and the emergent Roman Empire was an incarnation, in political form, of nature itself: one world state (Rome/the universe), governed by one power (the emperor/God), under one law (the law of nations/the law of nature). Moreover, the ethical doctrines of Stoicism resonated well with traditional Roman attitudes. Stoic *apatheia* bore a resemblance to Roman *severitas*. The idea of a natural "social instinct" that bound all people together paired agreeably with the Roman sense of duty to serve the "common good."

## Cicero and Latin Philosophy

### *The Life of Cicero*

If the above fairly captures the character of Roman philosophy, then Marcus Tullius Cicero (106–43 BCE) best epitomizes the Roman philosopher. Born of a noble father in Arpinum, Italy, Cicero rose to political prominence during his consulship in 63 BCE, when he exposed the Catilinarian conspiracy and (in his words) delivered the Roman Republic from ruin.[17] Later exiled by Piso (58 BCE), he returned to politics in the late 50s. As tensions now grew between the all-powerful generals Pompey and Julius Caesar, Cicero threw his support behind Pompey. Unfortunately, Caesar emerged victorious and, though Cicero was pardoned, he had no recourse but to withdraw from politics yet again. Forced into retirement and bereaved by both a divorce and the loss of a beloved daughter, he devoted himself to philosophy; between late 46 and 44 BCE, he produced an impressively prolific collection of philosophical dialogues. A year later, he was executed at the command of Marcus Antony.

This brief biographical sketch omits an aspect of Cicero's career that, he believed, even his contemporaries overlooked: his lifelong interest in philosophy. In his introduction to *On the Nature of the Gods*, he remarks that during his prolific period of writing between 46 and 44 BCE, his peers voiced surprise at his "sudden outburst of philosophical interest." Their impression, he assures his readers, is misinformed, for he had devoted "no small amount of time and energy" to philosophy even from his youth. Evidence of his interest had appeared in his many forensic and deliberative speeches over the years—for which he was admittedly better known—and he had in fact been pursuing philosophy intensely at the very periods when he "least appeared" to be doing so.[18]

His earliest pursuit of philosophy followed a quest for truth pattern that characterized the young careers of many aspiring philosophers.[19] In his youth, he

17. Cicero, *Oration Against Catiline.*

18. *Nat. d.* 1.3.6–7 (LCL, Rackham).

19. For such sampling, note the examples of Galen (*On the Passions of the Soul* 8), Apollonius of Tyana (*Vit. Apoll.* 1.7.1–3), Justin Martyr (*Dial.* 29.1, 3), and Josephus (*Vita* 1.10), the last of whom presents the Jewish "sects" as if they were philosophical schools.

"sampled" all the major schools by studying with teachers from each of them before finally settling on the school whose doctrines he found most agreeable. Before the age of twenty, he studied with Phaedrus the Epicurean (whom he continued to admire throughout his life), Diodotus the Stoic (who lived for many years at Cicero's house), and Philo the Academic (who had fled to Rome during the siege of Athens 88–86 BCE).[20] The impact of Cicero's studies during this early period is already evident in what may have been his very first publication—namely, *On Invention*—which, while treating the theory of rhetoric, prefaces by emphasizing the necessity of combining eloquence (rhetoric) with wisdom (philosophy).[21] Sometime after his studies in Rome, he spent two years training with Greek philosophers and rhetoricians in Athens, studying with the founder of the Old Academy, Antiochus of Ascalon, as well as hearing the Epicurean Zeno of Sidon, among other philosophers.[22] Then at Rhodes he befriended Posidonius, the successor to the last of the Stoic heads in Athens—namely, Panaetius.[23] In his temporary retirement in the late 50s, he returned to Athens where he became acquainted with the Academic philosopher Aristus. In Mitylene, he befriended the Peripatetic Cratippus, who became the teacher of his son.[24] Several works from this period of retirement—particularly his dialogues *On the Republic* and *On the Laws*—further illustrate that even when he was not writing about philosophy, philosophy deeply shaped his thinking.

### *Cicero's Philosophical Views*

Despite the diverse affiliations of his philosophical acquaintances over the years, Cicero developed an affinity early on for the views of the Academy and remained a partisan of Academic views throughout his life.[25] One suspects that this attraction had partly to do with the unique traditional emphasis of the Academy on oratory (and arguing both sides of an issue),[26] in which Cicero demonstrated precocious talent. Although his study with Antiochus suggests a period of predilection for the views of the Old Academy (see chapter 10), he must have quickly returned to the views of Philo, to whom he had been committed in his youth.[27] As a representative of Philo's (fourth) Academy, Cicero rejected the Stoic idea of "cognitive impressions," or self-evident knowledge (see chapter 7), while equally rejecting Carneades's skeptical ideal of final "suspension of judgment," rather committing

20. Phaedrus in *Fam.* 13.1.2; Diodotus in *Tusc.* 5.39.113; Philo in Cicero, *Brut.* 306; *Tusc.* 2.11.26; cf. *Acad.* 1.12.43–1.12.46; *Nat. d.* 1.7.17; all three in *Nat. d.* 1.3.6.

21. *Cicero,* 1.1–5.

22. Antiochus in *Brut.* 315; *Tusc.* 3.25.59; *Nat. d.* 1.3.6; *Fin.* 5.1; Zeno in *Tusc.* 3.17.38.

23. *Tusc.* 2.25.61.

24. Aristus in *Tusc.* 5.8.21; Cratippus in *Off.* 3.5; with whom his son also studied, *Off.* 1.1.

25. In his later period: Cicero, *Nat. d.* 1.5.11; cf. *Tusc.* 2.3.9; 3.3.7; 5.4.11.

26. Cicero, *Nat. d.* 2.1.1; 2.67.168; Plutarch, *Cat. Maj.* 22.2–3; Lactantius, *Inst.* 5.14.3–5. Arcesilaus the Academic is said to have been the first of the Academics to advocate arguing on both sides of a question (Diogenes Laërtius, *Vit. phil.* 4.28).

27. Cicero dedicated himself to Philo wholly in his early years (*Brut.* 306). In the 50s BCE, he studied for six months with Antiochus (*Brut.* 315; cf. *Fin.* 5.1.1). At the end of his life, he staunchly defended the views of Philo (*Acad.* 1.12.43–46; *Nat. d.* 1.7.17).

himself to a more constructive quest for the truth. Like Philo, Cicero believed that while the truth cannot be known for certain, one is justified in affirming what is *probably* the truth, or what seems "most like the truth (*veri simillima*)," and in allowing this probable truth to serve as a basis for conduct.[28] Cicero emphasized that the blind allegiance of partisans of the dogmatic schools, by contrast, restricted their freedom to affirm the most probable (*probabile*) argument on any given issue, as he and his "probabilist" associates were free to do.[29]

The result of Cicero's outlook was an inclination sometimes toward Platonism and sometimes toward Stoicism, but always a strong antipathy for Epicureanism.[30] In his ethics, he fittingly represented the spirit of the transitional period. In a move toward conciliation between Stoicism, Peripateticism, and Platonism (or toward a common moral tradition), Cicero emphasized that all these traditions affirmed the sufficiency of virtue for happiness. In fact, he said, their ethical accounts disagreed not in content but merely in their form of expression.[31]

### *Cicero's Philosophical Works*

Cicero's philosophical works are immensely valuable as conduits of the Hellenistic philosophical traditions. Since little besides fragments survives from Hellenistic writers, Cicero's works offer our earliest and most holistic accounts of the views of the Hellenistic schools. In composing, he generally worked directly from some Greek authority, borrowing selectively but often merely translating.[32] This practice helps explain how he was able to write so rapidly during his most prolific period when he produced—to the astonishment of his contemporaries—some dozen philosophical works in just two years, some of them quite lengthy. On the other hand, Cicero affirms that his translations did not represent slavish equivalents but were rather "imitations," or *mimēseis*, based on specific Greek prototypes but contrived as genuinely new productions (as Latin poets, such as Virgil, imitated Greek poets, such as Homer).[33] While his rapidity and close adherence to his models earned Cicero in modern times a reputation as a popularizer or amateur rather than an original philosopher, recent reassessment has expressed growing appreciation for the originality and uniqueness of his philosophy, and for Roman philosophy generally.[34]

---

28. *Cicero, Tusc.* 1.11.23; cf. "like the truth (*veri simile*)" (2.3.9); "appearance of the truth (*species vertitatis*)" (5.29.82); "likeness to the truth (*veritatis similitudo*)" (*Nat. d.* 3.40.95); as a basis for conduct (*Nat. d.* 1.5.12).

29. *Tusc.* 4.4.7.

30. Platonism on the immortality of the soul (*Tusc.* 1.12.26–1.49.119); Stoicism on the emotions (*Tusc.* 4.38.84), on the sufficiency of virtue for the happy life (*Tusc.* 5.1.1–4), and on the nature of the gods (*Tusc.* 3.40.95). Cicero's remarks on Epicureanism are consistently critical, although he had admired his teacher Phaedrus (*Fam.* 13.1.2).

31. *Tusc.* 5.11.32; 5.41.120; *Fin.* 3.12.41; *Off.* 1.2.6; *Acad.* 1.12.43–1.12.46.

32. *On Duties* is based on a work of Panaetius, and the Stoic portion of *On the Nature of the Gods* on the work of Posidonius.

33. *Cicero, Acad.*, 1.3.10; cf. *Off.* 1.2.6.

34. On Ciceronian scholarship, see Maso, *Cicero's Philosophy*; on Roman philosophy, see Williams and Volk, *Roman Reflections*.

### *Cicero as Roman Philosopher*

Cicero admits that he was not the first to write Latin philosophy. Philosophical literature originating from certain circles of Roman philosophers already existed and was known, as he says, to "anyone of even moderate learning."[35] He complains, however, that disregard for style of expression in these compositions left no reason for these books to be read "except in the circle of those who hold the same views and read their books to one another." For Cicero, everything in writing should "approve itself to the taste of all educated readers"—that is to say, even if one doesn't agree with the ideas, these writings should be worth reading on grounds of elegant style.[36]

The centrality of politics in Cicero's biography demonstrates what kind of philosopher he, and the Roman philosopher generally, was. Like most philosophers in the centuries before him, Cicero believed that philosophy was thoroughly practical on a personal level, especially as therapy for the soul.[37] Unlike the Hellenistic philosophers, however, he believed that philosophy's most critical sphere of application was that of politics. Cicero wrote explicitly for the benefit of his countrymen,[38] not only making Greek philosophy available to them in Latin but also reshaping it for direct application to statecraft. The idea of a natural "social" instinct, or mutual benefit, bent him toward Stoicism. He believed that if nature has so designed us as to join instinctively into "political" bodies (i.e., cities), then we who are equipped through liberal education have a duty to serve the body's interest through civic administration.[39] Philosophy rendered moral formation necessary to make the public servant suited to his office. Thus Cicero urged that statesmen should possess wisdom alongside eloquence and that citizen education—which for a long time focused on oratory—should include an equal emphasis on philosophy.[40] Put differently, Cicero emphasized that the statesman should not only be eloquent; he should also be "good."

## Notes on the Primary Sources

Cicero's philosophical treatises and dialogues are among the earliest complete sources of Latin philosophy available. His dialogues follow Plato's dialogical style, though generally with more continuous speech, less back and forth, and less interruption. His early dialogues, written between 55 and 52 BCE, include *On the Orator* (on the philosophically trained orator), *On the Republic* (on political philosophy), and *On Laws* (on civic and natural law). Cicero composed most of his philosophical works late in life, between 46 and 44 BCE during his forced retirement under Julius Caesar. Among other dialogues from this period are his lengthy *On Ends*

35. Cicero, *Tusc.* 2.3.7 (LCL, King).
36. Cicero, *Tusc.* 2.3.8 (LCL, King).
37. Cicero, *Nat. d.* 1.4.9; *Acad.* 1.3.11; cf. *Tusc.* 3.1.1; 5.2.5.
38. Cicero, *Acad.* 1.3.11; *Nat. d.* 1.4.7.
39. Cicero, *Acad.* 2.2.6; *Off.* 1.1.1; 1.6.19. Cicero here departs from the prevailing attitude of the Hellenistic philosophers.
40. Cicero, *Inv.* 1.1; *Or.* 3.16.61; *Off.* 1.1.1.

*of Goods and Evils* and *On the Nature of the Gods* (each summarizing the views of the Epicureans, Stoics, and Academics, respectively), *Tusculan Disputations* (a dialogical discussion about the value of philosophy as medicine for the soul), and his final treatise *On Duties* (about the obligation of the philosopher-orator to serve the state).

Among other extant Latin writings are Lucretius's *On the Nature of the Gods* (first half of the first century BCE), an Epicurean poem summarizing Epicurus's treatise *On Nature*; the moral letters and moral treatises of the Stoic Seneca the Younger; and Apuleius's Platonic treatise *Phaedo*. Representing Roman Stoicism, but written in Greek, are the *Discourses* of Musonius Rufus and Epictetus as well as Marcus Aurelius's *Meditations*.

## For Further Study

Atkins, Jed W., and Thomas Bénatouil, eds. *The Cambridge Companion to Cicero's Philosophy*. Cambridge Companions to Philosophy. Cambridge: Cambridge University Press, 2022.

Furhrer, Therese. "Philosophy in Rome." Pages 545–71 in *Ancient Philosophy: Textual Paths and Historical Explorations*. Edited by Lorenzo Perilli and Daniela P. Taormina. New York: Routledge, 2017.

Garani, Myrto, David Konstan, and Gretchen Reydams-Schils, eds. *The Oxford Handbook of Roman Philosophy*. New York: Oxford University Press, 2023.

Long, A. A. "Roman Philosophy." Pages 184–210 in *The Cambridge Companion to Greek and Roman Philosophy*. Edited by David N. Sedley. Cambridge: Cambridge University Press, 2003.

Maso, Stefano. *Cicero's Philosophy*. Trends in Classics 3. Berlin: De Gruyter, 2022.

Remer, Gary. *Ethics and the Orator: The Ciceronian Tradition of Political Morality*. Chicago: University of Chicago Press, 2017.

Sellars, John. "Marcus Aurelius and the Tradition of Spiritual Exercises." *The Oxford Handbook of Roman Philosophy*. Edited by Myrto Garani, David Konstan, and Gretchen Reydams-Schils. New York: Oxford University Press, 2023.

Williams, Gareth D., and Katharina Volk, eds. *Roman Reflections: Studies in Latin Philosophy*. New York: Oxford University Press, 2016.

# 13

# Development and Revival

For Greek philosophy, the post-Hellenistic period was not just a time of change. It was also a time of revival (see table 9 below).[1] As Platonism began to thrive in the form of Middle Platonism and Stoicism passed its peak, several philosophical movements that had virtually disappeared in the Hellenistic era returned, seemingly out of nowhere. Aristotle returned from the grave (his works literally did, as the story goes). Cynics multiplied like a pestilence (as some felt). Pythagoras, from pre-Socratic days, began to pique renewed interest. Pyrrhonism returned as an alternative to Academic skepticism, though the Academic tradition did not disappear. Although Middle Platonism was now gaining steadily on Stoicism, the latter remained strong for a time but with some new doctrinal tweaks of its own. Devotees of Epicurus remained plentiful. Philosophy was more prevalent and widespread than ever, making its presence felt in every region of the empire from east to west.

## Neo-Pythagoreanism

### *Pythagoras*

Among the pre-Socratic philosophers, only one lent his name to a following worthy of being counted among the most relevant philosophical groups more than a half a millennium later. They called themselves Pythagoreans (*Pythagorikoi*), though in truth their Pythagoras was as much legend as he was history.[2] Reportedly, Pythagoras was born on the Aegean island of Samos in the mid-sixth century BCE. At a young age, he studied the mysteries known in Greece and abroad. He traveled to Egypt, where he learned the Egyptian language, and then to Chaldea to study with the Magi. In time, he came to Croton in Italy, where he established a constitution for the Italian Greeks. In the Roman era, the Romans laid double claim to him as a Trojan in lineage and as the bearer of philosophy to Rome itself (see chapter 11). Tradition made him into a virtually mythical figure: a son of either Apollo or Hermes who worked miracles, saw the future, talked to animals and mountains,

1. Adapted from Richard Goulet, "Ancient Philosophers: A First Statistical Survey," in *Philosophy as a Way of Life: Ancients and Moderns; Essays in Honor of Pierre Hadot*, ed. Michael Chase, Stephen R. L. Clark, and Michael McGhee (Oxford: Wiley-Blackwell, 2013), 10–39, chart 2.

2. For the life of Pythagoras, see Diogenes Laërtius, *Vit. phil.* 8.1–50.

remembered his past lives, and had a golden thigh. However exaggerated this description, his impact in his day must have been enormous, for his known followers from the fifth century BCE outnumbered the followers from any other school in any century from then on.[3]

TABLE 9. Attested Philosophers by schools and centuries

| SECOND CENTURY BCE | | FIRST CENTURY BCE | | FIRST CENTURY CE | |
|---|---|---|---|---|---|
| 1. Academicians | 74 | 1. Epicureans | 54 | 1. N/A | 74 |
| 2. Stoics | 55 | 2. N/A | 52 | 2. Stoics | 63 |
| 3. N/A | 26 | 3. Stoics | 37 | 3. Platonists | 16 |
| 4. Epicureans | 23 | 4. Academicians | 25 | 4. Epicureans | 15 |
| 5. Aristotelians/ Peripatetics | 14 (1 and 13) | 5. Aristotelians/ Peripatetics | 15 (2 and 13) | 5. Cynics | 10 |
| 6. Pythagoreans | 3 | 6. Pythagoreans | 6 | 6. Pythagoreans | 9 |
| 7. Platonists | 1 | 7. Cynics | 3 | 7. Aristotelians/ Peripatetics | 5 (0 and 5) |
| 8. Pyrrhonists | 0 | 8. Platonists | 2 | 8. Academicians | 1 |
| 9. Cynics | 0 | 9. Pyrrhonists | 0 | 9. Pyrrhonists | 1 |

## *The Twofold Pythagorean Legacy*

As a philosopher, Pythagoras's legacy was twofold.[4] He was remembered, on the one hand, as a leader of a certain esoteric philosophical circle and author of a unique set of religious beliefs and practices. He was apparently the first philosopher to promote the doctrine of the transmigration of the soul, or "metempsychosis," famously associated later with Plato. He himself alleged that he had been Patroclus, comrade of Achilles, in a previous life. He required his followers to take a five-year vow of silence, during which time they listened to him teach through a veil. After this, they took an examination that, if passed, permitted them to see him face to face in his own house. As noted (chapter 3), his teachings included a strong ethical component that involved special dietary restrictions on foods like meat and beans—the former being prohibited on grounds of metempsychosis (an animal corpse might have embodied the transmigrated soul of a human being), the latter

3. Goulet, "Ancient Philosophers," chart 2.2.

4. Aristotle is an important early witness to Pythagoras's practices and beliefs. He addresses these at some length in his *Politics* (community practices) and *Metaphysics* (ontology, the soul).

for reasons not fully understood (but often speculated about).[5] Ethical requirements were reinforced by members of his circle through a practice of routine self-examination, exercises that facilitated self-improvement, and the administration of mutual accountability.

Pythagoras was remembered, on the other hand, for his metaphysical speculation concerning especially the cosmic significance of numbers. According to this tradition, Pythagoras held that the universe itself was made of numbers and was organized and knowable through them. Supposedly, he posited two chief numerical principles known as "Oneness" (the Monad) and "Plurality" (the Dyad). Oneness constitutes the origin of all things, and Plurality the differentiation of things derived from the One. The influence of scientific/mathematical Pythagoreanism is evident in the writings of Plato, who imbibed Pythagorean ideas about cosmic numbers, perhaps finding inspiration here for his doctrine of transcendent "forms" (see chapter 5).

Pythagoras left nothing in writing, so it is difficult to determine to what extent "Pythagoreanism" derives from Pythagoras and to what extent it derived from the later developments of his followers. In view of his popularity and influence, it is interesting that the Pythagoreans are not included in traditional lists of the ancient philosophical sects,[6] particularly since their unwavering commitment to his authority—best expressed in their mantra "He himself said it" (*autos epha/ ipse dixit*)—was upheld as an example of the allegiance typical of the dogmatic schools.[7] Their omission, however, is explicable on several grounds. On the whole, Pythagoreanism never materialized in a continuous institutional form overseen by renowned teachers who acted as authoritative heads of school.[8] Moreover, this failure to institutionalize surely followed not only from the fact that Pythagoras left nothing in writing, but also from the bifurcating of his legacy into two relatively separate traditions.

## *The Pythagorean Revival*

Very little literature in the Pythagorean tradition survives from the Hellenistic period. Some of what remains is attributed, pseudonymously, to Classical-era Pythagoreans Philolaus and Archytus and consists mostly of an amalgamation of Platonic and Aristotelian ideas. It was therefore a genuine revival of Pythagoreanism when, in the early post-Hellenistic era, P. Nigidius Figulus (praetor 58 BCE) revived Pythagorean teaching in Rome and Eudorus (fl. ca. 25 BCE) revived it in Athens. The neo-Pythagoreanism of this period utilized (the largely pseudonymous) texts

---

5. Lucian's satire *The Dream, or The Cock* provides a comical answer. Pythagoras's soul, having transmigrated into a rooster, admits that if he had made only ordinary rules, then no one would ever have wondered at him. His obscure regulation about beans kept them guessing and ever perplexed (§18). It was also said that he abstained from beans because they caused flatulence: Cicero, *Div.* 1.62; Diogenes Laërtius, *Vit. phil.* 8.24, and reporting in 8.34 that Aristotle relayed several reasons. See also Pliny, *Nat.* 18.118–19.

6. Diogenes Laërtius, *Vit. phil.* 1.16–21. See table 1 in chapter 2.

7. Cicero, *Nat. d.* 1.10. For the slogan, see also Quintilian, *Inst.* 11.1.27; Diogenes Laërtius, *Vit. phil.* 8.46.

8. Katharina Volk, "Roman Pythagoras," in *Roman Reflections*, 33–49, esp. 45.

from the Hellenistic period as authorities for Pythagorean doctrine. Yet in its new, systematic form, neo-Pythagoreanism in fact represented a harmonization of Platonic and Aristotelian ideas, on the one hand, with traditional Pythagorean ideas centering around the cosmic importance of numbers, on the other, supplemented also by some new innovations. In particular, Eudorus, an Academic who shared Antiochus's affinity for dogmatic Platonism (see chapter 10), infused scientific Pythagoreanism with elements of Platonism. As a self-identifying Academic, Eudorus will be treated further under "Middle Platonism" below.

### *Late Ancient Sources*

Late Ancient sources offer a mixture of history and legend about Pythagoras, as well as a mixture of authentic doctrines and later incrustations. Sources include the Late Ancient biographies of Diogenes Laërtius on Pythagoras (*Lives* 8.1–50) and his followers (*Lives* 8.51–91), Iamblichus's *On the Pythagorean Way of Life*, and Porphyry's biography *The Life of Pythagoras*, along with Porphyry's neo-Platonic treatises. Many traditional elements of Pythagoras's biography, and some of his teachings, are also preserved in Lucian's satire *The Dream, or the Cock*. By this time, the historical character of Pythagoras had been built up with legendary accretions (see above) that elevated him to the stature of the quintessential "divine man." In this capacity, Pythagoras became the paradigm in whose mold Philostratus, in the third century CE, depicted Apollonius of Tyana (*Life of Apollonius*), a first-/second-century CE figure who devoted himself to the Pythagorean way of life. Made in the image of a legend (Pythagoras), Philostratus's Apollonius took on a legendary quality of his own.

## Middle Platonism

### *The Return of Dogmatic Platonism*

Less than a century after Plato's death, the Academy that had preserved his teachings under the headship of Speusippus and on until Crantor veered decidedly away from dogmatic Platonism. It took up a stance of skepticism that, consistently applied, impugned not only the dogmatic views of rival schools but even dogmatic thinking itself (see chapter 10). Plato's Academy was no longer his but a "New" Academy. The Academy's skeptical phase was not short-lived and yet the skeptical takeover did not altogether vanquish dogmatic Platonism. Largely latent during the Hellenistic period,[9] dogmatic Platonism returned with a vengeance in the transitional period (ca. 100 BCE–100 CE), reemerging in the Academy under Antiochus of Ascalon (b. ca. 130 BCE), and from there not only growing steadily in strength but also seeming to acquire its mass by depleting the strength of its rivals.

Antiochus provides a chronological marker for a new phase of dogmatic Platonism generally known as Middle Platonism. Once a member of the New Acad-

9. People continued to read Plato: Hatzimichaeli, "The Texts of Plato and Aristotle in the First Century."

emy, Antiochus had studied with Philo of Larissa for longer and—it is said—with greater fervor than any other student. He had fled Athens during the siege of 86 BCE, in the tumult of which the site of the Academy was destroyed. After returning to Athens in 84 BCE, he established a school of his own, now advocating a return to dogmatic Platonism and recanting from his own skeptical view, which he got from his teacher with whom he had studied so long, as if the tragedy of the war had shaken his skepticism as abruptly as it had shaken his city.[10]

As discussed in chapter 10, though Antiochus's Academy was newer than the Skeptical Academy, he called it the Old Academy,[11] for it was his aim to recover the dogmatic philosophy of Plato and his earliest successors, before the New Academy went a different way. On the other hand, institutionally, Antiochus did not represent the return of the Academy to Platonism. Rather, he represented a break between a Platonist and the (New) Academy.[12]

It was Eudorus of Alexandria (fl. ca. 25 BCE) who introduced the doctrines that transformed early Platonism into Middle Platonism. Although Eudorus was named an "Academic" like Antiochus,[13] he based his philosophical views on the doctrines of Plato, whom he considered the sole basis of doctrinal authority. In truth, Eudorus read Plato through the lens of Pythagoreanism. Central for Eudorus were numbers. Fundamental to reality as we know it, numbers derive from two basic ontological principles (*Stoicheiai*), the Monad and the Dyad (referenced earlier). Above both principles, however, was a higher principle known as the *Archē*, which Eudorus identified with Plato's "Good," calling it "the One," or "God."

## *Plato as Nonexclusive Authority*

From the time of Antiochus and Eudorus, an identifiable school of thought began to take shape, decentralized and nonmonolithic to be sure, but united by a common commitment to Plato. The driving assumption of this movement was this: "Plato *is right*."[14] That is, for dogmatic purposes, Plato was always the final authority.

On the other hand, those of this persuasion did not consider Plato to be an *exclusive* authority. Other philosophers shared bits of the truth, often affirming the same things as Plato. According to Antiochus in Cicero, Plato, the Peripatetics, and the Stoics actually said the same thing, just in different words.[15] Or rather, what Aristotle and the Stoics said was already *implicit* in Plato.[16]

---

10. The abruptness of the change is indicated by Cicero's facetious remark, "I am curious to know the exact date of the day whose dawning light revealed to him [Antiochus] that mark of truth and falsehood which he had for many years been in the habit of denying" (*Acad.* 2.69). For more on Antiochus, see Cicero, *Acad.* 2.69–71.

11. Cicero, *Acad.* 1.4.13–1.12.46.

12. G. R. Boys-Stones argues that Middle Platonism was not a continuation of the Academy. *Platonist Philosophy 80 BC to AD 250*, 13.

13. Boys-Stones, *Platonist Philosophy 80 BC to AD 250*, 3.

14. Boys-Stones, *Platonist Philosophy 80 BC to AD 250*, 16.

15. Cicero, *Nat. d.* 1.7.16; cf. Cicero, *Tusc.* 5.11.32; *Fin.* 3.41.

16. Cicero, *Tusc.* 4.2.3; 5.8.22.

The openness of Middle Platonists to the Stoics and Aristotle could tend in one direction more than the other.[17] Although Antiochus prioritized the framework of Plato, many accused him of being a Stoic.[18] Eudorus and Philo of Alexandria are also examples of Stoicizing Platonists.[19] Then there were Middle Platonists who opposed Stoic views while welcoming those of Aristotle, and especially Pythagoras. Platonists in this line include the second-century CE figures Galen, Plutarch, and Alcinous.

It may be asked why the Middle Platonists attributed this absolute authority to Plato.[20] In one way, his authority can be understood as deriving from Pythagoras, from whom he borrowed his key tenets. Thus even a "Pythagorean" like Numenius (second century CE) was happy to draw from Plato as one who allegedly was wholly consistent with Pythagoras.[21] Tracing Plato's authority back to Pythagoras, however, only pushes back the question; and in any case, those who acknowledged the authority of Plato do not seem to have located their justification in his indebtedness to his predecessor. If one were to pinpoint the foundational justification, it would rather be this: Plato had discovered an all-encompassing theory that could explicate what so many other people had grasped only in part.

### *Transcendent Causes as a Unifying Doctrine*

Along with the assumption of Plato's comprehensive correctness was another assumption—that Plato's works formed an integral body of doctrine and its various parts cohered in perfect agreement. Students could therefore come to Plato's works expecting consistency in every respect. It would take some laborious spadework, but it was possible to synthesize his body of work, and in so doing, uncover the whole of his penetrating, all-explaining theory of what is. This synthetic construction constituted the essence of the Middle Platonist system.

The doctrine that was believed to bring Plato's whole system together was that of transcendent causes, or principles.[22] Since Plato referred to transcendent causes in various ways—while also referring apparently to various transcendent causes—interpreters labored to sort out the references scattered throughout his works into a system that, as presupposed, underlay the parts. Interpreters basically agreed in identifying two distinct transcendent principles, one higher and the other lower. (1) The highest principle was God, or rather the "God *above* the heavens." This God was unknowable and ineffable, too transcendent even for reason to comprehend. (2) Beneath this God was a God "*in* the heavens" who, unlike the God above the heavens, could be grasped by the human intellect. Correlating with this second

17. For studies that trace the Stoic versus anti-Stoic/Aristotelian lines of Middle Platonism, see Boys-Stones, *Platonist Philosophy 80 BC to AD 250*, 16. See also Dillon, *Alcinous*, xxxviii–xxxix.

18. Sextus Empiricus, *Pyr.* 1.235.

19. Boys-Stones, *Platonist Philosophy 80 BC to AD 250*, 18.

20. Addressed in Boys-Stones, *Platonist Philosophy 80 BC to AD 250*, 31–37.

21. Boys-Stones, *Platonist Philosophy 80 BC to AD 250*, 9.

22. Boys-Stones, *Platonist Philosophy 80 BC to AD 250*, 29.

God were Plato's forms that were, in mythical terms, also identical with the demiurge. This second God also went by the name of the *logos* or the mind of the world soul. In any case, this God—the demiurge—fashioned the world as an imitation of the form of all forms; that is, in imitation of himself. In the world, the demiurge then set a world soul, which although preexistent had now been awakened so that it could bring coherence and order to the created world. Here, then, is the Middle Platonic hierarchy of being:

1. God above the heavens
2. God in the heavens, the demiurge, the form, *logos*, or mind of the world soul
3. The world soul[23]

## *The End in Middle Platonism*

Evident in the Middle Platonic distinction between the God above the heavens, the God in the heavens, and the world soul is a move arguably toward greater complexity in Plato's doctrines than Plato himself had meant to affirm. In the same way, Plato's ethics now came to be explained more systematically and with sharper specificity. Plato's ethical *end* (*telos*) was now articulated more determinately as "assimilation to God (*homoiōsis tōi theōi*) insofar as is possible," or alternatively as "following God (*to hepesthai theōi*)."[24] In this regard, by contemplating God (the God *in* the heavens, that is), the human being came to share in God's knowledge and virtue and thus became *like* God.

With regard to the end, Middle Platonists like Alcinous took a thoroughly anti-Stoic stance. Whereas the Stoics held that there are no *degrees* of virtue; that there is nothing intermediate between virtue and vice; and that one either has all the virtues or one has none, these Middle Platonists emphasized the counter notion of *progress*. From this perspective, a person moves gradually toward virtue by developing good habits, by following rules, and by undergoing education (especially in the precepts of the correct philosophical system). Achieving virtue requires restraining the passions, which if left unchecked seduce the mind to succumb to the demands of the body. The Middle Platonists emphasized that one can counter and ultimately weaken the influence of the body by undertaking ascetic practices that habituate the body to denial and thus wean it from its "unreasonable" impulses—that is, the passions.

23. The Middle Platonic sources themselves, however, are difficult to harmonize. See Lee's table in *Moral Transformation*, 134, table 3.

24. "Assimilation to God": Alcinous, *Handbook* §28; "following God": Plutarch, *Mor.* 37d. Plato alternately described the end as "likeness to God," "following God," "imaging oneself to God," and "participating in God." For the sources, see Lee, *Moral Transformation*, 104–5.

TABLE 10. "The End" according to the Classical and Hellenistic schools

| SCHOOL | "THE END" |
|---|---|
| Old Academy | Living according to virtue while enjoying the bodily goods that nature recommends |
| Stoics | Living in accordance with nature (= living virtuously) |
| Epicureans | Pleasure (= absence of pain) |
| Skeptical Academy | Suspension of judgment |
| Platonists/ Middle Platonists | Likeness to God |

### *Representatives and Sources*

By the second century CE, Middle Platonism had well outstripped Stoicism in representation, with attested Platonists skyrocketing as the number of Stoics plummeted.[25] Known Platonists from the second century CE include Galen the physician, Alexander of Aphrodisias, Apuleius, Albinus, Atticus, the Platonizing Pythagorean Numenius, the Platonizing Peripatetic Aspasias, and the Platonizing sophist Maximus of Tyre. In the late second century CE, when Emperor Marcus Aurelius established four chairs of philosophy in Athens representing four different schools, one of the chairs was reserved for the Platonists.[26] Platonism remained the unrivaled and dominant philosophy throughout the rest of antiquity.

The apparent prevalence of Middle Platonic activity during this period is incommensurate with the quantity of extant sources from Middle Platonists. Middle Platonic views are relayed largely through non-Platonist writers. Cicero preserves the views of Antiochus in his dialogues discussing the New and Old Academy (especially *Academica*). Eudorus's treatise on ethics is preserved in summary in Arius Didmyus's epitome of philosophical views. The best-known representative of Middle Platonism in the first century CE was the Hellenistic Jewish philosopher Philo of Alexandria, who represented Plato in the all-wise person of Moses (*Life of Moses*). Our most complete source on Middle Platonism is the *Didaskalikos* or *Handbook of Platonism* attributed to Alcinous, a second-century CE Platonist about whom nothing else is known. This short handbook offers an epitome of (Middle)

25. Goulet, "Ancient Philosophers," chart 2.2. Stoic representation dropped from sixty-three individuals in the first century CE to twenty-two in the next, while Platonists rose from seventeen to fifty-five. See table 12 here.

26. One position each for the Stoics, Platonists, Peripatetics, and Epicureans (Philostratus, *Vit. Soph.* 2.566; Lucian, *Eun.* 3).

Platonism divided into the departments of the theoretical (theology, physics, mathematics), the practical (ethics, economics, politics), and the dialectical (demonstrative, epicheirematic, rhetorical).

## Aristotelianism

### *The Transmission of Aristotle's Writings*

After the Classical period, things initially went no better for Aristotle than they did for Plato. Following Aristotle's death, his school at the Lyceum fell to the leadership of Theophrastus (372/371 or 371/370–288/287 or 287/286 BCE) and thereafter to Strato (head of Lyceum ca. 287–269 BCE). Theophrastus and Strato carried on Aristotle's line of inquiry into all subjects, with Strato narrowing the focus more intently to the natural sciences, especially botany. Neither man, however, took interest in systematizing Aristotle's teachings, and both were willing to disagree with him. At this point, "Peripatetic" and "Aristotelian" were by no means synonymous.[27]

Interest in the writings of Aristotle seems to have waned considerably during the Hellenistic era. The Lyceum remained active but dwindled into obscurity for much of the period. Peripatetic activity nevertheless bustled in Alexandria, where Peripatetics led the way in devising a system of classification for the world's most extensive library by assigning books to respective branches of specialization. As for Aristotle himself, like Plato, he made a surprising return as an authoritative figure in the first century BCE. Although his comeback was weaker than Plato's, it was much more sensational—if the story is to be believed. According to Strabo (ca. 64 BCE–after 21 CE), Aristotle's writings passed through Theophrastus and then to their student Neleus. Neleus bequeathed the books to his patrimonial heirs, who then buried them in fear that the Attalic kings would commandeer them for the libraries in Pergamum. Later, Neleus's descendants sold the books, damaged, to Apellicon of Teos (first century BCE), who restored them and made new copies, though he incorrectly filled in the gaps (being a bibliophile rather than a philosopher) and published the books fraught with errors. The Roman general Sulla then pillaged the books in his sack of Athens (86 BCE) and carried them back to Rome, where they fell into the hands of booksellers who reproduced them with the aid of bad copyists.[28] In this way, Aristotle again came to light, ripe for philosophical analysis and serious text-criticism.

### *Systematization of Aristotle*

Although a strong current of philosophers found Aristotle a useful supplement to Plato (Antiochus, Eudorus, and other Middle Platonists above), there also arose a formidable Peripatetic movement committed to the authority of Aristotle himself, in the same way that Stoics were committed to Zeno and Epicureans were to Epicurus. Whereas the Stoics and Epicureans (and to some extent, the Platonists)

---

27. Note the distinction in table 9 in this chapter and table 12 in chapter 14.
28. Strabo, *Geogr.* 13.1.54.

had already systematically codified the teachings of their founders in the generations of the first successors, only now did followers of Aristotle attempt to devise such a system, based on exacting interpretation of his corpus, that had recently been made available. Prerequisite to this, they had first to restore the texts that had been corrupted by time and careless copying. These challenges gave rise to a flourishing commentary tradition in which devotees strove to restore Aristotle's original texts, to divine from these his doctrines, to arrange them into a coherent whole with discrepancies removed, and at the same time to defend him against detractors. After a seminal commentary by Andronicus of Rhodes in the first century BCE, Peripatetic commentaries appeared prolifically in the second century CE, of which the commentary of Alexander of Aphrodisias eclipses all. Devotees of Aristotle, having fully joined the culture of philosophical allegiance (see chapter 9), could now rightly be called "Aristotelians."[29]

This new wave of interest in Aristotle continued strong for more than two centuries. When Marcus Aurelius established the four chairs of philosophy in Athens, he reserved one of the seats for a Peripatetic. Yet through the post-Hellenistic period, Aristotelianism was always the most poorly represented of the four philosophies (see table 9 above).[30] At this time, the Peripatetics still enjoyed prominence among the ancient schools, but this would not last much longer. Like Stoicism, Aristotelianism was soon eclipsed by Platonism before disappearing altogether.

### *Ancient Sources*

Primary sources from Peripatetics during the Hellenistic and post-Hellenistic periods are scarce. Diogenes Laërtius covers the lives of Theophrastus and Strato in *Lives* 5.36–57 and 5.58–64, respectively, and lists their works in 5.42–50 and 5.59–60. Antiochus's appropriation of Aristotle in the Old Academy is discussed throughout Cicero's dialogues (especially *Academica*). Stobaeus excerpts Arius Didymus's (first century BCE) coverage of Peripatetic ethics. Many commentaries of Alexander of Aphrodisias remain. Testimonia and fragments are plentiful and are collected in Sharples (2010).

## Pyrrhonism

### *Pyrrho*

Whether Pyrrhonism can rightly be called a philosophical school (or *hairesis*) is debatable, for Pyrrho (365–275 BCE) himself had no doctrines.[31] And hav-

---

29. Cicero refers to "certain Aristotelian (*Aristotelios*) commentaries" (*Fin.* 3.10). In the second century, Galen refers to "those from Aristotle (*tois ap' Aristotelous*)" (*De libris propriis liber* [C. G. Kühn, *Claudii Galeni opera omnia*, vol. 8. (Leipzig: Knobloch, 1824; repr. Hildesheim: Olms, 1965): 493–765; repr. Cambridge, 2011)], and in the second/third, Dio Cassius refers to "those called Aristotelian (*tous Aristoteleious*) philosophers" (*Hist.* 77.7.3). However, there were still those known as "Peripatetics" (e.g., Philostratus, *Vit. Soph.* 566; Lucian, *Eun.* 3).

30. Goulet, "Ancient Philosophers," chart 2.2; graph 2.4a; 2.4.b.

31. Diogenes Laërtius mentions the debate over whether they could be called a *hairesis* (*Vit. phil.* 1.20).

ing no doctrines, he wrote nothing. Pyrrho's reputation as a philosopher was tied merely to a few core convictions, which happened to overlap partly with the views later held in the Skeptical Academy. Like the New Academics, Pyrrho held that nothing could be known for certain and thus advocated for suspension of judgment in all things. His skepticism owed something to Democritus as well as the Gymnosophists with whom he had spent time in India. Yet, Pyrrho's brand of skepticism uniquely attributed the problem of indeterminability, not to limitation of the senses—as other skeptics did—but to the *nature of things themselves*. That is, for Pyrrho, the world contained no facts or any objective values; it simply *is* indeterminate. Hence, whereas other skeptics called for suspension of judgment on grounds that, for any given question, there exists a balance of competing evidence, impossible for the senses to adjudicate with certainty, Pyrrho called for suspension of judgment based on the nature of things themselves.

For Pyrrho, however, this state of affairs need not reduce one to *aporia*. Quite the contrary; relinquishing the desire to know liberates a person from the agony of not knowing and from the desire to attain the objects that they consider good but that are in fact indifferent. By suspending judgment, one frees oneself from passions like distress, and indeed from all disturbance, thus attaining the state in which one can be truly considered a "wise man."

TABLE 11. Succession up to Pyrrho[32]

| | |
|---|---|
| Democritus of Abdera or<br>Nessas of Chios | b. ca. 460 BCE<br>fifth–early fourth c. BCE |
| Metrodorus of Chios | fourth c. BCE |
| Diogenes of Smyrna | ? |
| Anaxarchus of Abdera | mid- to late fourth c. BCE |
| Pyrrho | ca. 365–275 BCE |

Tradition remembers Pyrrho as one who lived consistently with his doctrines and relays that he took no precautions. He is said to have defied every appearance of danger, whether he stood directly in the path of a moving cart or was headed straight toward a precipice, and that he was kept from harm's way only by the constant intervention of his friends. He lived, however, to be ninety. Later adherents of his views inform us that, while his philosophy promoted suspension of judgment, he nevertheless heeded foresight in his everyday actions. In fact, his doing so was—contrary to initial impressions—consistent with his philosophy. For Pyrrho insisted that despite the elusiveness of certainty, we have no reason to deviate from convention in our responses to "appearances" as they strike us. Regardless of whether our perceptions are true, how things appear to us provides sufficient grounds for action.

32. Diogenes Laërtius, *Vit. phil.* 9.58, 61.

### The Fall and Rise of Pyrrhonism

What we know of Pyrrho comes primarily through his only notable disciple, Timon of Phlius (320–230 BCE).[33] Unlike his master, Timon wrote, and in addition to canonizing Pyrrho's ideas, he produced several books that satirize the dogmatic philosophers. Timon left his school without a successor and the school became defunct; though according to some accounts, it revived more than a century later.[34] In any case, the Pyrrhonist movement was never strong.[35] It faded after Timon and by the Late Roman Republic virtually ceased to exist.

The disappearance of Pyrrhonism, however, would not be permanent. Like Platonism, Pyrrhonism returned in the late Hellenistic period, and again the champion of this revival was an Academic. Just as Antiochus had broken away from the Academy in advocacy of dogmatic Platonism, so Aenesidemus (first century BCE) defected from the Academy in advocacy of Pyrrhonism, regretting that Academics too often abandoned their skepticism to side with the Stoics and that they were dogmatic even in their skepticism.[36]

### Skepticism versus Pyrrhonism

In reality, the new Pyrrhonists regarded the Academics and themselves as two different types of skeptics. The best-known post-Hellenistic representative of Pyrrhonism, Sextus Empiricus (late second century CE), explains that the differences were twofold.[37] First, the Academy affirmed "negative dogmatism," holding that, while we cannot know anything for certain, we can at least know that we don't know. The Pyrrhonist brand of skeptic objected that we cannot know even that. In short, the Academic skeptics treat the truth as inapprehensible, while the Pyrrhonists "keep searching"; thus they are considered "zetetic" skeptics.[38] Second, while the Academic skeptic recognized degrees of plausibility (thus leading to probable belief), the Pyrrhonists suspended judgment entirely. Consequently, the Pyrrhonist skeptic refused not only to say that they "know" anything; they also refused to say that they "believe" anything, even about phenomenological *appearances*. That is, they denied that they "believe" *in* the phenomena that appear to them, saying that they "believe" only in how the phenomena *appear*. Based on these differences, Sextus split the traditional classification that divided philosophers into Dogmatists and Skeptics into the threefold classification of Dogmatists, Academics, and Skeptics (Pyrrhonists).

### A Post-Hellenistic Account of Pyrrhonism

As our best-known representative of Pyrrhonism, Sextus lays out the most extensive account of Pyrrhonism available in his treatise *Outlines of Pyrrhonism*. The

33. Other disciples included Hecataeus of Abdera and Nausiphanes of Teos, the latter a teacher of Epicurus.

34. Diogenes Laërtius, *Vit. phil.* 1.115.

35. Nevertheless, Diogenes Laërtius (*Vit. phil.* 7.115–16) records claims of succession reaching from Timon all the way to Sextus Empiricus (on Sextus see below).

36. LS §71c.

37. Sextus Empiricus, *Pyr.* 1.1–4.

38. *Zētētikoi* (Sextus Empiricus, *Pyr.* 1.4).

account goes as follows. Skepticism is an ability (*dynamis*) by which we examine appearances (*phainomena*) and judgments (*noumena*) in every which way so that we might expose the "equipollence" (*isostheneia*) of possible interpretations and so induce "suspension of judgment" (*epochē*), by which we achieve "freedom from disturbance" (*ataraxia*),[39] the highest end (*telos*).[40]

Regarding the end of *ataraxia*, Sextus reasons as follows. The Dogmatist type of philosopher establishes firm opinions about what is good and bad. In doing so, he makes happiness dependent on attaining the good things and avoiding the bad things as he defines them. He is then either crestfallen when he cannot attain the desired goods or fearful that he will lose them if he attains them. Likewise, he fears suffering the things that he has determined to be bad, or else experiences these things *as* bad because he has so determined them to be. The wise man—the Pyrrhonist skeptic—is immune to such solicitudes. As the Pyrrhonist determines nothing to be good or bad, nothing that he either possesses or lacks can cause him disturbance.[41] In this way, it happens just as it did for the painter Apelles when, failing to produce the effect of foam in a horse's mouth, he flung his sponge at his work, thereby producing the effect of foam in the very act of no longer trying to produce it.[42] So also does one attain freedom from disturbance by no longer trying to attain it.

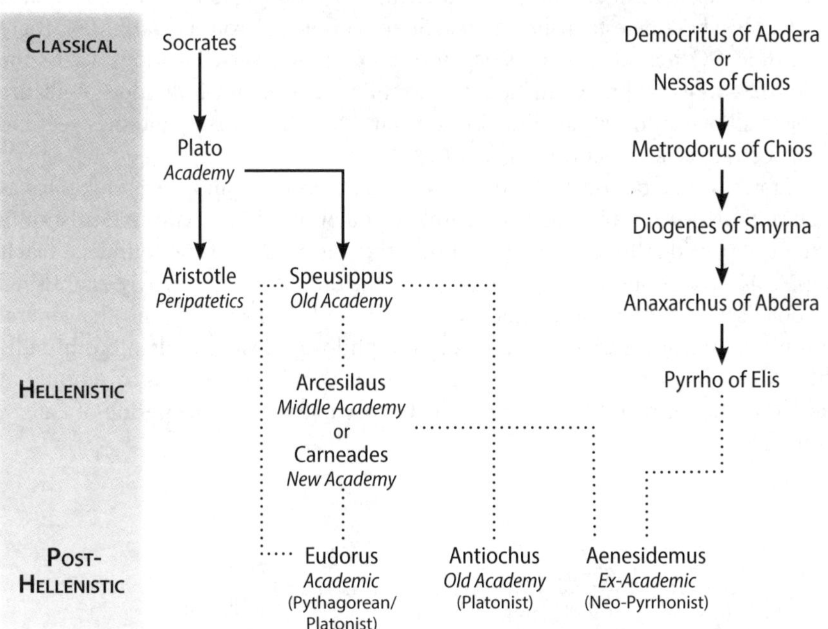


Figure 6. Succession and adherence according to tradition.[43]

39. Sextus Empiricus, *Pyr.* 1.8–9.
40. Sextus Empiricus, *Pyr.* 1.25.
41. Sextus Empiricus, *Pyr.* 1.27–28.
42. Sextus Empiricus, *Pyr.* 1.28–29.
43. Diogenes Laërtius, *Vit. phil.* 1.14–15; 9.58, 61.

### *Ancient Sources*

The fragments and testimonia of Pyrrho and Timon are available in Long and Sedley (1987: §1–2), including those witnessing to the polemics of Timon against the Dogmatists (§3). Excerpts are also available in Inwood and Gerson (1997). Diogenes Laërtius includes the biographies of Pyrrho (*Vit. phil.* 9.61–108) and Timon (*Vit. phil.* 9.109–16) in his *Lives of Eminent Philosophers*. Long and Sedley (1987) collect fragments and testimonia from the post-Hellenistic Pyrrhonist revival in §71–72. While Sextus's Pyrrhonism differed from that of his predecessors (including Pyrrho himself), his three-book account (*Outlines of Pyrrhonism*) became the normative representation of Pyrrhonist thought in Late Antiquity.

## Roman Stoicism

### *The Beginning of Roman Stoicism*

Rome's incursion into Athens in 86 BCE had a similar effect on the Stoics as it did for the Academics: It sent them scattering. Posidonius (135–51 BCE) migrated to Rhodes where he established a local Stoic school. Cicero was his student there for a time.[44] Other Stoic schools began to crop up in diverse locations across the Empire. Schools are known in Tarsus, Alexandria, and Rome. Individual Stoics are attested all over, most abundantly in Rome and the Greek east,[45] and they seem to have been especially plentiful in Tarsus.[46]

Stoics of this period continued to look back to Zeno and the early Stoics as their authorities. On the other hand, the termination of the chain of headship in Athens deprived adherents of an authoritative interpreter of the founders' teachings. This lapse of succession, together with the diffusiveness of newly established schools, continued interaction between Stoics and rival schools, and the general culture of transition that was affecting the philosophical schools more broadly provoked some new developments in Stoicism. Thus began what is commonly regarded as the third and final stage in the history of Stoicism: the period of Late or Roman Stoicism.[47]

---

44. Cicero, *Tusc.* 2.61; *Fin.* 1.2.6; *Nat. d.* 1.3.6; cf. 2.34.88.

45. Goulet, "Ancient Philosophers," 10–39.

46. First-century BCE Stoics from Tarsus include Zeno of Tarsus, Antipater of Tarsus, and two Stoics chosen as governors during the reign of Augustus; namely, Athenodorus and Arius Didymus.

47. Jacques Brunschwig and David Sedley ("Hellenistic Philosophy," in *The Cambridge Companion to Greek and Roman Philosophy*, ed. David N. Sedley [Cambridge: Cambridge University Press, 2003], 151–83) divide the school's history into the phases "early," "middle," and "imperial" or "Roman" Stoicism (165). Sedley ("The School, from Zeno to Arius Didymus," 7) notes that this is the usual way of dividing Stoicism's history, although he himself divides it into five periods. Inwood (*Later Stoicism*, 2–3) challenges the standard divisions.

## *Representatives and Sources*

From this period come some of antiquity's most celebrated Stoics, who in turn left some of our most valuable sources for the study of ancient Stoicism. Among known Roman Stoics were Athenodorus, Arius Didymus, Cornutus, Seneca, Lucan, Musonius Rufus, Euphrates, Epictetus, Hierocles, Thrasea, Helvidius Priscus, and Marcus Aurelius, along with many lesser lights. Substantial literature survives from many of these representatives. Stobaeus preserves lengthy fragments of Stoic ethics from the doxography of Arius Didymus. A Stoic allegorical reading of the Greek poets by Cornutus also remains. Among our best sources are Marcus Aurelius's *Meditations* (personal reflections from a Stoic perspective), the *Discourses* of Epictetus and Musonius Rufus (preserved by their students), and most extensive of all, the one hundred and twenty-four "moral epistles" and twelve "moral treatises" of Seneca, along with his lengthy work *On Nature* and a number of tragedies imbued with Stoic themes.

## *Philosophical Allegiance and Doctrinal Innovations*

Despite decentralization of the Stoic school and the geographical isolation of its representatives, Stoics remained united translocally through an attitude of philosophical allegiance to the school's original founder (Zeno) and his early successors (especially Chrysippus), chiefly through common study of their founders' texts.[48] While the Roman Stoics did introduce some modifications to Stoic theory, these did not ultimately contradict the precepts of the early masters, even where they stood in some tension with them.[49]

The chief innovations were restricted to two main areas.[50] The first was in the area of moral psychology. The early Stoics had argued—opposite Plato's view—that errors of judgment were actual movements of a person's *reasoning* faculty, not movements of the *irrational* part of the soul impelled by the influence of bodily stimuli, or the passions. Put differently, the Stoics argued that nothing *external* to the reasoning faculty was capable of causing action. The reasoning faculty was autonomous, and any error of judgment could be attributed to one thing alone: reason's own miscalculation. As opponents pointed out, however, this theory seemed to make people utterly impervious to sense experience. In this regard, hunger, exhaustion, sickness, or even torture should theoretically be able to wield no power

48. See ch. 7 (Sedley vs. Snyder) on philosophical allegiance. Boys-Stones has recently argued that Stoics were united translocally as a "textual community" dedicated to study of the early scholarchs' texts (*L. Annaeus Cornutus:* Greek Theology, *Fragments, and Testimonia*, WGRW [Atlanta: Society of Biblical Literature Press], 9–12).

49. Christopher Gill has catalogued several areas of innovation ("The School in the Roman Imperial Period," in *The Cambridge Companion to the Stoics*, ed. Brad Inwood [Cambridge: Cambridge University Press, 2003]," 33–53, esp. 38–50). Seneca's deviations from orthodoxy in the area of psychology owe a debt to the Stoic scholarch Posidonius (J. M. Rist, "Seneca and Stoic Orthodoxy," *ANRW* 2.36: 1993–2012, esp. 2011–12). For a longer discussion of innovations, see Lee, *Moral Transformation*, 271–331 (moral psychology) and 332–74 (habit, practice, and mentoring).

50. Lee, *Moral Transformation*, 271–331.

of influence over the movement of the will. Reflexive reactions—as when one turns pale at the sudden appearance of something frightful—ought not occur. Pleasurable sensations like those induced by soothing music or a beautiful poem should add no impetus to act in one direction or another.

Conceding the problem, Roman Stoics answered not by abandoning orthodox teaching but by adding to it. They persisted in the view that every decision is "rational;" i.e., a choice for which the "reasoning" faculty—not bodily stimuli or external powers like the passions—is responsible. However, the new Stoics introduced a special qualification to explain reflexive movements that, admittedly, resembled acts of "passion." The sudden sensation of pain or the unexpected arrival of tragic news, yes, could strike you with the *involuntary* shock of distress or grief. This instant of shock, however, does not represent a "choice" in the direction of passion but rather a "pre-passion" (*praeparatio affectūs*)—a reflexive reaction that reason overcomes the moment you stop reeling from the blow.

Just as they found an explanation for the impingement of negative bodily stimuli, so they found one for the apparent impact of positive stimuli. They refused to abandon the view that the will of the wise man is autonomous, buffered from the influence of bodily stimuli. They conceded, however, that there do exist certain "noncognitive aids" (like music or poetry) that might help bend the reasoning faculty in the right direction.[51] Even so, it is the reasoning faculty that was responsible for the final judgment.

The second innovation concerned the impact of habit, practice, and mentoring on moral improvement. The early Stoics argued that there are no *degrees* of virtue. Hence, the transition from vice to virtue is not gradual but instantaneous. In theory, this implies that good habits or moral exercises contribute nothing to strengthening virtue—that is, progressively—since virtue represents an all-or-nothing state. While the Roman Stoics did not relinquish the traditional view, they conceded to the value of training as a mechanism for strengthening the soul, thus increasing the soul's *potential* to cross over the threshold from vice to virtue. In this way, they admitted the possibility of progress without abandoning the idea of virtue as an absolute state.

### *From Stoicism to Platonism*

Stoicism continued to flourish through the first century of the common era and into the second. At the close of the second century, it still held sufficient eminence among the schools for Marcus Aurelius to include a Stoic seat among the four state-sponsored chairs newly established in Athens. On the other hand, Stoicism had been gradually losing ground to Middle Platonism since the first century BCE (see table 12). As Middle Platonism established itself as the new champion among philosophies, Stoicism finally faded away. Although its influence is evident in later writers and its doctrines continued to be discussed, no notable Stoics are known after the second century, and after the third they virtually disappear from the record.[52]

---

51. See the discussion of "noncognitive aids" in Lee, *Moral Transformation*, 315–31.
52. Goulet, "Ancient Philosophers," chart 2.2.

## Epicureanism

### Continuity and Popularity

The school that Epicurus left in Athens persevered under the guidance of a long line of successors, which remained intact even after the Roman invasion of 86 BCE. Perhaps due to this continuity, the kind of philosophical allegiance that was typical of the dogmatic schools seems to have remained stronger among Epicureans than any other school of the post-Hellenistic era.[53]

Although it was no close rival with Stoicism or Middle Platonism, Epicureanism remained widely popular in this period in Rome and abroad.[54] The one-time head of school in Athens, Phaedrus (ca. 140–70 BCE), took up residence in Rome, where he became the teacher of Cicero. Epicurean communities are also known in Naples (under Siro) and Herculaneum (under Philodemus). In general, Roman statesmen found Stoic values more congruous with the Roman sense of duty to the common good, in contrast with the Epicurean ideal of seclusion among friends and their aversion to politics as a hindrance to *ataraxia* ("freedom from disturbance"). Nonetheless, Epicureanism drew many advocates from the higher Roman orders. The conspirators Brutus and Cassius admired Epicureanism, Virgil was among the students of Siro in Naples, Horace's writings reflect the strong influence of Epicureanism, and Cicero's dialogues name still other representatives.[55] Moreover, epigraphical evidence evinces that Epicureanism made a considerable impact on a population much larger than the circles of elites known from literary sources. The distinctly Epicurean formula *non fui, fui, non sum, non curo* ("I was not, I was, I am not, I care not")—in reference to the deceased's nonexistence—was recurrent in epitaphs, and due to its commonness was occasionally even abbreviated *n.f.f.n.s.n.c.*[56]

### Ancient Sources

Our best Epicurean sources from this period also represent the greater part of our sources for ancient Epicureanism. Due to the strength of Epicurean commitment to the teachings of their founder (Epicurus was a "savior" and a "god"), adherents of Epicurus's views during this period can be taken as faithful representatives of earlier, i.e., Hellenistic, Epicureanism. As noted in chapter 9, sources from the post-Hellenistic period include Lucretius's poem "On the Nature of Things"; several treatises of Philodemus, including *On Frank Criticism*; and the lengthy Lycian inscription sponsored by Diogenes of Oenoanda. There are also the (sometimes hostile) treatises of outsiders, including those of Cicero, Plutarch, and Sextus Empiricus.

---

53. Like a "god" (*deus*) in Cicero, *Tusc.* 1.48; *Nat. d.* 1.43; Lucretius, *Rer. nat.* 3.1–30; 5.8–10; "savior" in Philodemus, *Lib.*//fr. 40; cf. 43.

54. Goulet, "Ancient Philosophers," chart 2.2.

55. Velleius was a Roman senator (*Nat. d.* 1.6.15).

56. Ahlholm, *Philosophers in Stone*, 24–37; with the inscriptions catalogued in appendix 2.

### *Late Epicureanism*

Epicureanism remained prominent enough through the second century CE to merit action on the part of more than one Roman emperor to establish Epicurean teachers in official state positions. Hadrian (ruled 117–138 CE) sanctioned the headship of Popillius Theotimus as the successor to Epicurus in the school in Athens.[57] An Epicurean post was included among the four state-sponsored chairs in Athens instituted by Marcus Aurelius. Lucian's biography of the charlatan prophet Alexander of Abonoteichus (or Alexander "the False Prophet"), depicting events around 150–170 CE, recounts how Epicureans in Abonoteichus played a prominent role in efforts to debunk Alexander's religious cult by exposing his methods of trickery.[58] Other writers of the late second century and after continued to discuss Epicureanism, though often to oppose it.[59] Epicureans remained a major target of criticism from Skeptics in the latter's opposition to the dogmatic schools, which were said to be attached unconditionally to the precepts of their founders.[60] Beginning in the third century CE, Epicureans become extremely scarce in the record, and by the sixth century, they disappear entirely.[61]

## Cynicism

The Cynic way of life that—with the help of his endearingly raffish personality—Diogenes had made attractive to several noteworthy followers apparently looked less attractive in the absence of his example. Hardly a generation after his death, Cynicism produced no more figures of the stature of a Diogenes, a Crates, or a Hipparchia.[62] In fact, little Cynic activity is known in the next two or three centuries that followed. Around the turn of the common era, however, Cynicism made a strident comeback. In the first and second centuries CE, the Cynic revival reached a high point,[63] now achieving a popularity it had not enjoyed since the days of Diogenes and Crates. Evidence survives of Cynic activity in all the great cities of the empire, including Athens, Corinth, Rome, Alexandria, and cities throughout Asia Minor and the Decapolis.

The popularity of Cynicism at this time, though, was more than matched by its unpopularity. Several sources remark—with sometimes trenchant contempt—how populous the Cynics had become,[64] making themselves the more conspicuous by

57. Hadrian's permission for Popillius to be head in *IG* II[2] 1099.

58. Lucian, *Alex.* 25; 43–47; cf. 38.

59. Cf. Sextus Empiricus, *Pyr.* 1.3.

60. Cf. Sextus Empiricus, *Pyr.* 1.3; Origen, *Cels.* 1.10.

61. Goulet, "Ancient Philosophers," chart 2.2.

62. Though some evidence exists; see Goulet-Caze, *Cynicism and Christianity in Antiquity*, 16–17.

63. See Goulet, "Ancient Philosophers," chart 2.2.

64. In one dialogue, Zeus asks (*Bis. acc.* 6), "Do not you see how many short cloaks and staves and wallets there are? On all sides there are long beards. . . . The public walks are full of people. . . . There is nobody who does not . . . ," etc. (LCL, Harmon); cf. *Fug.* 3–4, 17.

posting themselves on street corners and railing at passers-by.[65] To the chagrin of the other philosophers, these wandering Cynics gave philosophy a bad name,[66] dressing the part but not living it,[67] and some allegedly even adopting the Cynic life of begging in order to avoid plying a toilsome trade.[68] Lucian of Samosata, a bitter opponent of Cynicism, composed a wholly negative biography of a Christian turned Cynic named Peregrinus (*The Passing of Peregrinus*), whom he despised so greatly that he laughed at his death.[69]

Negative reactions to Cynicism, however, may have in some cases represented elite contempt for the lower classes more than for the Cynic philosophy per se. The Cynics who intentionally quit their trades to live freely off of society's resources were, as sources often note, drawn precisely from the order of the uneducated and illiterate.[70] This socioeconomic correlation may explain why some of the same writers who expressed harsh disdain for the Cynics as a group also expressed admiration for a more idealized type of Cynic.[71] Elite writers who found value in Cynic principles but found the lifestyle of popular Cynicism undignified substituted a version of Cynicism stripped of its more immodest features.[72] While Lucian expressed consummate disdain for the street Cynics, he was also able to express his deepest admiration for a Cynic like Demonax (second century CE)—an educated man of polite demeanor.[73] There were also other Cynics of this ilk, such as Demetrius, Oenomaus, Peregrinus, and Maximus of Tyre. This contrast of representatives justifies a distinction between what can be considered two different strands of Cynicism: a "popular Cynicism" and a "literate Cynicism."[74] The Cynic Epistles (largely dating from the post-Hellenistic period) likely stem from the more popular movement and may represent a defense of classic Cynicism against elite criticisms.[75]

Most of our sources for ancient Cynicism derive from the post-Hellenistic era. The pseudonymous Cynic Epistles are especially important and include letters attributed to Diogenes, Crates, Socrates, and others. These fictive letters are products of various authors and date largely from the first century BCE through Late Antiquity. Discussion of Cynics and Cynicism can also be found scattered throughout the works of Cicero, Varro, Horace, Plutarch, Galen, Aelius Aristides, Maximus of Tyre, Philo of Alexandria, Seneca, and Julian the Apostate. These sources often

65. Philo, *Plant.* 151; Dio, *Or.* 32.9; Lucian, *Bis acc.* 6; *Peregr.* 3; Origen, *Cels.* 3.50; cf. Dio, *Or.* 72.4; Lucian, *Fug.* 3–4.

66. Dio, *Or.* 32.9; Lucian, *Fug.* 3–4, 21; cf. Seneca, *Ep.* 5.2, 4.

67. Lucian, *Fug.* 4; 13–20; cf. Seneca, *Ep.* 5.2. For the dress: Diogenes, *Epistle 30*, 25–34; Diogenes, *Epistle 7*, 17–21; Lucian, *Peregr.* 15; 24; 36; cf. Epictetus, *Diatr.* 3.1.24; Lucian, *Dem.* 13.

68. Lucian, *Bis acc.* 6; *Vit. auct.* 7–11; *Fug.* 13–14, 17.

69. Lucian, *Peregr.* 31; 34.

70. Origen (*Cels.* 3.50) mentions criticisms of this kind. Cf. n68 above.

71. Dio, *Or.* 4; 6; 8; 9; 10; 73; etc.; Epictetus, *Diatr.* 3.22; Lucian's *Demonax*.

72. As presented, for example, in Epictetus, *Diatr.* 3.22.

73. Note also the contrast in Seneca's allusion to street Cynics (*Ep.* 5.2, 4) and his high respect for the eloquent Demetrius (*Ben.* 7.8.2).

74. See discussion in Goulet-Cazé, *Cynics and Christian Origins*, 77–88.

75. Goulet-Cazé, *Cynics and Christian Origins*, 85–87.

depict Cynicism negatively. In a number of Lucian's works, including especially his satires (*The Runaways*; *Vit. auct.* 7–11) and a biography of Peregrinus (*The Passing of Peregrinus*), Cynics are a subject of derision and sometimes shocking disdain. More positive depictions appear in Dio Chrysostom's orations (*Or.* 4; 6; 8; 9; 10; 73; etc.). Despite Lucian's wholly negative biography of Peregrinus, he composed an appreciative portrait of the Cynic Demonax (in *Demonax*), as well as an ironic eulogy of the Cynic lifestyle in *The Dream, or the Cock*. Positive portrayals tended to Stoicize Cynicism, as seen in the plentiful Cynic Epistles and in a diatribe of Epictetus discussing the "ideal Cynic" (*Diatr.* 3.22). The diatribes of Musonius Rufus exude Cynic tendencies, though he is usually considered to have been a Stoic.

## Neoplatonism

The final chapter in the story of ancient philosophy has at its center the philosophy of Neoplatonism. The emergence of Neoplatonism not only coincided with the historical transition from the Roman era into Late Antiquity (mid-third century CE); it also marked both the final chronological development in the history of ancient philosophy and virtually the end of the other philosophies as palpable presences in the ancient landscape.

Platonism began to gain on Stoicism in the first century BCE, and over the next couple of centuries it steadily advanced to become the most dominant philosophical tradition, as it partly absorbed and partly bettered its competitors. By the early third century CE, it had successfully displaced them all. It was at this time that a Platonist named Plotinus (205–269/270 CE) carried Platonism into its final phase. Plotinus is known primarily through his student Porphyry (234 ca.–305 CE), who collected and edited his teacher's writings, arranging them into six *Enneads* (groups of nine) and publishing them around 300 CE.

Plotinus's developments stemmed from the central tenet that every being in the world descends from a single principle. This principle was *the* principle, the *archē*, which was synonymous with the "One," or with Plato's "good." From the One, Plotinus traced the origins and hierarchy of being. After the One were the world mind (the *nous*), the world soul (the *psychē*), nature (*physis*), and matter (*hylē*). Plotinus said that each entity, including each composite in the world, "participates" in the One and so is a "one" in itself.

Neoplatonists were explicitly indebted to Pythagoras for certain central metaphysical ideas, including especially the traditional Pythagorean conception of number symbolism. Fittingly, Porphyry wrote *Life of Pythagoras*, and the later Neoplatonist Iamblichus (ca. 245–ca. 325 CE) wrote *On the Pythagorean Way of Life*. The relationship between Neo-Pythagoreanism and Neoplatonism was intimate, for the view of the Middle Platonists remained: While Plato had gotten everything right, he was only agreeing with Pythagoras.

In addition to his other writings, Porphyry produced a treatise targeted at the "superstition" (*deisidaimonia)* of the Christians (titled *Against the Christians*). Porphyry's attention to Christianity at this time is both consistent with and evidence of Christianity's emergence—coincident with the disappearance of rival philosophies in the shadow of Neoplatonism—as the last and most formidable threat to Neoplatonism's supremacy.

## Key Terms and Concepts

### *Middle Platonism*

- Assimilation to God
- God above the heavens
- God in the heavens
- *Logos*
- Transcendent causes
- World soul

### *Pyrrhonism*

- Appearances (*phainomena*)
- Equipollence (*isotheneia*)
- Freedom from disturbance (*ataraxia*)
- Suspension of judgment (*epochē*)

### *Neo-Stoicism*

- Roman Stoics
- Pre-passions
- Noncognitive aids

## For Further Study

### *General*

Adamson, Peter. *Philosophy in the Hellenistic and Roman Worlds: A History of Philosophy Without Any Gaps*. Vol. 2. Oxford: Oxford University Press, 2015.

Long, A. A. *From Epicurus to Epictetus: Studies in Hellenistic and Roman Philosophy.* Oxford: Oxford University Press, 2006.

Shields, Christopher. *Ancient Philosophy: A Contemporary Introduction.* 2nd ed. New York: Routledge, 2023.

### *Neo-Pythagoreanism and Neoplatonism*

Dillon, John M., and Wolfgang Polleichtner, eds. *Iamblichus of Chalcis: The Letters.* Writings from the Greco-Roman World. Atlanta: Society of Biblical Literature Press, 2009.

Hadot, Ilsetraut. *Simplicius the Neoplatonist in Light of Contemporary Research: A Critical Review*. Academia Philosophical Studies 67. Baden-Baden: Academia Verlag, 2020.

Volk, Katharina. "Roman Pythagoras." Pages 33–49 in *Roman Reflections: Studies in Latin Philosophy*. Edited by Gareth D. Williams and Katharina Volk. New York: Oxford University Press, 2016.

### *Middle Platonism*

Boys-Stones, George R. *Platonist Philosophy 80 BC to AD 250: An Introduction and Collection of Sources in Translation*. Cambridge Source Books in Post-Hellenistic Philosophy. Cambridge: Cambridge University Press, 2018.

Dillon, John. *Alcinous: The Handbook of Platonism; Introduction, Text and Commentary*. Oxford: Oxford University Press, 2002.

Dillon, John. *The Middle Platonists*. Rev. ed. Ithaca, NY: Cornell University Press, 1996.

Engberg-Pedersen, Troels, ed. *From Stoicism to Platonism: The Development of Philosophy, 100 BCE–100 CE*. Cambridge: Cambridge University Press, 2017.

Lee, Max J. *Moral Transformation in Greco-Roman Philosophy of Mind*. Wissenschaftliche Untersuchungen zum Neuen Testament 2/515. Tübingen: Mohr Siebeck, 2020.

Tarrant, Harold, Danielle A. Layne, Dirk Baltzly, and François Renaud, eds. *Brill's Companion to the Reception of Plato in Antiquity*. Brill's Companions to Classical Reception 13. Leiden: Brill, 2018.

### *Aristotelianism*

Baltussen, H. *The Peripatetics: Aristotle's Heirs, 322 BCE–200 CE*. Abingdon: Routledge, 2017.

Schofield, Malcolm, ed. *Aristotle, Plato and Pythagoreanism in the First Century BC: New Directions for Philosophy*. Cambridge: Cambridge University Press, 2013.

Sharples, Robert W. *Peripatetic Philosophy, 200 BC to AD 200: An Introduction and Collection of Sources in Translation*. Cambridge Source Books in Post-Hellenistic Philosophy. Cambridge: Cambridge University Press, 2010.

### *Pyrrhonism*

Long, A. A., and David N. Sedley. *The Hellenistic Philosophers*. 2 vols. Cambridge: Cambridge University Press, 1987.

### *Roman Stoicism*

Bartsch, Shadi, and Alessandro Schiesaro, eds. *The Cambridge Companion to Seneca*. Cambridge: Cambridge University Press, 2015.

Damschen, Gregor, and Andreas Heil, eds. *Brill's Companion to Seneca: Philosopher and Dramatist*. Leiden: Brill, 2014.

Fitch, John G., ed. *Seneca*. Oxford Readings in Classical Studies. Oxford: Oxford University Press, 2008.

Inwood, Brad, ed. *The Cambridge Companion to the Stoics*. Cambridge: Cambridge University Press, 2003.

Lee, Max J. *Moral Transformation in Greco-Roman Philosophy of Mind*. Wissenschaftliche Untersuchungen zum Neuen Testament 2/515. Tübingen: Mohr Siebeck, 2020.

Long, A. A. *Epictetus: A Stoic and Socratic Guide to Life*. Oxford: Oxford University Press, 2002.

Sellars, John. *Marcus Aurelius*. Philosophy in the Roman World. Abingdon: Routledge, 2020.

### *Epicureanism*

Davis, Gregson, and Sergio Yona, eds. *Afterlives of the Garden: Receptions of Epicurean Thought in the Early Empire and Late Antiquity*. Cicero 8. Berlin: de Gruyter, 2023.

Erler, Michael, Jan Erik Hessler, and Federico M. Petrucci, eds. *Authority and Authoritative Texts in the Epicurean Tradition*. Epicurea 5. Basel: Schwabe Verlag, 2021.

Hammerstaedt, Jürgen, Pierre-Marie Morel, and Refik Güremen, eds. *Diogenes of Oinoanda Epicureanism and Philosophical Debates*. Diogène d'Œnoanda Épicurisme et controverses. Ancient and Medieval Philosophy. Series 1, 55. Leuven: Leuven University Press, 2017.

Konstan, David, D. Clay, C. E. Glad, J. C. Thom, and J. Ware. *Philodemus: On Frank Criticism*. Texts and Translations 43. Atlanta: Scholars, 1998.

### *Cynicism*

Billerbeck, Margarethe. "The Ideal Cynic from Epictetus to Julian." Pages 205–21 in *The Cynics: The Cynic Movement in Antiquity and Its Legacy*. Edited by R. Bracht Branham and Marie-Odile Goulet-Cazé. Los Angeles: University of California Press, 1996.

Branham, R. Bracht, and Marie-Odile Goulet-Cazé, eds. *The Cynics: The Cynic Movement in Antiquity and Its Legacy*. Berkeley: University of California Press, 1996.

Goulet-Cazé, Marie-Odile. *Cynicism and Christianity in Antiquity*. Grand Rapids: Eerdmans, 2019.

# 14

# Philosophy as a Popular and Social Phenomenon

As the foregoing chapters have shown, ancient philosophy was not an armchair exercise pursued in isolation and leisure by a tiny, educated elite. Philosophy was (theoretically) a practical discipline, lived out in life and made visible in public, sometimes by direct and even obtrusive confrontation between philosophers and the people they strove to reform. Moreover, although our best surviving sources are products of elite writers, the teachings of philosophy actually reached a vast population of people who, while more difficult to find in the literary record, come more fully to light in sources less easily accessed.

Hence, the purpose of this chapter is twofold: First, to survey the wider population of those in the post-Hellenistic era who identified with philosophy, as well as their social locations; and second, to briefly explore philosophers' varied orientations toward public involvement and their preferred styles of social integration.

## Defining Popular Philosophy

Academic studies have used the term "popular philosophy" in several senses. While these senses overlap, it is important to distinguish them. First, in one sense, popular philosophy refers to a basically common ethical tradition, shared among multiple philosophical sects and distinctive to none of them.[1] Second, popular philosophy is sometimes identified specifically with Cynicism or Cynic-Stoicism.[2] As discussed, Cynicism was not a "philosophical sect" defined by an elaborate set of doctrines. Rather, it was a "way of life" that could be paired with the doctrines of any number of schools or even practiced free of doctrinal baggage altogether (this was the Cynic "shortcut"). Often mentioned as an example of this sort of popular philosopher is Dio Chrysostom (ca. 40/50–after 110 CE), a Sophist-turned-philosopher who took on the lifestyle of an itinerant Cynic and orator.

In a third sense, popular philosophy is equated with philosophical content that worked its way directly or indirectly into nonphilosophical cultural domains, like politics or the arts (the latter including the stage and literature). The ancient purveyor of popular philosophy in this sense likely would not have identified as a

1. Cf. Malherbe, *Paul and the Popular Philosophers*, esp. 11–24; Divjanović, *Paulus als Philosoph*, 2n2; Engberg-Pedersen, "Setting the Scene," 23.

2. Downing (*Cynics and Christian Origins*, 24) cites literature that equates "popular philosophy" with Cynicism or Cynic-Stoicism.

"philosopher" per se (*philosophos*/*philosophus*), even if they acknowledged their indebtedness to philosophy. For instance, Roman statesmen, whose political philosophy or ethics were sometimes consciously shaped by philosophy, generally refused to call themselves "philosophers," as they felt this conflicted with their primary identity as statesmen (see chapter 12). At an even weaker level, literary works in the genres of historiography or epic poetry might reflect common philosophical themes or common places. Such themes appear in both Greco-Roman (e.g., Virgil) and Hellenistic-Jewish literature (e.g., 4 Maccabees).

All three of these definitions define the essence of "popular" philosophy in terms of degree of philosophical purity. That is, "popular" designates a type of reception in which the philosophical content is not identifiable with the unique doctrines of a particular philosophical sect in any technical or systematic way, or is sporadic rather than integrated in its representation, or is in some other way diluted.

It is important to distinguish "popular" in the above senses from another sense of the word *popular*. In this sense, rather than referring to degree of philosophical *purity*, "popular" refers to the *reach* of philosophy within culture—that is, to philosophy's "popularity."[3] In this regard, popular philosophy can be understood as a phenomenon encompassing people—including but not limited to professional philosophers and teachers—who viewed philosophy as an important part of their identity construction, possibly even to the extent of identifying with a specific philosophical sect. Popular philosophy in this sense thus represents a broad phenomenon that encompasses sectarian philosophers, nonsectarian self-proclaimed "philosophers" (*philosophoi*/*philosophi*), and other non-sectarians or even semi-sectarians who considered philosophy an important part of their identity.

## Channels of Influence

In the Roman era, outside of local centers of study, philosophy reached a wider public through various channels, literary and nonliterary.

The literate were exposed to philosophy through both formal education and various other written media. (1) Literary sources from the Roman period—primarily addressing elite parents—regularly advocated for exposure to philosophy even from the early stages of formal education.[4] On the other hand, school exercises in surviving papyri—largely representing nonelite students—suggest that, for most children, philosophy rarely featured as a major part of the curriculum.[5] What little exposure they had came primarily through the copying of sayings (*sententiae*, *gnōmai*), with Diogenes the Cynic featuring most frequently among philosophers. (2) Available to the avid reader were the philosophical "epitomes" of the schools'

3. This understanding in Ahlholm, "Philosophers in Stone," 13, cf. 38, 65.

4. E.g., literary tractates frequently recommend the study of philosophy as part of students' training: Quintilian, *Inst.* 1.pr.9–20; 10.1.35–36, 81–84, 131; Cicero, *Or.* 1.52–57; *Inv.* 1.1; Ps.-Plutarch, *Lib. ed.* 7d–e; Ps.-Cicero, *Rhet.* 1.1.1; 4.55.69; Theon, *Prog.* pr.

5. See Teresa Morgan's tabulation of authors in *Literate Education in the Hellenistic and Roman Worlds* (Cambridge: Cambridge University Press, 1998), 122–23, and table 15 on p. 313.

doctrines. These offered basic summaries of key doctrines and memorable maxims to reinforce proper behavior. Serious philosophers, however, lamented that the epitomes were a weak substitute for in-depth study of the primary sources.[6] (3) Philosophers made occasional efforts to reach the public through inscriptions consisting of quotations from historic philosophers, maxims for daily living, or even lengthy messages promulgating the life-changing doctrines of some school or another.[7] (4) Surviving epitaphs communicate recognizably "philosophical attitudes." Especially popular was the distinctly Epicurean epitaph "I was not, I was, I am not, I care not"[8] in reference to the deceased's nonexistence. (5) Historiography, poetry, satire, comedy, orations, and other literature contained philosophical ideas, if in more diluted form (see definition 3 above).[9]

Philosophy reached the public also through nonliterary channels. (6) Philosophical schools sometimes met in public spaces (temples, clubrooms, gymnasia, multipurpose rooms attached to shops, shops themselves, etc.) and might have been open to the philosophical "inquirer."[10] Although the schools, under the tutelage of a teacher, would be reliable sources of doctrine, inquirers would only get out of instruction what they put into it. (7) For more casual listening, there were the street corner preachers who sought to reform the masses and the wandering charlatans who peddled philosophy for a living.[11] (8) Social dinners in the homes of the well-to-do were often occasions for "table talk" featuring educated conversation about various topics of inquiry, including philosophical topics.[12] (9) Seneca remarked that even tragedy, drama, mime, and the stage—popular forms of public entertainment—conveyed the same ideas as philosophy.[13] (10) Conventional social networks (patron-client relationships, master-slave relationships) and the nature of city life (public baths, the forum, temples, intermingled housing) connected people representing disparate socioeconomic classes, creating channels for philosophy to percolate down from the formally educated to the uneducated classes.[14]

In sum, even apart from the tutelage of a qualified teacher, philosophy could be easily accessed through various other kinds of exposure. Thus, while serious ac-

---

6. Seneca, *Ep.* 33.4–8; 39.1.

7. In the second century CE, the Epicurean philosopher Diogenes of Oenoanda left a 25,000-word inscription that included doctrines and sayings of Epicurus.

8. See ch. 9, n56.

9. For instance, Cicero states (*Nat. d.* 1.3.6–7) that his public speeches throughout the years were full of philosophical themes.

10. Raffaella Cribiore, *Gymnastics of the Mind: Greek Education in Hellenistic and Roman Egypt* (Princeton: Princeton University Press, 2001), 21–22. Loveday Alexander ("Paul and the Hellenistic Schools: The Evidence of Galen," in Paul in His Hellenistic Context, ed. Troels Engberg-Pedersen [London: T&T Clark, 1995], 76) notes that philosophical schools often consisted of an inner circle of core students and an outer circle of inquirers.

11. On such figures, see Dio, *Or.* 32.9; 72.4; Lucian, *Fug.* 3–4; Philo, *Plant.* 151; Lucian, *Bis acc.* 6; Origen, *Cels.* 3.50; Stoics: Epictetus, *Diatr.* 2.12.17; Horace, *Sat.* 2.3. For discussion in the secondary literature, see Malherbe, *Paul and the Popular Philosophers*, 38–39.

12. Plutarch, *Quaes. conv.* 723a–724b; Lucian's *Symposium*; cf. *The Dream, or the Cock* 11.

13. Seneca, *Ep.* 8.8.

14. Downing (*Cynics and Christian Origins*, 107–8) mentions transference of information through eavesdropping slaves, nurses, teachers, and pedagogues.

quaintance with the doctrines of the schools often implied literacy and leisure, and therefore relatively high social standing,[15] philosophy touched a large percentage of people outside this circle of representatives. Indeed, an abundance of commonly overlooked evidence shows that people with philosophical pretensions could be found at all social levels, and not just among the highly educated. This evidence reveals that the population of those who fancied themselves philosophers was vastly greater in number than our more accessible evidence suggests.

## The Prevalence of Philosophy

Were modern readers asked to name philosophers of the post-Hellenistic era, they are likely to think first (if they could name any at all) of iconic Stoics like Seneca and Epictetus, Middle Platonists like Philo of Alexandria and Plutarch, or maybe even an Epicurean like Lucretius or Philodemus. The reason for our familiarity with these philosophers is that they were elite writers who produced copious amounts of philosophical literature that has been preserved up to the present day. Slightly less known are other elite writers whose writings survive, though generally in smaller quantities and often in fragments: for instance, the Stoics Hierocles, Cornutus, and Arius Didymus; the Middle Platonist Alcinous; and the Pyrrhonist skeptic Sextus Empiricus. Elite literature also preserves the names of philosophers whose writings are not extant: for example, the Stoic Helvidius Priscus, the Cynic Demetrius, or the Pythagorean Apollonius of Tyana.[16]

Such known individuals, however, represent only the tiniest fraction of those who considered themselves philosophers of some sort. Any philosophical teacher had students, most of whom never reached any level of renown in their own times; and even of those who did, many if not most have not been remembered in history. There were also those who acquired knowledge of philosophy apart from a definite attachment to a teacher or school. The number of people who fell into this category cannot be calculated. Perhaps, though, one gets some sense of the philosopher population from remarks about philosophers as a *class*. Lucian's observation that bearded men, cloaked and carrying a staff and wallet (i.e., Cynic philosophers), appeared everywhere one cast an eye is exaggerated but nonetheless telling.[17] In any case, the fate of most of these people was the same as almost any other person in antiquity—they were forgotten. Such is history.

Still, the surviving record of identifiable philosophers from antiquity is much more extensive than elite literature by itself suggests. Philosophers are amply attested in papyri, in coins, busts, herms, statues, and mosaics, and most extensively in the epigraphic record. Several studies have begun to gather this evidence.

---

15. For the literacy rates, see William V. Harris, *Ancient Literacy* (Cambridge, MA: Harvard University Press, 1989); see also more recently, the reassessment in W. A. Johnson and H. N. Parker, eds., *Ancient Literacies: The Culture of Reading in Greece and Rome* (Oxford: Oxford University Press, 2009).

16. For first-century CE Stoics in the literary record, see Timothy A. Brookins, *Rediscovering the Wisdom of the Corinthians: Paul, Stoicism, and Spiritual Hierarchy* (Grand Rapids: Eerdmans, 2024), 281–82.

17. See chapter 6, n64.

In 1957, Marcus Tod made a first effort to glean this evidence, with a view to looking at "how deeply and in what directions philosophic teachings affected the thought and speech and life of the common people of the Greek and Greco-Roman world."[18] From epigraphic and archeological records, Tod cataloged a wealth of "sidelights" referring to Pythagoreans, Platonists, Epicureans, Stoics, and other philosophers, mostly from the Hellenistic and post-Hellenistic periods.

In a more recent study (2017),[19] Tuuli Ahlholm observed that even until now "philosophy as a 'popular' phenomenon in imperial Roman society has largely been neglected."[20] Ahlholm's study considers popular philosophy primarily in terms of identity criteria (similar to definition 4 above). Hence, she is interested in examining how people marked themselves as philosophers—or at least as philosophically inclined—using epigraphy as her primary evidence. She finds that most people who declared themselves "philosophers" in name (*philosophoi*) were people with Roman *citizenship*—including especially magistrates in the Greek east—and therefore people of elite or near-elite status. Ahlholm's survey, however, includes not only those who *called* themselves "philosophers" (*philosophoi/philosophi*), but also those who exhibited "philosophical attitudes" sufficient to indicate that philosophy was an essential part of their "identity construction."[21] Ahlholm admits into this category the many Roman magistrates who engaged in philosophical activity and whose lives were clearly shaped by philosophy but who may have been reticent to declare themselves *philosophi* by name lest they appear distracted from the obligations of their public duties.[22] She also cites here instances where philosophical attitudes appear on the tombstones of less prominent individuals, whereby philosophy is shown to have played a prominent role in defining their sense of personal identity.[23] As noted earlier, the distinctly Epicurean epitaph *non fui, fui, non sum, non curo* ("I was not, I was, I am not, I care not") was a fairly common epitaph.[24] In all, the result of Ahlholm's study is an extensive collection of inscriptions that encompasses examples of not only elite male philosophers but also an even *greater* number of philosophically inclined people who belonged to the lower social orders (freedmen and slaves) and ordinarily less visible demographic categories (youth, women, children).[25]

The online database known as the *Hairesis* project has gathered philosopher inscriptions dating between the sixth century BCE and the fourth century CE.[26] The database includes 326 philosophers known from nonliterary sources across this period.

The most comprehensive repository available—the monumental seven-volume *Dictionnaire des philosophes antiques* (1989–2018) edited by Richard Goulet—

18. Marcus N. Tod, "Sidelights on Greek Philosophers," *JHS* 77 (1957): 132–41, esp. 141.
19. Ahlholm, "Philosophers in Stone."
20. Ahlholm, "Philosophers in Stone," 13.
21. Ahlholm, "Philosophers in Stone," 38.
22. Ahlholm, "Philosophers in Stone," 38–45. See here chapter 12.
23. Ahlholm, "Philosophers in Stone," 20–37.
24. Ahlholm, "Philosophers in Stone," 24–37; inscriptions catalogued in appendix 2.
25. Ahlholm, "Philosophers in Stone," 46–64.
26. *Hairesis*, Ancient Philosophical Schools and Their Representatives in Greek and Latin Inscriptions (6th century BC–4th century AD), https://hairesis.msh-lse.fr/?menuIndex=0&submenuIndex=-1.

includes a list of nearly three thousand philosophers attested between the sixth century BCE and the sixth century CE in literary, epigraphical, and papyrological sources.[27] Thankfully, in an essay-length study, Goulet distills this information into an array of highly illuminating statistical charts and graphs (this study including a total of 2,463 historical philosophers).[28] The following highlights may be noted with regard to philosophers of the post-Hellenistic period (see table 12 in this book):[29]

- In the first century BCE, Epicureans and Stoics are by far the best represented groups.
- In the first century CE, the tally of Epicureans drops precipitously to make them the second most prevalent group, with Stoics skyrocketing to surpass all the other schools by a substantial margin. Academicians fall off steeply as well.
- In the second century CE, Platonism and Stoicism swap places as the tally of Platonists rises and that of Stoics falls.
- By the fourth century CE, Platonism and Neoplatonism become the unrivaled favorites. While Cynicism experiences a modest revival, the other schools vanish almost entirely.
- Between the first century BCE and the second century CE, the most common geographical region of study is Greece, followed by Italy, Asia Minor, and Egypt, though more philosophers had their origins in Asia Minor than elsewhere.
- Eighty-five of the 2,463 philosophers are women. During the post-Hellenistic period, these women apparently identify almost exclusively as Epicureans, Platonists, or Stoics.

TABLE 12. Attested philosophers by schools and centuries[30]

| FIRST CENTURY BCE | | FIRST CENTURY CE | | SECOND CENTURY CE | |
|---|---|---|---|---|---|
| 1. Epicureans | 54 | 1. N/A | 74 | 1. N/A | 118 |
| 2. N/A | 52 | 2. Stoics | 63 | 2. Middle Platonist/ Platonist | 53 (14 and 39) |
| 3. Stoics | 37 | 3. Platonists | 16 | 3. Stoics | 22 |
| 4. Academicians | 25 | 4. Epicureans | 15 | 4. Epicureans | 20 |
| 5. Aristotelians Peripatetics | 15 (2 and 13) | 5. Peripatetics | 5 | 5. Aristotelians/ Peripatetics | 17 (3 and 14) |
| 6. Platonists | 2 | 6. Academicians | 1 | 6. Academicians | 1 |

27. Richard Goulet, *Dictionnaire des Philosophes Anciennes*, 7 vols. (Paris: CNRS éditions, 1994–2018).

28. Goulet, "Ancient Philosophers," 10–39.

29. See Goulet, "Ancient Philosophers," charts 2.1 ("Women Philosophers by Schools and Centuries"); 2.2 ("Philosophers by Schools and Centuries"); chart 2.7 ("Philosophers by Schools and by Geographical Areas of Study").

30. Adapted from Goulet, "Ancient Philosophers," chart 2.2.

Goulet's data furnishes further support for Ahlholm's conclusion that a great many people considered themselves philosophers who did not commit themselves to philosophy wholly and professionally. Indeed, Goulet's collection uncovers many who in addition to identifying with philosophy also pursued other intellectual interests (Goulet identifies 405 such people). Also corroborating Ahlholm's study, Goulet's data reveals a large number of aspiring philosophers who practiced non-elite occupations. Among the attested are cart drivers, tanners, painters, sculptors, pantomimes, wrestlers, boxers, shoemakers, barbers, and many others.[31]

As far as initial impressions go, a count of 2,463 philosophers may perhaps strike one subjectively as a large number of historical individuals to be captured in the ancient record from this walk of life. On the other hand, the fact that this tally is drawn from an overall population of people in antiquity over the course of a millennium raises questions as to how plentiful philosophers were relative to the population at any given time. We seem to be enlightened, however, if we compare the prevalence of the professional "philosopher" with the prevalence of the professional "rhetorician" or "sophist." Interestingly, a search of the *Lexicon of Greek Personal Names* by profession reveals that individuals who are identifiable as professional "philosophers" are almost double those who can be identified as "rhetors"/"sophists" (combined).[32] Limiting attention to the post-Hellenistic period—when rhetorical theory had become the almost exclusive subject of school curriculum and public display rhetoric was immensely popular—still more professional philosophers are attested than rhetoricians /sophists. Only in the second century CE do sophists become more prevalent, during the height of the Second Sophistic (see chapter 15).

The city of Corinth offers an interesting case example of the comparison geographically. Evidence from Roman Corinth attests to slightly more philosophers than orators/sophists through the first two centuries of the common era. Itinerants of both types are known to have spent time in Corinth. Among itinerant philosophers were the Cynic-Stoic Dio Chrysostom, the neo-Pythagorean Apollonius of Tyana, the Middle-Platonist Plutarch, and Favorinus the Philosopher, who had Pyrrhonist and Academic leanings, and several other philosophers.[33] Attested among itinerant sophists are Herodes Atticus, Aelius Aristides, and others mentioned as a group.[34] Among more permanent residents—all attested in inscriptions—are several philosophers. Two date to the middle of the first century CE and are identifiable as Stoics. A statuary inscription dating between 1 and 67 CE refers to a

31. Goulet, "Ancient Philosophers," 38.

32. A search by "profession" in the Lexicon of Greek Personal Names (www.lgpn.ox.ac.uk) includes forty-two individuals identified as "philosophers" (plus one instance of a philosopher/doctor) but only twenty-three total individuals identified as either "rhetors" (seven, plus one called a rhetor/Asiarch) or "sophists" (sixteen).

33. Dio (*Or.* 31.121); Apollonius (Philostratus, *Vit. Apoll.* 4.25; 7.10); Plutarch (*Quaes. conv.* 8.4; cf. 9.5); Favorinus (Dio, *Or.* 37.8; Philostratus, *Vit. Soph.* 489, 491).

34. Herodes Atticus (Plutarch, *Quaes. conv.* 723; also mentioned in *IKorinthKent* 128), Aelius Aristides (*For Poseidon* 23), other unnamed sophists (Dio, *Or.* 8.9); as well as the Sophistic philosophers Dio Chrysostom and Favorinus (Dio in Dio, *Or.* 8; Favorinus in Dio, *Or.* 37; cf. Philostratus, *Vit. Soph.* 489, 491, 492).

"Corinthian Stoic philosopher" (*philosophon Stōikon Korinthion*) and Roman citizen named Lucius Peticius Propas.[35] The base of the statue indicates that the statue was dedicated by Lucius's mother Occia Prisca "because of his virtue and wisdom" (*aretēs heneka kai sophias*). Another Corinthian philosopher dating to the mid-first century CE is a Stoic named Bassus, attested in Philostratus's *Life of Apollonius* and in several epistles attributed to Apollonius.[36] This Bassus may be one and the same as the Gellius Bassus named as a magistrate in several Corinthian inscriptions.[37] Other resident philosophers in the record include a Lucius Flavius Arrianus, a multiply-attested Lucius Gellius Menander, and two other individuals identified as a philosophers.[38]

We find somewhat fewer rhetors, among whom were Herodes Atticus (also identified above), Publius Aelius Sospinus, [Lucius?] Maecius Faustinus, and Marcus Valerius Taurinus (also described as a "philosopher").[39] In all, evidence attests to some dozen philosophers—just exceeding the number of attested orators—in Corinth between the first and second centuries CE.[40] The orators date almost exclusively to the second century CE.

## The Social Lives of Philosophers

As plentiful as they were, philosophers could be as hidden as they were visible, depending on their attitude toward public involvement and their preferred style of social integration. Some of the most visible philosophers were also the most antisocial. The average street philosopher, despite their conspicuousness, lived relationally in isolation, being leery of the negative influence of the masses and assured of their self-sufficiency, after the example of the esteemed Diogenes. The withdrawn philosopher, on the other hand, could still exhibit a keen sense of social obligation. Many people (including other philosophers) criticized some philosophers for withdrawing from public involvement to indulge privately in philosophical speculation.[41] Some philosophers, however, were among the most devoted public servants and persistently emphasized that withdrawal was appropriate only under

35. *IvO* 453. On the dating, see also A. D. Rizakis and S. Zoumbaki, *Roman Peloponnese I. Roman Personal Names in Their Social Context (Achaia, Arcadia, Argolis, Corinthia and Eleia)*, Meletemata 31 (Athens: Research Centre for Greek and Roman Antiquity, 2001), who list the inscription as "second half of 1st c. A.D." (512).

36. Philostratus, *Vit. Apoll.* 4.24; 26; Apollonius, *Ep.* 36; 37; 74; cf. 60; 77.

37. *IG* IV$^2$ 1, 694; *IG* V 2.518.

38. Lucius Peticius (*IvO* 453); Lucius Flavius (*SEG* 30.159; 31.285); Lucius Gellius Menander (*IKorinthMeritt* 82; 125; *PIR*$^2$ c 670, 675); Gellius Bassus (*IG* IV$^2$ 1, 694; *IG* V 2.518); an unnamed individual (*IKorinthKent* 124).

39. Herodes Atticus (*IKorinthKent* 128); Publius Aelius Sospinus (*IKorinthKent* 226); [Lucius?] Maecius Faustinus (*IKorinthKent* 264); Marcus Valerius Taurinus (*IKorinthKent* 268). Peducaeus Cestianus is described as an "Apollonian orator" (*IKorinthKent* 269).

40. By my count, twelve philosophers, nine orators, and one identified as both a philosopher and an orator.

41. Plutarch, *Mor.* 1043b; Cicero, *Off.* 1.6.19; implicit defense in Seneca, *Ot.* 3.3–5; *Tranq.* 3.3–4.8; *Ep.* 14.14; 68.1–2; cf. Cicero, *Acad.* 2.2.6; *Off.* 1.1.1.

exceptional circumstances.[42] While both Cicero and Seneca, for instance, were forced into political retirement, even then they aimed to improve the lives of humanity by writing philosophy for public consumption.[43]

Social philosophers joined together in various kinds of fellowships. The classic school community found a setting in both private and public spaces, from private homes to temples, multipurpose buildings, and even open spaces like the Stoic colonnade.[44] Cicero's philosophical dialogues also offer clear examples of the phenomenon of discussion circles, in which men of leisure spent mornings, afternoons, or all hours of the day discussing philosophical topics with more focused attention and in sometimes very serious mode, often with participants representing different viewpoints. Less formally, the philosophically educated gathered for special occasions in the homes of the well-to-do to share a meal and engage in philosophical table talk.[45] Even after the Athenian schools disbanded in the first century BCE and philosophers scattered abroad, adherents of some school traditions maintained a sense of translocal connectivity as members of a sort of "textual community" that shared a common dedication to study of their founders' texts.[46]

In their most social configuration, philosophers formed *collegia*, or associations, akin to other religious or professional clubs.[47] In this configuration, philosophical circles were not only scholastic communities but also truly social organizations. As in the typical association, membership was voluntary and likely came with certain economic benefits (like mutual assistance or covering cost of burial for the deceased). Even as philosophers, these groups might share certain religious practices, especially practices centering around a patron deity; the Muses were a common focus of devotion for philosophers. They would have gathered according to a schedule to share a common meal. Members would consent to certain organizational rules and rituals. Perhaps in their most contented moments, they even felt that their communities represented the ideal that philosophers often mused about: a community of wise men.[48]

---

42. Cicero, *Off.* 1.21.71; on Seneca, see n41.

43. Cicero, *Nat. d.* 1.7–9. Seneca asserts that philosophers can benefit humanity even in their retirement (*Tranq.* 3.3–5).

44. Homes in Epictetus, *Diatr.* 3.23; Seneca, *Ep.* 76.4; Lucian, *Herm.* 11; Aulus Gellius, *Noct. Att.* 2.2; Philostratus, *Vit. Soph.* 604; Suetonius, *Life of Persius* 24–28; cf. Plutarch, *Quaes. conv.* 5.3.1–3; 8.4.1, 3. On other spaces, see Teresa Morgan, *Literate Education*, 28; cf. Harris, *Ancient Literacy*, 236.

45. Plutarch, *Quaes. conv.* 723a–724b; Lucian's *Symposium*; cf. *The Dream, or the Cock* 11.

46. Boys-Stones, *L. Annaeus Cornutus:* Greek Theology, *Fragments, and Testimonia*, 9–12.

47. Note an Epicurean synod in Lycia (*GRA* 146), an Epicurean *hetairos* in Bithynia (Lucian, *Alex.* 25; 43), and an association of Stoic philosophers in Bithynia (*IPrusaOlymp* 17–18). Philip A. Harland discusses a number of other philosophical associations, in *Greco-Roman Associations: Texts, Translations, and Commentary*, vol. 2, North Coast of the Black Sea, Asia Minor, BZNT 204 (Berlin: de Gruyter, 2014), 2:367–85.

48. E.g., Seneca, *Ben.* 7.12.2; Diogenes Laërtius, *Vit. phil.* 7.124; cf. Diogenes Laërtius, *Vit. phil.* 10.148//*Kur. Dox.* 28.

## For Further Study

Ahlholm, Tuuli. "Philosophers in Stone: Philosophy and Self-Representation in Epigraphy of the Roman Empire." MPhil thesis, Oxford University, 2017.

Brookins, Timothy A. "Educational Infrastructure." *Early Christian Centers. Vol. 3. Corinth.* Tübingen: Mohr Siebeck. Forthcoming.

Goulet, Richard. "Ancient Philosophers: A First Statistical Survey." Pages 10–39 in *Philosophy as a Way of Life: Ancients and Moderns; Essays in Honor of Pierre Hadot*. Edited by Michael Chase, Stephen R. L. Clark, and Michael McGhee. Oxford: Wiley-Blackwell, 2013.

Goulet, Richard. *Dictionnaire des Philosophes Anciennes*. 7 vols. Paris: CNRS éditions, 1994–2018.

Tod, Marcus N. "Sidelights on Greek Philosophers." *The Journal of Hellenic Studies* 77 (1957): 132–41.

# 15

# The Second Sophistic and Philosophy

If Plato could have returned from the grave around the year 150 CE, he would surely have been pleased to hear that "Platonism" was alive and well. He might have been disappointed, however, to learn that sophistry was flourishing too. Indeed, in the second half of the first century CE, a new kind of sophistry emerged. It was inspired by the old, but it now added the practice of oratory as a form of public entertainment to the earlier emphasis on public oratory as a practical skill. Flourishing between roughly 60 and 230 CE, this period came to be known, appropriately, as the "Second Sophistic." As in the former days, the "sophist" continued to find definition against the figure of the "philosopher."

## Philostratus's *Lives of the Sophists*

Flavius Philostratus was born in 170 CE to a prominent family residing on the Aegean island of Lemnos. A sophist and the son of a sophist, Philostratus in his later years wrote a book of *Lives of the Sophists*, which covered the lives of some of the most prominent sophists in history, ranging from the time of Plato until the publication of Philostratus's book sometime in the 230s CE.

In tracing the Sophistic movement historically, Philostratus made two important distinctions pertinent to his understanding of the relationship between sophistry and philosophy. The first distinction is a *chronological* one.[1] Rooted in the Classical period, "ancient" (*archaia*) sophistry, Philostratus stated, consisted in the practice of eloquently expounding on philosophical themes such as the nature of virtue or how the universe was fashioned.[2] From this kind of sophistry, Philostratus distinguished another, which although later than the first was by no means "new"; for it too had originated in the Classical period. This he called "second" (*deutera*) sophistry—whence is derived the historians' moniker "Second Sophistic" as an era of Classical history. Philostratus explained that, in distinction from the earlier kind of sophistry, second sophistry consisted in the extempore handling of "definite and special themes for which history shows the way."[3] What Philostratus is describing is a style of display oratory for which students prepared in the rhetorical schools through the exercise of "declamation," in which teachers assigned speech topics

1. Philostratus, *Vit. Soph.*. 481.

2. He also refers to ancient sophistry as "philosophic rhetoric (*rhētorikēn . . . philosophousan*)" (*Vit. Soph.* 480).

3. Philostratus, *Vit. Soph.* 481.

and students then expounded on their topics extempore. The words "for which history shows the way" indicate that the topics concerned famous events of the past. In this regard, after being assigned their topic, students might attempt to make a deliberative argument in favor of the most expedient course of action, as if speaking from the vantage point of the given historical moment. As a product of this kind of training, the Second Sophistic was therefore characterized largely by this type of display rhetoric.

Philostratus's second distinction was similar but not identical to his first. This one was not primarily chronological, but personal. Here, Philostratus distinguished between those philosophers who spoke eloquently and "sophists properly so called."[4] While this distinction overlaps partially with the first one, it cuts across the chronological divide between "ancient" and "second" sophistry.[5] In short, for Philostratus, there were eloquent philosophers and proper sophists in the second period of sophistry, just as there were in the first.

## Philosophers Versus Sophists

### *Historical Separation*

With these distinctions in the background, Philostratus's work reprises the theme of conflict between sophists and philosophers that were featured, either centrally or peripherally, in so many of Plato's dialogues centuries earlier. It seems that, once established, Plato's distinction (see chapter 4) persisted. Indeed, although Cicero (first century BCE) was both an orator and a philosopher, he never let us forget that he was an anomaly in this regard.[6] He was the ideal, a new kind of Roman intent on reconciling the "tongue and the brain"—i.e., rhetoric and philosophy.[7] The watershed of wisdom, Cicero regretted, had "divided in two" in the days of Socrates, with philosophers and rhetoricians going their separate ways so that each "never touched anything from the side of the other study except what this group borrowed from that one, or that one from this."[8] This narrative was echoed later by the Roman rhetorician Quintilian (first century CE),[9] who with Cicero made an appeal for philosophy and rhetoric to reunite.[10] In this regard, it is noteworthy that both Cicero and Quintilian reserve special, and clearly conventional, terminology to distinguish the proper domains of philosophy and rhetoric, the philosopher and the rhetorician. By their account, when wisdom "divided in two," the philosophers won the claim to wisdom in name. Indeed, in the post-Hellenistic era, philosophy commonly went by the lexical designation of "wisdom" (*sapientia*),

---

4. Philostratus, *Vit. Soph.* 479; cf. 484.
5. Philosophers from the Classical period through the Second Sophistic are covered in *Philostratus, Vit. Soph.,* 484–92.
6. Cicero, *Off.* 1.1.3–4.
7. Cicero, *Or.* 3.61; cf. *Tusc.* 1.1–7; *Off.* 1.1.1–2; *Inv.* 1.1.
8. Cicero, *Or.* 3.69–73, esp. 72.
9. Quintilian, *Inst.* 1.pr.13, 17–19; 12.2.5, 8; cf. 2.21.13.
10. Quintilian, *Inst.* 1.pr.9–20; 12.2.1–23.

just as rhetoric went by the designation of "eloquence" (*eloquentia*);[11] likewise, the philosopher held the title of the "wise man" (*sapiens*), while the rhetorician held the title of the "eloquent man" (*eloquens*).[12] Alternatively, manifold Latin sources use the circumlocution "pursuit of wisdom" (*studium sapientiae*) as a substitute for "philosophy," and "the one who pursues wisdom" (*studiosus sapientiae*) as a substitute for the "philosopher." On the other hand, these sources use "pursuit of eloquence" (*studium eloquentiae*) as a substitute for "rhetoric."[13]

Cicero and Quintilian were rhetoricians who recognized this split. The philosophers felt no differently. Although many philosophers over the centuries contributed to the study of grammar and rhetoric,[14] they insisted that their respective interests, on the whole, were very different. For example, Philo of Alexandria often set the philosopher and the sophist in direct antithesis.[15] Philosophers commonly captured the rhetoric-philosophy dynamic in terms of an opposition between "words" and "things."[16] From their perspective, orators were interested in "words" (form) while philosophers were interested in "things" (truth content).

### *Philostratus's Taxonomic Distinctions*

In Philostratus's *Lives*, Plato's distinction between sophists and philosophers is reaffirmed but now from the perspective of a sophist in the Second Sophistic. Here, keeping Philostratus's first distinction distinct from his second is vital for understanding the significance of the nominal distinction he wished to maintain between philosophers and sophists. Together, the two distinctions—the chronological and the personal—result in a *fourfold*, if overlapping, taxonomy of persons. To begin with, although "ancient" sophistry was primarily "philosophic," Philostratus insisted on a distinction in the ancient period between the sophists who expounded on philosophical themes and philosophers who discoursed eloquently.[17] In the "second" period, moreover, according to Philostratus, sophistry was not philosophic but rather exhibitive. Here again, Philostratus insisted on a distinction between eloquent philosophers and sophists properly so called. In short, Philostratus was adamant that in either period, the philosophers were "not actually sophists" or "sophists properly so called."[18]

---

11. Cicero, *Inv.* 1.1–3; Quintilian, *Inst.* 2.14.1–3; 12.2.8; 12.6.7; cf. Tacitus, *Agr.* 4; Seneca, *Ep.* 89.4, 6.

12. Quintilian, *Inst.* 1.pr.13.

13. Quintilian, *Inst.* 1.pr.14; 12.2.8; Cicero, *Off.* 2.5; *Inv.* 1.1.1–3; *Tusc.* 1.1; 4.3.5; *Vit. beat.* 24.4; Tacitus, *Agr.* 4; cf. Lucretius, *Rer. nat.* 5.7–12, 1.635–44.

14. In addition to Aristotle's treatise *On Rhetoric*, note Stoic influence on grammatical theory, in Morgan, *Literate Education*, 169–74; and Stoic adaptations to rhetorical theory in J. R. Butts, "The Progymnasmata of Theon: A New Text with Translation and Commentary" (Ph.D. dissertation, Claremont Graduate School, 1986), 6–7.

15. Philo, *Cher.* 1.10; *Sobr.* 1.9; *Praem.* 1.58.

16. Using a variety of terms for the antithesis: Dio Chrysostom, *Or.* 18.17; Musonius Rufus, *Diatr.* 5; Seneca, *Ep.* 20.2; 34.4; Musonius Rufus, *Diatr.* 1; 5; 6; 8.

17. The latter is treated in *Vit. Soph.* 484–6.

18. The latter phrasing in *Vit. Soph.* 479; both in 484.

In this regard, Philostratus's account may imply that an even stronger—or at least more established—distinction existed between philosophy and sophistry in his own day than in Plato's. Indeed, in contrast to the earlier period, Philostratus is able to name from the Second Sophistic only two philosophers who ranked with the sophists.[19] Regarding Dio of Prusa (ca. 40–120 CE; later called Chrysostom, "Golden-mouthed"), Philostratus pretends to be at a loss: "I do not know what one ought to call him, such was his excellence in all departments."[20] Philostratus includes Dio, nonetheless, in the group of those (two people) who ranked as sophists due to their eloquence but in truth were philosophers.

Interestingly, other accounts explain Dio's ambiguity differently, although they come to a similar conclusion. It seems that Dio had a fluctuating relationship with philosophy. He had been a student of the Cynic-Stoic philosopher Musonius Rufus[21] and, accordingly, his own discourses exhibited extensive Cynic and Stoic qualities. Yet it appears that at one time, he had actually been critical of Musonius.[22] Adding to this tension, Dio was eloquent like the sophists, and certain of his discourses could be described as more trifling, in the style of the sophists.[23] Moreover, while in exile, he is said to have sustained himself with just two books: *Phaedo* by Plato (a philosopher) and *On the False Embassy* by Demosthenes (an orator).[24] A later tradition reconciles this assortment of facts—Dio's sophist-like abilities, his critical stance toward philosophy, his association with philosophers, and his predilection for philosophical themes in his discourses—by posing that Dio had a crisis of sudden conversion in which he turned from sophist to philosopher.[25] According to this tradition, Dio's conversion occurred during his period of exile during Domitian's persecutions of the philosophers in Rome.[26] Whether his break from sophistry was as clean as this account suggests, the very possibility of depicting a transition from one profession to the other as a matter of "conversion" illustrates how distinct from one another these professions must have been viewed.[27] In any case, even for Philostratus, Dio was not among the "sophists properly so called," eloquent though he was.

The other philosopher that Philostratus included among sophists from the Second Sophistic is Favorinus (ca. 85–155 CE), whom he actually calls "Favorinus the Philosopher."[28] Favorinus wrote on philosophical subjects, considered himself

---

19. Philostratus, *Vit. Soph.* 486–8. While not included by Philostratus, other philosophizing declaimers include the Middle Platonists Apuleius and Maximus of Tyre.

20. Philostratus, *Vit. Soph.* 486.

21. Fronto, *To Marcus Antoninus* 4; cf. Dio, *Or.* 32.122; Lucian, *Peregr.* 18.

22. Dio apparently expressed his criticism in a nonextant work called *To Musonius* and in two letters to Musonius.

23. Philostratus (*Vit. Soph.* 487) mentions the *Tale of Euboea* and the *Encomium of a Parrot*.

24. Philostratus, *Vit. Soph.* 488.

25. Synesius of Cyrene, *In Praise of Baldness*.

26. On Dio's "exile" see Philostratus, *Vit. Soph.* 488 (although Philostratus points out that it was voluntary); cf. Dio, *Or.* 3.13.

27. Note also Lucian's suggestion of a choice of loyalty between rhetoric and philosophy: *Bis acc.* 32.

28. Philostratus, *Vit. Soph.* 489.

to be a philosopher, and identified with the New Academy.[29] Yet in speech, he was eloquent and utilized the ornate "Asianist" style. A bitter rivalry arose between him and the famous sophist Polemo, fed by the envy of each at the other's popularity. Philostratus explained that it was based on this rivalry that Favorinus, despite being a philosopher, could also be called a sophist.[30]

### *The Differences Defined*

At the outset of his *Lives*, Philostratus established the main difference on which his taxonomic distinction was based. The philosopher, on the one hand, purports to know nothing but then presents step-by-step arguments as if leading toward some known truth. The sophist, on the other hand, "assumes a knowledge of that whereof he speaks" and hence speaks in a way that implies a "clear grasp of the truth."[31]

Undoubtedly, Plato would have taken exception to this formulation, for Philostratus seems to directly reverse Plato's definitions of the respective classes (see chapter 3). There seems, however, to be a simple explanation for this contradiction. Philostratus's characterization of philosophy here describes the approach of the Skeptical philosophers, not of the Dogmatic schools (see chapter 10). Moreover, his description confines attention to philosophers who were active in oratory. Out of all the philosophical schools, it was the Skeptical Academy that most emphasized training in rhetoric; and like the early sophists, the Skeptical Academics also emphasized the importance of training in pro-and-contra argument.[32] This interpretation of Philostratus's remark is corroborated when one takes note of the philosophical commitments of the "philosophical sophists" he treats in the *Lives*: They almost invariably identify with the Academy.[33]

### *The Outsider's Perspective*

It is apparent, then, that the traditional distinction between sophists and philosophers Plato had succeeded in establishing in the fourth century BCE was still being observed in the post-Hellenistic era by practitioners of the respective professions, who generally (though not always) defined self-identity in terms of one profession to the exclusion of the other.[34] As Philostratus attests, this attitude of opposition continued into the Second Sophistic.

---

29. Philostratus, *Vit. Soph.* 491.

30. Philostratus, *Vit. Soph.* 491.

31. Philostratus, *Vit. Soph.* 480; in reference to "ancient" sophistry.

32. Cicero, *Nat. d.* 2.168; Diogenes Laërtius, *Vit. phil.* 4.28; LS §68m; Plutarch, *Cat. Maj.* 22.2–3.

33. Eudoxus, Dias of Ephesus, Carneades (Philostratus, *Vit. Soph.* 484; 485; 486), and Favorinus (Philostratus, *Vit. Soph.* 489–91) are identified as Academics. Dio seems to have had Stoic and Platonic leanings, though tradition holds that he had previously been a sophist.

34. It was possible to be described as both "philosopher" and "orator"; e.g., Marcus Valerius Taurinus in *IKorinthKent* 268. The former title, however, was perhaps less appropriately paired with "sophist."

One could, however, view the matter of identity from a different perspective—i.e., an *etic*, or outsider's, perspective. Indeed, the definite sense of self-identity claimed by practitioners (from their *emic* perspective) did not guarantee that the outside observer would perceive or characterize the subject in keeping with the latter's self-understanding. Contradictory identification could arise from either of two scenarios. In one scenario, the observer "misidentifies" the subject either because they cannot tell or because they do not know the difference between a philosopher and a sophist, being ignorant of the definitions adhered to by each.[35] For the average citizen, a Cynic street preacher and an itinerant sophist, for instance, might appear to be cut from a similar cloth. In another scenario, an observer—or better, a critic—might intentionally brand the subject with a contrary label as a means of insult. Generally, this kind of slander would involve branding a philosopher a sophist, with the latter term likely functioning as a pejorative label in which the target is branded as a pretender to wisdom or as a charlatan who employs a sly or deceitful style of argument.[36] The reviler in this case would presumably know the conventional distinction, since the intent to slander is achieved precisely in the "misapplication."

### *Legal Distinction*

The distinction between the philosopher and rhetorician or sophist also had legal significance. When the emperors at various times exiled the philosophers from Rome (see chapter 12), they did not include sophists with them.[37] The distinction between the two also came into play in matters related to state sponsorship of public education. Under the empire, states increasingly supported education with public subsidies: for instance, by instituting a limited number of salaried professorships in each city or province. Appointees enjoyed certain exemptions from taxes and other forms of public service. These positions were almost invariably reserved for secondary-level teachers and rhetoricians or sophists and excluded elementary teachers and philosophers.[38]

## For Further Study

Richter, Daniel S., and William A. Johnson, eds. *The Oxford Handbook of the Second Sophistic*. Oxford: Oxford University Press, 2017.

Schmidt, Thomas, and Pascale Fleury, eds. *Perceptions of the Second Sophistic and Its Times/Regards sur la Seconde Sophistique et son époque*. Phoenix Supplementary Volumes 49. Toronto: University of Toronto Press, 2011.

---

35. G. R. Stanton shows that the distinction held even when the difference was hard for the outside observer to discern "Sophists and Philosophers: Problems of Classification," *AJP* 94 (1973): 350–64.

36. For instance, used of philosophers in Lucian, *Iupp. conf.* 19; *Gall.* 4; *Par.* 43. For the pejorative denotation, see Pierre Chantraine, *Dictionnaire étymologique de la langue grecque: Histoire des mots* (Paris: Klincksieck, 2000), 1031.

37. On Dio Chrysostom as philosopher, see above.

38. Justinian, *Dig.* 27.1.6.2; Pliny, *Ep.* 4.13.3; Philostratus, *Vit. Soph.* 524; cf. Juvenal, *Sat.* 7.203–206. Pliny (*Ep.* 10.58.1) describes a scenario in which a philosopher's claim to exemption was suspect.

# Part 4

# Christianity and Philosophy

# 16

# Christianity and Philosophy in the Second Through Fourth Centuries

Writing to one of his pupils in the early third century CE, the Christian theologian Origen of Alexandria offered his student the following advice:

> I wish to ask you to extract from the philosophy of the Greeks what may serve as a course of study or a *preparation for Christianity*, and from geometry and astronomy what will serve to explain the sacred Scriptures, in order that all that the sons of the philosophers are wont to say about geometry and music, grammar, rhetoric, and astronomy, as fellow-helpers to philosophy, we may say about philosophy itself, in relation to Christianity.[1]

It is not difficult to see why Origen found such value in pagan philosophy as preparation for the Christian faith. As the foregoing chapters repeatedly noted, philosophy in some ways found its genesis as a negative reaction to traditional polytheism with its conventional conception of the gods as petty, vindictive, jealous, and dissentious superhumans. If the gods were real, the philosophers objected, then they would be the most perfect kinds of beings conceivable, not just more powerful than human beings but altogether more virtuous. Among the earliest philosophers, moreover, many speculated that there was perhaps just one ultimate, ordering mind governing everything, a view that in essence most later philosophical traditions shared. Further still, when Socrates "brought philosophy from heaven to earth," as Cicero said, the dominant philosophical traditions that followed him elevated ethics to the level of highest importance on the philosophical agenda and almost invariably concluded that the best kind of life finds its fulfillment in virtue above all else.

In ways that the philosophers themselves recognized, these convictions set up philosophy as a kind of alternative to religion, or better, as an alternative *type* of religion. It was sometimes said that among common conceptions, there were three different kinds of "gods": mythical gods, civil gods, and natural gods.[2] The first type correlated with the gods of poetic myth, the second with the gods of the state

1. Origen, *Ep. Greg.* 1 (*ANF* 4); my italics.

2. Augustine draws this distinction (*tria genera tradita deorum*, "three kinds of gods") in *The City of God* (6.5–8) based on a lost work of the Roman philosopher Varro, who in turn drew the distinction from Scaevola (Augustine, *Civ.* 4.27). Augustine refers here to "three kinds of theology" (*tria genera theologiae*).

cults, and the third with the gods, or God, of philosophy. From most philosophers' perspective, mythic religion was impious and cultic religion (besides assuming the gods of mythic religion) was unproductive of virtue. Therefore, the best kind of religion was that of philosophy—a way of life concerned with virtuous conduct, understood as conformity with nature or the perfect being that moves it.

On this basis, it may be suggested that—as Origen would probably have agreed—ancient philosophy in many ways shared less in common with traditional folk or state religion than it did with the Judeo-Christian tradition. Hence, it is unsurprising that as Christians more fully elaborated their theology over the second and third centuries CE, Christianity came to be understood as a "philosophy" in its own right and—as often happens with things most alike—eventually became Greek philosophy's greatest rival.

## Moses, the Prophets, and the Philosophers

From Cain and Abel to Esau and Jacob, the Jewish scriptures are rife with stories about people who were at the same time blood relatives and bitter rivals. Through analogy, these stories of rivalry offer a fitting antecedent to the way that many Jews, following the Hellenization of Israel and Judea in the second century BCE, viewed the relationship between Jewish theology and Greek philosophy. They were both relatives and rivals. Through the light of divine reason, Greek philosophy claimed to unlock the deepest truths about the nature of the universe and our place within it. While many Jews trained in philosophy were willing to concede that the philosophers had indeed grasped much, they commonly argued that their realizations had not come about purely through the light of natural revelation. Rather, for some of their best insights, the Greeks had actually borrowed from the wisest and most inspired of the Jewish people: Moses. This idea appears frequently in the writings of the most Hellenized Jewish writers from the Hellenistic and Roman periods, including Aristobulus (second century BCE), Philo of Alexandria (early first century CE), and Josephus (37–ca. 100 CE). From their perspective, Moses was the source of the truths affirmed by all the best philosophers—Socrates, Pythagoras, Zeno, and most of all, Plato, who had grasped more truth than any other.[3] Despite the many authentic truths that the philosophers had derived from Moses, however, they had badly missed the big picture. That is, the *Greeks* had missed badly, not philosophers per se. One philosophy got it right. It was the philosophy of Moses—the *Jewish* philosophy.[4]

## Christian Attitudes Toward Philosophy

Unsurprisingly, early Christian writers shared similar views to Philo and other Hellenistic Jewish writers. Christian writers, however, were less interested in Moses as

3. Aristobulus, *fr.* 2.4; 3.1; 4.4; Philo, *Prob.* 57; Josephus, *Ag. Ap.* 2.168, 279–81. Even the Neoplatonist Numenius (second century CE) seems to acknowledge a connection: *fr.* 8.

4. Philo, *Praem.* 43–44; *Spec.* 2.44–48; 4 Macc 1:1; 8:15; cf. Josephus, *Ant.* 18.11.

a legislator than in Moses and the other writers of Scripture as inspired prophets. On this view, the prophets of Israel were philosophers themselves and the source of all the best doctrines affirmed by the Greeks—from the immortality of the soul to punishments after death, to truths about the heavenly realms.[5] While natural revelation contributed to Greek understanding, this was insufficient in itself to lead them to the whole truth; it only enlightened them to understand what they had read from the prophets themselves.[6]

Although from the Christian perspective Greek philosophy was only partly true, it did, from Origen's perspective, provide useful preparation for the study of Christian theology in the same way as for Plato geometry and music were preparatory for the study of philosophy.[7] In short, while non-Christian thinkers possessed part of the truth, Christianity possessed the *whole* truth. Justin Martyr aptly captured this view in a saying adapted, fittingly, from the philosophers themselves: "Whatever has been well said by anyone belongs to us Christians."[8]

Among the philosophers, Christians had some favorites. Near the top of the list was Seneca the Stoic. Tertullian refers to him as "Seneca, who is often our own" (*Seneca saepe noster*).[9] Two centuries later, Jerome named him "our Seneca" (*Seneca noster*) without qualification.[10] Lactantius even averred that Seneca would have been a "true worshiper" of God had someone shown him the way.[11] Another Stoic of sorts, Musonius Rufus, received honorable mention on account of his moral teaching.[12] Socrates was admired for holding fast to the truth even in the face of death.[13] Eventually, Plato earned first place.

Yet it seems to be a rule of nature that people will clash most bitterly with those who are most like them. As highly as many Christian theologians regarded such figures as Seneca and Plato, they were equally critical of them. Christian discussions of Stoic doctrines, for instance, tended to be characterized by a tension of "supportive and combative attitudes."[14] Within the history of ancient philosophy, this kind of interaction had a familiar ring: It was almost as if the Christians were philosophers fighting with other philosophers.

---

5. Justin, *Dial.* 44.8–9. See also Justin, *1 Apol.* 59.1–5; Clement of Alexandria, *Strom.* 1.22.4.

6. Justin, *1 Apol.* 44.10. See also Clement of Alexandria, *Strom.* 1.7; Gregory of Nazianzus, *Or.* 28.25.

7. Origen, *Ep. Greg.* 1.

8. Justin, *2 Apol.* 13; echoing Seneca, *Ep.* 16.7: "Whatever is well said by anyone is mine"; who was apparently echoing Epicurus (*fr.* 201).

9. Tertullian, *An.* 20.1.

10. Jerome, *Jov.* 1.49; cf. *Vir. ill.* 12.

11. Lactantius, *Inst.* 6.24.14.

12. Justin, *2 Apol.* 8; Origen, *Cels.* 3.66.

13. Justin, *1 Apol.* 5.

14. Marcia L. Colish, "Stoicism and the New Testament: An Essay in Historiography," *ANRW* 2.26.1:334–79, Part 2, Principat, 33.1, ed. H. Temporini and W. Haase (New York: de Gruyter, 1989), esp. 336–39. For an account of the relationship between Christianity and Stoicism for the first two thousand years, see Harry M. Hine, "Seneca and Paul: The First Two Thousand Years," in *Paul and Seneca in Dialogue*, ed. Joseph R. Dodson and David E. Briones, Ancient Philosophy and Religion 2 (Leiden: Brill, 2017), 22–48.

## Christianity as a Philosophy

### *From a Christian Perspective*

The memorable question asked by the Christian theologian Tertullian around the early third century CE, "What hath Athens to do with Jerusalem?,"[15] was as much a statement about Christianity's rejection of Greek philosophy as it was about the inevitable necessity of engaging it on its terms. Indeed, the Christian rivalry with philosophy was soon articulated as a rivalry *between* philosophies. As early as the mid-second century CE, Justin Martyr described Christianity as the "only philosophy" that is secure and beneficial, and he identified himself as a "philosopher" of that school.[16] He had been a philosopher prior to his conversion and now continued to wear the philosopher's characteristic dress.[17] A conception of Christianity as a philosophy—the best philosophy—became common among later Christian writers.[18]

If Christianity was to contend as a philosophy, then it behooved its theologians to render a Christian account of the Supreme Good, or *end*, as they soon did. Due to Platonism's dominance by the third century CE, accounts of the Christian end unsurprisingly echo the language of Plato and Middle Platonist writers.[19] Clement of Alexandria (ca. 150–215 CE), after reviewing Plato's view that the end is "assimilation to God as far as possible,"[20] showed from the Scriptures that this view aptly describes the Christian End—in a way. Appealing to 1 Cor 11:1, "Be my *imitators*, as I also am *of Christ*," Clement asserts that Paul holds the "aim [*skopos*] of faith" to be "assimilation to God . . . so that as far as possible a man becomes righteous and holy with wisdom" and "the end" (*telos*) to be "restitution of the promise which is effected by faith." From these doctrines, Clement says, "gush the fountains . . . of those [philosophers] who have dogmatized about the end."[21]

Two centuries later, Saint Augustine in his *City of God* identified 288 views on the Supreme Good that were conceivable based on all possible permutations of philosophical opinions.[22] Against all of these views, Augustine set the Christian view of the end: everlasting life,[23] or more precisely, peace in life everlasting in the Heavenly City.[24] Both Clement and Augustine mention the wording of the apostle Paul in Rom 6:22: "and the end [*telos*]—everlasting life."

---

15. Tertullian, *Praescr.* 7.

16. Justin, *Dial.* 8.1.

17. Justin, *Dial.* 1. On the dress, see ch. 6, n19.

18. Tertullian, *Pall.* 6.4; Tatian, *Or. Graec.* 31, 42; Clement, *Strom.* 6.8.1; Augustine, *Civ.* 19.

19. Plato alternately describes the end as "likeness to God," "following God," "imaging oneself to God," and "participating in God." For the sources, see Lee, *Moral Transformation*, 104–5.

20. See ch. 13 on the Middle Platonists and the end.

21. Clement, *Strom.* 2.22 (*ANF* 2); my italics.

22. Augustine based his calculation on Varro (an adherent of the Old Academy and student of Antiochus of Ascalon) in his book *On Philosophy.*

23. Augustine, *Civ.* 19.4.

24. Augustine, *Civ.* 19.11.

Many Christian theologians were clearly conversant with, or even highly educated in, Greek philosophical traditions. To take an early example, Justin Martyr adduced in his *1 Apology*, addressed to Emperor Antoninus Pius in the 150s, ample parallels to illustrate that Christian beliefs were no more absurd than those of their Greek or Roman counterparts. From the domain of religion, Justin compared theophanies in the Jewish scriptures with theophanies in Greek and Roman myths, the Christian conception of Jesus' divinity with traditional conceptions of demigods and the resurrection of Jesus with apotheosis traditions. Drawing from Stoic philosophy, Justin presented Jesus as the divine *Logos*, or reason, and acknowledged that God has sown a "seed of reason" (*logos spermatikos*) in all people. He observed that Christians share with Plato belief in a transcendent and immutable God, a providentially ordered universe, and punishment after death. Justin even appealed to traditional Epicurean and Skeptical arguments against pagan myth and worship practices. He quoted or alluded to famous maxims of many other philosophers. He also advised that not all who go by the name of "Christian" are true Christians, just as philosophers insisted that not all who go by the name of "philosopher" are true philosophers.

This tension between early Christian rejection of Greek philosophy and their appropriation of it was not self-contradictory. Rather, Christianity was now replicating the kind of interschool interaction that had increasingly characterized rival philosophies from the beginning of the post-Hellenistic era (see chapter 11). In this regard, Christian theologians appropriated philosophical material, not mechanically but creatively, integrating it with Christian beliefs to construct a new kind of philosophical, or theological, framework.[25] This endeavor reached its high point in the late fourth century with Augustine, who creatively adapted Neoplatonism to this end.[26] Far from representing Christian concession to Neoplatonism, Augustine's project represented a final tour de force that aimed to appropriate Neoplatonism—the last philosophy to defeat—against itself.

## *From an Outsider's Perspective*

Even from the outsider's perspective, Christian groups could look like philosophical schools as they gathered together in homes to study texts with teachings stemming from ancient authorities. Galen the physician (second century CE) identified Christians as "those from Moses and Christ" (*tous apo Mōsou kai Christou*), here employing the same formula used to identify devotees of other founding figures while echoing the old Skeptical critique of the Dogmatic schools by depicting Christians as unconditional adherents of their founders' teachings.[27] Similar is Lucian's description of Christians.[28]

25. George Karamanolis, *The Philosophy of Early Christianity*, Ancient Philosophies (Durham: Acumen, 2013; New York: Routledge, 2014), 168, 171, 193, esp. 26.

26. Shields, *Ancient Philosophy*, 269–86.

27. Galen, *De puls. diff.* 3.3, or "the school of Moses and Christ" (*De puls. diff.* 2.4). Early Christian texts, in turn, depict the philosophical schools in kind: Justin Martyr, *Dial.* 1.2; Origen, *Cels.* 1.10. On Galen, see Alexander, "Paul and the Hellenistic Schools," 60–83.

28. Lucian speaks of their commitment to Christ: "receiving such doctrines traditionally without any definite evidence" (*Peregr.* 13 [LCL, Harmon]).

## Christianity, Platonism, and Gnosticism

If the interaction of the orthodox fathers with Greek philosophy can be considered creative and intelligent, then Saint Irenaeus is not so generous in describing the "Gnostic sect" (*Gnōstikē hairesis*).[29] According to Irenaeus, the Gnostics (*Gnōstikoi*) drew their ideas from the philosophers, but in piecemeal fashion like a garment sewn together out of many rags, and these of the worst imaginable quality. To be sure, the Gnostics brought in their own novelties, but the pieces were not their own and were in any case, Irenaeus scoffed, "old and useless" and "redolent of ignorance and irreligion."[30]

Whether or not the Gnostics can be considered a philosophical sect (*hairesis*) in exactly the same way as the schools of the Stoics, Epicureans, or Academics, Irenaeus used this very same term to describe them as a group. That the Gnostics represented a relatively well-defined school of thought is corroborated by Neoplatonist thinkers of the early third century CE. In Porphyry's collection of Plotinus's "Enneads," Porphyry titles one of the tractates "Against *the* Gnostics" (*pros tous gnōstikous*).

While elements of incipient Gnosticism appear in the first century CE (and are perhaps combated by the author of the Johannine literature), Gnosticism did not reach full maturity until the century that followed. What is known about Gnosticism is conveyed primarily through its opponents, including chiefly the orthodox church fathers, but also some Neoplatonists. Irenaeus purports to offer a full account of its doctrines in *Against Heresies*. His account demonstrates that Gnostics drew abundantly from Jewish and Christian writings (hence his inclusion of Gnosticism among the Christian "heresies"). Their account of cosmic origins involved a complicated ancestry of deities known as "Aeons," many of whose names were borrowed from Christian names or titles for God (Father) or Christ (Christ, Only-Begotten, *Logos*, Savior), from abstract theological concepts associated with Christianity (grace, truth, wisdom), or from other Christian-associated terminology (*ecclēsia*). Within this mythology, Christ played the role of Savior, who descended from the *Plērōma* (heavenly fullness) to divulge esoteric knowledge, through which a person became liberated from the evil prison of the body.

The non-Christian elements of Gnosticism, on the other hand, derived predominantly from Platonism. This connection is not only noted by the church fathers. It is also evident from Neoplatonic responses to the Gnostics that the latter were both reading and indebted to Plato's writings. For historians, the Platonic connection received further confirmation in 1945 when a library of thirteen codices written in the Coptic dialectic around 350 CE was discovered. These contain not only a number of Gnostic Christian texts (the Gospel of Philip, the Gospel of Truth, and the Gospel of the Egyptians, among others) but also a portion of Plato's *Republic*.

From Irenaeus, Porphyry, and other available sources, many of the Gnostics' affinities for Platonism are clearly evident: The world was created by a lower deity

---

29. The term was introduced in Irenaeus, *Haer.* 1.11.1.

30. Irenaeus, *Haer.* 2.14.2.

known as the demiurge, matter is the "principle" of evil in the world, lower principles in the hierarchy of divine emanations are images of the higher ones, the human soul is pre-existent, and humans should strive to transcend the body through the divine intellect. Among the Gnostic Aeons, moreover, many of them bore names drawn from Platonic designations for the principles of the universe, including (in addition to the name of the demiurge) the terms "*logos*," "intellect" (*nous*), and "understanding" (*ennoia*). Porphyry, however, hastened to point out that although Plotinus identified matter as the principle of evil, he also maintained that matter does not have an independent existence separate from the One, or the good; nor does it represent an equal counterbalancing principle to the One. The good was supreme, and everyone—not just a Gnostic elite—had the ability to attain knowledge of it through the innate human intellect.

## For Further Study

Adamson, Peter. *Philosophy in the Hellenistic and Roman Worlds: A History of Philosophy Without Any Gaps*. Vol. 2. Oxford: Oxford University Press, 2015.

Bosman, Philip R., and Gideon R. Kotzé. *Ancient Philosophy and Early Christianity: Studies in Honor of Johan C. Thom*. Supplements to Novum Testamentum 188. Leiden: Brill, 2022.

Colish, Marcia L. "Stoicism and the New Testament: An Essay in Historiography." *ANRW* 2.26.1:334–79. Part 2, Principat, 33.1. Edited by H. Temporini and W. Haase. New York: de Gruyter, 1989.

Goulet-Cazé, Marie-Odile. *Cynicism and Christianity in Antiquity*. Grand Rapids: Eerdmans, 2019.

Karamanolis, George. *The Philosophy of Early Christianity*. Ancient Philosophies. Second ed. New York: Routledge, 2021.

Malherbe, Abraham J. "Hellenistic Moralists and the New Testament." *ANRW* 2.26.1:267–333. Part 2, Principat, 33.1. Edited by H. Temporini and W. Haase. New York: de Gruyter, 1989.

Stead, Christopher. *Philosophy in Christian Antiquity*. Cambridge: Cambridge University Press, 1994.

Van Unnik, W. C. "Corpus Hellenisticum Novi Testamenti." *Journal of Biblical Literature* 83 (1964): 17–33.

# 17

# Philosophy and the New Testament

In the New Testament period, the extent of Christian interaction with Greek philosophy is much more difficult to discern. In fact, prior to Justin Martyr in the middle of the second century CE, no clear evidence exists of Christian writers wrestling rigorously or systematically with Greek philosophical questions or engaging in overt polemic with Greek philosophy.[1] In all the New Testament, the only passage that refers explicitly to philosophers is the Areopagus scene in Acts 17:16–34, where the apostle Paul, preaching in Athens about the resurrection, wooed the attention of "some of the Epicurean and Stoic philosophers" (17:18). Here, being seized and taken up to the Areopagus, Paul makes a defense that until the closing remarks adheres superficially though consistently to generically Greek philosophical categories. In this same speech is included one of only two clear citations of Greek philosophers (Aratus and Cleanthes) in the New Testament: "We are also his [God's] offspring."[2]

The historian, however, should not jump to the conclusion that the NT's absence of overt discussion of philosophy indicates a total lack of engagement. It cannot be ruled out from the start (though it is questionable) that some NT writers may have had some exposure to philosophy through firsthand study (Luke, Paul, and the author of Hebrews would be the best candidates). In any case, the New Testament writers all wrote in Greek, and most if not all of them in diasporic contexts. If Lucian of Samosata is to be even remotely believed—that philosophers were unavoidable in public (see chapter 14)—then it would have been impossible for these writers to avoid encountering philosophers and absorbing at least a smattering of their doctrines and manner of speech. At its most basic level of influence, Greek philosophy made a substantial contribution to the intellectual culture of the times and, as noted, made its way into many forms of cultural discourse, from literature and the arts to politics. As a competitor in this marketplace of religions, ideologies, and philosophies, Christianity would have needed quickly to adapt its message into terms intelligible to contemporary audiences and to prove itself an equal or superior option to its alternatives, especially Greek philosophy.

On these grounds, it is justifiable that modern scholarship over the last century and a half has closely analyzed the NT writings for traces of philosophical

1. Karamanolis, *The Philosophy of Early Christianity*, 2–3.

2. The quotation is from the Stoic Aratus, *Phaen.* 5; a similar line occurs in the Stoic Cleanthes's "Hymn to Zeus" (*SVF* 1.537 [p. 121, line 37]). The other quotation is from the pre-Socratic Epimenides, *de Oraculis*, found in Titus 1:12: "Cretans are always liars, evil beasts, lazy gluttons."

interaction, noting, on the one hand, its writers' appropriation of and allusions to philosophical arguments, verbiage, and commonplaces, and even evidence of influence; and on the other hand, subversive engagement of the NT writers with philosophical ideas, as well as the possibility of the influence of philosophy on the writers' audiences. It has not been the purpose of this book to review this scholarship. However, I provide in appendix 1 an annotated bibliography of such research over especially the last half century to offer an entry point into these discussions or material for further research. In addition, this book itself is offered as a further contribution to what seems to be a new wave of interest in this line of research (see chapter 1). Hopefully it serves as further stimulus for movement along this trajectory.

## For Further Study

Adamson, Peter. *Philosophy in the Hellenistic and Roman Worlds: A History of Philosophy Without Any Gaps*. Vol. 2. Oxford: Oxford University Press, 2015.

Colish, Marcia L. "Stoicism and the New Testament: An Essay in Historiography." *ANRW* 2.26.1:334–79. Part 2, Principat, 33.1. Edited by H. Temporini and W. Haase. New York: de Gruyter, 1989.

Goulet-Cazé, Marie-Odile. *Cynicism and Christianity in Antiquity*. Grand Rapids: Eerdmans, 2019.

Karamanolis, George. *The Philosophy of Early Christianity*. Ancient Philosophies. 2nd ed. New York: Routledge, 2021.

Malherbe, Abraham J. "Hellenistic Moralists and the New Testament." *ANRW* 2.26.1:267–333. Part 2, Principat, 33.1. Edited by H. Temporini and W. Haase. New York: de Gruyter, 1989.

Van Unnik, W. C. "Corpus Hellenisticum Novi Testamenti." *Journal of Biblical Literature* 83 (1964): 17–33.

# APPENDIXES

# Appendix 1: An Annotated Bibliography of New Testament Research

Over the last century, scholarship has produced a profusion of articles, chapter essays, and monographs that juxtapose Greco-Roman philosophical traditions with New Testament writings, with the letters of Paul attracting by far the lion's share of attention. These studies cover the full gamut of major philosophical schools. They focus sometimes on select themes, and sometimes on major departments of philosophical systems, or even whole systems of thought. The following is an annotated bibliography of some such studies, organized by individual philosophers or philosophical school.

## Comparative Methodology

This line of NT scholarship is largely comparative. That is, to juxtapose Christian writings with philosophical writings is to ask questions about similarity, difference, genealogy, and uniqueness. As noted in chapter 1, these questions have been of keen interest to modern interpreters since the days of the *Religionsgeschicthliche Schule* and the inception of the Corpus Hellenisticum project in the late nineteenth and early twentieth centuries.

The soundness of this line of inquiry has also been challenged. It has been many decades since Samuel Sandmel delivered his classic, and critical, SBL Presidential Address titled "Parallelomania." While the purpose of Sandmel's paper was not to deny the value of "parallels" and comparative inquiry, he noted a concerning lack of methodological rigor in the way parallels were often used in biblical scholarship.[1] His concerns have been echoed by others.[2]

Recent scholarship has made major strides toward greater methodological sophistication. Contributing to the field of religious studies more broadly, Jonathan Z. Smith introduced an important methodological distinction between "genealogical" and "illustrative" comparison.[3] According to Smith, genealogical comparison seeks

---

1. Samuel Sandmel, "Parallelomania," *JBL* 81 (1962): 1–13; a published version of his 1961 Society of Biblical Literature Presidential Address.

2. Van Unnik, "Corpus Hellenisticum," 17–33; and L. Michael White and John T. Fitzgerald, "*Quod est comparandum*: The Problem of Parallels," in *Early Christianity and Classical Culture*, ed. J. T. Fitzgerald, T. H. Olbricht, and L. M. White (Leiden: Brill, 2003), 13–39.

3. Notable contributions by Jonathan Z. Smith include *Map Is Not Territory: Studies in the History of Religions* (Chicago: University of Chicago Press, 1982); *Drudgery Divine: On*

to demonstrate "real" similarities between comparanda (things that are compared) attributable to an alleged genetic relationship. Illustrative comparison, on the other hand, is "heuristic" and serves as a means through which the inquirer discovers something new about one or both comparanda through the very exercise of juxtaposing them while assuming nothing about their "real" relationship.[4] The illustrative approach opens up wider opportunities for comparison, since it sidesteps questions concerning the concrete contexts of contact and even the question of whether a genetic relationship between comparanda existed at all. The exercise, rather, serves the goal of analysis by potentially enhancing insights about the comparanda in themselves. A number of recent studies in biblical scholarship explicitly advocate for or take an illustrative approach to analyzing NT texts.[5]

Further advances have occurred through the development of new taxonomies for analyzing "interactions" between ancient traditions like those of the philosophical schools. In chapter 11, we introduced a distinction between "irenic appropriation" (when philosophical schools appropriate foreign material with a conciliatory attitude toward it) and "polemical appropriation" (when schools reject elements of a competing philosophy or subversively reinterpret material within a new framework).[6] As recent scholarship illustrates, such acts of appropriation among the schools were not tantamount to simple genealogical derivation, since these acts involved creative usage and integration with one's own tradition.

Max Lee builds on the irenic-polemical appropriation distinction by offering a more variegated taxonomy of interaction types. In his monograph *Moral Transformation in Greco-Roman Philosophy of Mind*, Lee distinguishes six types:

1. *Eclecticism*. The subject assimilates or appropriates material from another school, but the rationale behind their appropriation remains unclear.
2. *Refutation*. The subject cites and proceeds to disprove the source philosophy or to demonstrate that their own philosophy is more correct.
3. *Competitive appropriation*. The subject takes over the meaning of the source's linguistic inventory and uses it in a "better" way.
4. *Irenic appropriation*. The subject critically supplements or synchronizes a rival's material.

---

*the Comparison of Early Christianities and the Religions of Late Antiquity* (Chicago: University of Chicago Press, 1990); and "Re: Corinthians," in *Redescribing Paul and the Corinthians*, ed. R. Cameron and M. P. Miller (Atlanta: Society of Biblical Literature, 2011), 17–34.

4. For a recent appeal to this distinction, see John S. Kloppenborg, "Disciplined Exaggeration: The Heuristics of Comparison in Biblical Studies," *NovT* 59 (2017): 390–414.

5. A collection of essays on the comparison in biblical studies can be found in John M. G. Barclay and B. G. White, *The New Testament in Comparison: Validity, Method, and Purpose in Comparing Traditions* (London: T&T Clark, 2020); see also Kloppenborg's article "Disciplined Exaggeration." For recent studies that take a heuristic approach, see Troels Engberg-Pedersen, "Stoicism in Early Christianity," in *Routledge Handbook of the Stoic Tradition*, ed. John Sellars (London: Routledge, 2016), 19–43, esp. 30, 40; and *John and Philosophy*, esp. vii, 32–34.

6. This distinction is based on Engberg-Pedersen's language of "irenic" and "polemical" or "subordinating appropriation" (*From Stoicism to Platonism*, 9–10).

5. *Concession.* The subject concedes to a rival school's teaching.
6. *Common ethical usage.* The subject appropriates language or concepts that belong to a common encyclopedia of philosophy or moral tradition.[7]

In a more recent essay, Lee adds a seventh interaction type:

7. *Doctrinal reformulation.* Adherents within a common tradition reinterpret their founder's teachings while intending to preserve the essential integrity of his original doctrines.[8]

While Lee develops this taxonomy initially with reference to the ancient philosophical schools, he sees it as prospectively useful for examining how the apostle Paul "appropriates the language of philosophical discourse in his moral exhortations to his gentile churches."[9]

## The Philosophical Traditions

### *Socrates*

A limited number of studies focus narrowly on Paul/the Pauline corpus and Socrates/Socratic literature. In a monograph-length treatment, Betz (1972) examines Paul's "apology" in 2 Corinthians 10–13 in light of the Socratic tradition. In another monograph, Fiore (1986) looks at the function of personal example in the Pastoral Epistles and the pseudonymous Socratic epistles.

### *Cynicism*

In a 1910 monograph, Bultmann offers a comparison between Paul's style of argument and Cynic-Stoic diatribe. Much more recently, Downing dedicates two monographs to the relationship between early Christianity and Cynicism, one focusing on Christian origins broadly (1992) and the other on Paul and the Pauline churches (1998). Along with Downing (1992), Kloppenborg (1987; 2000) and Mack (1993) propose a link between a Cynic stream of Christianity and the hypothetical Q document. Goulet-Cazet (2019) responds to the Q hypothesis by retracing evidence for Cynic contact with the Christian tradition, reexamining the comparison between the Cynic *chreia* genre and the hypothetical Q document, and surveying the relationship between Christianity and Cynicism in the second through fifth centuries.

7. Lee, *Moral Transformation*, 493–516.

8. Max J. Lee, "A Taxonomy of Intertextual Interactions Practiced by NT Authors: An Introduction," in *Practicing Intertextuality*, ed. Max J. Lee and B. J. Oropeza (Eugene, OR: Cascade, 2021), 3–16, esp. 5–6.

9. Lee, *Moral Transformation*, vii.

## *Stoicism*

Commensurate with the dominance of Stoicism in the first century CE, studies on the NT and Stoicism outnumber studies on all the other philosophical traditions combined. As an initiative of the Corpus Hellenisticum project, a series of articles by van der Horst catalogs parallels between several Stoics and various NT writings without much further comment; these cover the Stoics Musonius Rufus (1974), Hierocles (1975), and Cornutus (1981). Paul's letters have been perused in light of a number of Stoic themes in a host of articles and book chapters: self-sufficiency (Arnold 2017), freedom (Dautzenberg 1996), determinism (Malherbe 1994), indifferents (Deming 2003), the wise man (Thorsteinsson 2017), conscience (Wilson 2023), and even the whole department of ethics (Thorsteinsson 2006). A variety of monographs have covered these and other themes: law (Huttunen 2009; Wilson 2022); the self (Gorman 2023); freedom (Galloway 2004); indifferents (Jaquette 1995); marriage, celibacy, and indifferents (Deming 1995); and the diatribe style (Bultmann 1910). Engberg-Pedersen, who has been incomparably prolific in his examination of Stoicism and the NT, has produced a long list of narrowly focused thematic and exegetical studies on Paul and Stoicism, including studies on gift giving and friendship (2008), life after death (2017), virtue and vice (2003b), altruism (2003a), relationship with others (2005), along with many other topics. Several authors limit their attention to Paul and certain individual Stoics: Epictetus (Galloway 2004; Huttunen 2009; Gorman 2023); Seneca (Sevenster 1961; Dodson and Briones 2017); Seneca, Epictetus, and Marcus Aurelius (Rowe 2016).

A number of studies demonstrate connections between Stoicism and the views of the agitators, or "wise" people, addressed in 1 Corinthians, including articles by Grant (1951), Paige (1992), and Deming (2003), as well as monographs by Deming (1995), Garcilazo (2007), and myself (2014; 2024). In my 2024 book, I argue that certain Corinthian church members labeled themselves "wise men" after the paradigm of the Stoic philosophical "wise man" (*ho Sophos*), and that a similarity existed between the wise group's partisan allegiance to Paul and the philosophers' common practice of sectarian allegiance.

Many studies maintain a broader focus. Some pursue a comparison between Paul and individual Stoics holistically rather than thematically (Sevenster 1961; Rowe 2016). Lee's in-depth study (2020) of moral formation in Stoicism and Middle Platonism is written with a prospective interest in comparison with moral formation in Paul's theology. As part of a more ambitious project, Engberg-Pedersen adds to his resume of more narrowly focused studies several monographs arguing for more holistic comparison between Paul and the Stoics (2000; 2010), as well as between Stoicism and the theology of the Gospel of John (2017). Rasimus et al. (2010) takes a sweeping look at Stoicism in early Christianity, while Thorsteinsson (2010) compares Roman Stoicism and Roman Christianity.

## *Epicureanism*

Epicureanism has received far less attention than Stoicism. Yet several studies have compared Paul's pastoral strategies or techniques for fostering moral growth with the practices of Epicurean communities. Monographs on this subject include de Witt (1964), Glad (1995), and Allison (2020). In addition, Malherbe's study (1987) on pastoral care and the Thessalonian church gives special attention to Epicurean practices.

### *Middle Platonism*

In an article-length treatment, Atkins (2021) looks at the *logos* concept in John 1 through the lens of Middle Platonism. An article by Hubbard (2022) examines Paul's Areopagus discourse in Acts 17:16–34 in light of exegetical traditions on Plato's *Timaeus*. Galloway's monograph (2004) on Paul's appeal to his example in 1 Corinthians 9 puts Paul in conversation with Philo of Alexandria (a Middle Platonist) and Epictetus (a Stoic). Van Kooten (2008) argues for a consistency between Paul's anthropology and the Platonic idea of "assimilation to God." Lee's study (2020) on moral formation in the Greco-Roman philosophical tradition treats Middle Platonism alongside Stoicism, considering each with a prospective interest in comparison with moral formation in Paul's theology.

### *Aristotle and Other Philosophical Traditions*

A short chapter by Briones in Dodson and Briones (2019) juxtaposes Paul's views on friendship with Aristotle's, and an *ANRW* (1992) article by Balch examines New Testament texts in light of the neo-Pythagorean moralists.

### *Popular Philosophy*

Malherbe's career was virtually dedicated to the study of the NT and "popular philosophy," a phenomenon he identified chiefly with Cynicism and the common moral tradition of post-Hellenistic philosophy. Malherbe's 1989 volume on *Paul and the Popular Philosophers* is a collection mostly of his own previously published essays exploring various angles of comparison. Some essays overlap with the focus of his 1987 monograph on Paul's strategies of pastoral care and strategies of nurture in the philosophical schools, above all in Epicurean communities. Malherbe's research is condensed in his *ANRW* article (1992) on "Hellenistic Moralists and the New Testament."

### *General Studies*

Many studies cover philosophy as a wider tradition. A monograph by Divjanovic (2015) examines Paul "as philosopher" (*als Philosoph*). Fitzgerald (1988) examines Paul's hardship lists in the Corinthian correspondence in light of the philosophers' presentation of the character of the wise man. Barnes (2014) considers how philosophically educated women might have heard 1 Corinthians. Thorsteinsson (2018) looks at Jesus as a philosophical sage. Sharp (2022) considers Paul and ancient views on divination. Two collections of essays (1994; 2001) edited by Engberg-Pedersen and dedicated to the broader topic of Paul within his Hellenistic milieu include an assortment of essays on Paul and philosophy, including essays by Alexander on Christian communities and philosophical allegiance (1994) and on citation of authority in Paul and the Hellenistic schools (2001), and an essay by Stowers (2001) on the resemblance between Paul's communities and philosophical schools at the level of "central practices." Similar collections are available in Balch (1990), Sampley (2003; 2nd ed. 2016), and Holladay et al. (2013). Essays in Dodson and Briones (2019) survey a variety of philosophers and NT authors.

# Appendix 2: Major Philosophers by School[1]

## The Pre-Socratics and Socrates

Anaxagoras (probably 500–428 BCE)
Anaximander (d. sometime after 427 BCE)
Anaximenes (fl. 546–525 BCE)
Democritus (b. 460–457 BCE)
Empedocles (ca. 492–432 BCE)
Heraclitus (fl. ca. 500 BCE)
Leucippus (second half of fifth c. BCE)
Parmenides of Elea (fl. ca. 450 BCE)
Pythagoras (b. mid-sixth c. BCE)
Socrates (469–399 BCE)
Thales of Miletus (fl. early sixth c. BCE)
Xenophanes (mid-sixth–early fifth c. BCE)
Zeno of Elea (fl. early fifth c. BCE)

## The Academy

### *Classical Period*

Plato (ca. 429–347 BCE)
Speusippus (ca. 407–339 BCE)
Xenocrates (head 339–314 BCE)

### *Hellenistic Period*

Polemo (head 314/313–270/269 BCE)
Crates of Athens (early third c. BCE)
Arcesilaus (316/315–242/241 BCE)
Lacydes (ca. 235–ca. 160 BCE)

---

1. All dates are from the *Oxford Classical Dictionary*, ed. S. Hornblower and A. Spawforth, 3rd ed. (Oxford: Oxford University Press, 1996); supplemented by LS, *The Hellenistic Philosophers*.

Carneades (ca. 214/213–129/128 BCE)
Philo of Larissa (159/158–84/83 BCE)

### *Post-Hellenistic Period*

[Aenesidemus (first c. BCE)][2]
[Antiochus of Ascalon (b. ca. 130 BCE)]
Cicero (106–43 BCE)
Eudorus of Alexandria (fl. ca. 25 BCE)
Favorinus (ca. 85–155 CE)

## Aristotelians

Alexander of Aphrodisias (ca. 200 CE)
Andronicus of Rhodes (first c. BCE)

## Cynics

### *Classical and Hellenistic Cynics*

Antisthenes (mid-fifth–mid-fourth c. BCE)
Diogenes of Sinope (b. ca. 412/403, d. ca. 324/321 BCE)
Crates of Thebes (b. ca. 368–365, d. 288/285 BCE)

### *Post-Hellenistic Cynics*

Demetrius the Cynic (mid-first c. CE)
Demonax of Cyprus (second c. CE)
Oenomaus of Gadara (fl. 120 CE)
Peregrinus (d. 165 CE)

## Epicureans

### *Hellenistic Cynics*

Epicurus (341–270 BCE)
Hermarchus of Mytilene (early third c. BCE)

---

2. Bracketed names indicate either our uncertainty about the individual's school identity or ambiguous tendencies or a change in their affiliation at some point in their career.

*Post-Hellenistic Cynics*

Diogenes of Oenoanda (probably second c. CE)
Lucretius (first half of first c. BCE)
Phaedrus (ca. 140–70 BCE)
Philodemus of Gadara (ca. 110–ca. 40/35 BCE)

## Middle Platonists

Alcinous (second c. CE)
Antiochus of Ascalon (b. ca. 130 BCE)
[Eudorus of Alexandria (fl. ca. 25 BCE)]
Galen (129–?199/216 CE)
Numenius (second c. CE)
Philo of Alexandria (early to mid-first c. CE)
Plutarch (b. before 50, d. after 120 CE)

## Peripatetics

Aristotle (384–322 BCE)
Theophrastus (372/371 or 371/370–288/287 or 287/286 BCE)
Strato of Lampascus (head of Lyceum ca. 287–269 BCE)

## Neo-Platonists

Plotinus (205–269/270 CE)
Porphyry (234–ca. 305 CE)
Iamblichus (ca. 245–ca. 325 CE)

## Pyrrhonists

*Hellenistic Pyrrhonists*

Pyrrho of Elis (ca. 365–275 BCE)
Nausiphanes (fl. 340–320 BCE)
Timon of Phlius (ca. 320–230 BCE)

*Post-Hellenistic Pyrrhonists*

Aenesidemus (first c. BCE)
Sextus Empiricus (late second c. CE)

## Neo-Pythagoreans

Apollonius of Tyana (first c. CE)
[Eudorus of Alexandria] (fl. ca. 25 BCE)
P. Nigidius Figulus (praetor 58 BCE)
Numenius (second c. CE)

## Stoics

*Hellenistic Stoics*

Zeno of Citium (335–263 BCE)
Cleanthes of Assos (ca. 330–230 BCE)
Chrysippus (ca. 280–207 BCE)

*Middle Stoics*

Panaetius (ca. 185–109 BCE)
Posidonius (ca. 135–51 BCE)

*Post-Hellenistic Stoics*

Cornutus (mid-first c. CE)
Epictetus (mid-first to second c. CE)
Hierocles (early second c. CE)
Marcus Aurelius (121–180 CE)
[Musonius Rufus] (b. before 30, d. before 101/102 CE)
Seneca, Lucius Annaeus (b. 4 BCE–1 CE, d. 65 CE)

## Other Socratic Schools

Aristippus of Cyrene (late fifth–early fourth c. BCE)
Euclides of Megara (ca. 450–380 BCE)
Phaedo of Elis (fifth–fourth c. BCE)

# Appendix 3: Major Philosophers by Period

## Pre-Socratics and Socrates

Anaxagoras (probably 500–428 BCE)
Anaximander (d. sometime after 427 BCE)
Anaximenes (fl. 546–525 BCE)
Democritus (b. 460–457 BCE)
Empedocles (ca. 492–432 BCE)
Heraclitus (fl. ca. 500 BCE)
Leucippus (second half of fifth c. BCE)
Parmenides of Elea (fl. ca. 450 BCE)
Pythagoras (b. mid-sixth c. BCE)
Socrates (469–399 BCE)
Thales of Miletus (fl. early sixth c. BCE)
Xenophanes (mid-sixth–early fifth c. BCE)
Zeno of Elea (fl. early fifth c. BCE)

## Late Classical

Antisthenes (mid-fifth–mid-fourth c. BCE)
Aristippus of Cyrene (late fifth–early fourth c. BCE)
Aristotle (384–322 BCE)
Diogenes of Sinope (b. ca. 412/403, d. ca. 324/321 BCE)
Euclides of Megara (ca. 450–380 BCE)
Nausiphanes (fl. 340–320 BCE)
Phaedo of Elis (fifth–fourth c. BCE)
Plato (ca. 429–347 BCE)
Speusippus (ca. 407–339 BCE)
Xenocrates (head of academy 339–314 BCE)

## Hellenistic

Arcesilaus (316/315–242/241 BCE)
Carneades (ca. 214/213–129/128 BCE)
Chrysippus (ca. 280–207 BCE)
Cleanthes of Assos (ca. 330–230 BCE)
Crates of Athens (early third c. BCE)
Crates of Thebes (b. ca. 368–365, d. 288/285 BCE)
Epicurus (341–270 BCE)
Hermarchus of Mytilene (early third c. BCE)
Lacydes (ca. 235–ca. 160 BCE)
Panaetius (ca. 185–109 BCE)
Philo of Larissa (159/158–84/83 BCE)
Polemo (head of academy 314/313–270/269 BCE)
Posidonius (ca. 135–51 BCE)
Pyrrho of Elis (ca. 365–275 BCE)
Strato of Lampascus (head of Lyceum ca. 287–269 BCE)
Theophrastus (372/371 or 371/370–288/287 or 287/286 BCE)
Timon of Phlius (ca. 320–230 BCE)
Zeno of Citium (335–263 BCE)

## Post-Hellenistic

Aenesidemus (first c. BCE)
Alcinous (second c. CE)
Alexander of Aphrodisias (ca. 200 CE)
Andronicus of Rhodes (first c. BCE)
Antiochus of Ascalon (b. ca. 130 BCE)
Apollonius of Tyana (first c. CE)
Cicero (106–43 BCE)
Cornutus (mid-first c. CE)
Demetrius the Cynic (mid-first c. CE)
Demonax of Cyprus (second c. CE)
Diogenes of Oenoanda (probably second c. CE)
Epictetus (mid-first–second c. CE)
Eudorus of Alexandria (fl. ca. 25 BCE)
Favorinus (ca. 85–155 CE)
Galen (129–?199/216 CE)
Hierocles (early second c. CE)
Lucretius (first half of first c. BCE)
Marcus Aurelius (121–180 CE)
Musonius Rufus (b. before 30, d. before 101/102 CE)

P. Nigidius Figulus (praetor 58 BCE)
Numenius (second c. CE)
Oenomaus of Gadara (fl. 120 CE)
Peregrinus (d. 165 CE)
Phaedrus (ca. 140–70 BCE)
Philo of Alexandria (early–mid-first c. CE)
Philodemus of Gadara (ca. 110–ca. 40/35 BCE)
Plutarch (b. before 50, d. after 120 CE)
Seneca, Lucius Annaeus (b. 4 BCE–1 CE, d. 65 CE)
Sextus Empiricus (late second c. CE)

## Late Ancient

Plotinus (205–269/270 CE)
Porphyry (234–ca. 305 CE)
Iamblichus (ca. 245–ca. 325 CE)

# Appendix 4

SYRIA
Sinope
Citium
CYPRUS
EGYPT
Alexandria
ASIA MINOR
Rhodes
IONIA
SAMOS
CRETE
Aegean Sea
Athens
Corinth
Delphi
MACEDONIA
GREECE
Elis
Mediterranean Sea
Adriatic Sea
Elea
ITALY
SICILY
0 50 100 150 miles
0 100 200 km
City or Town

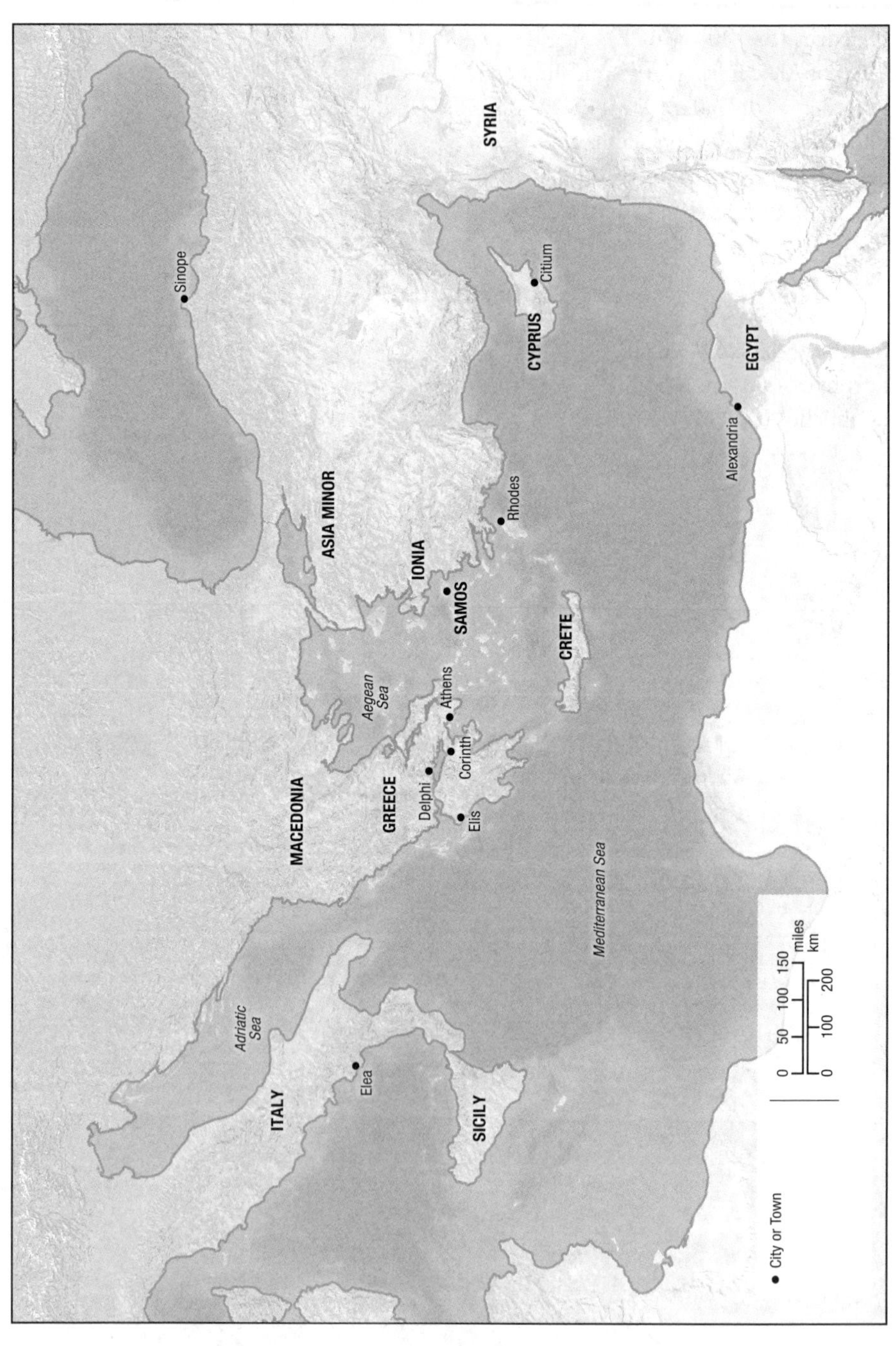

# Ancient Mediterranean World Maps

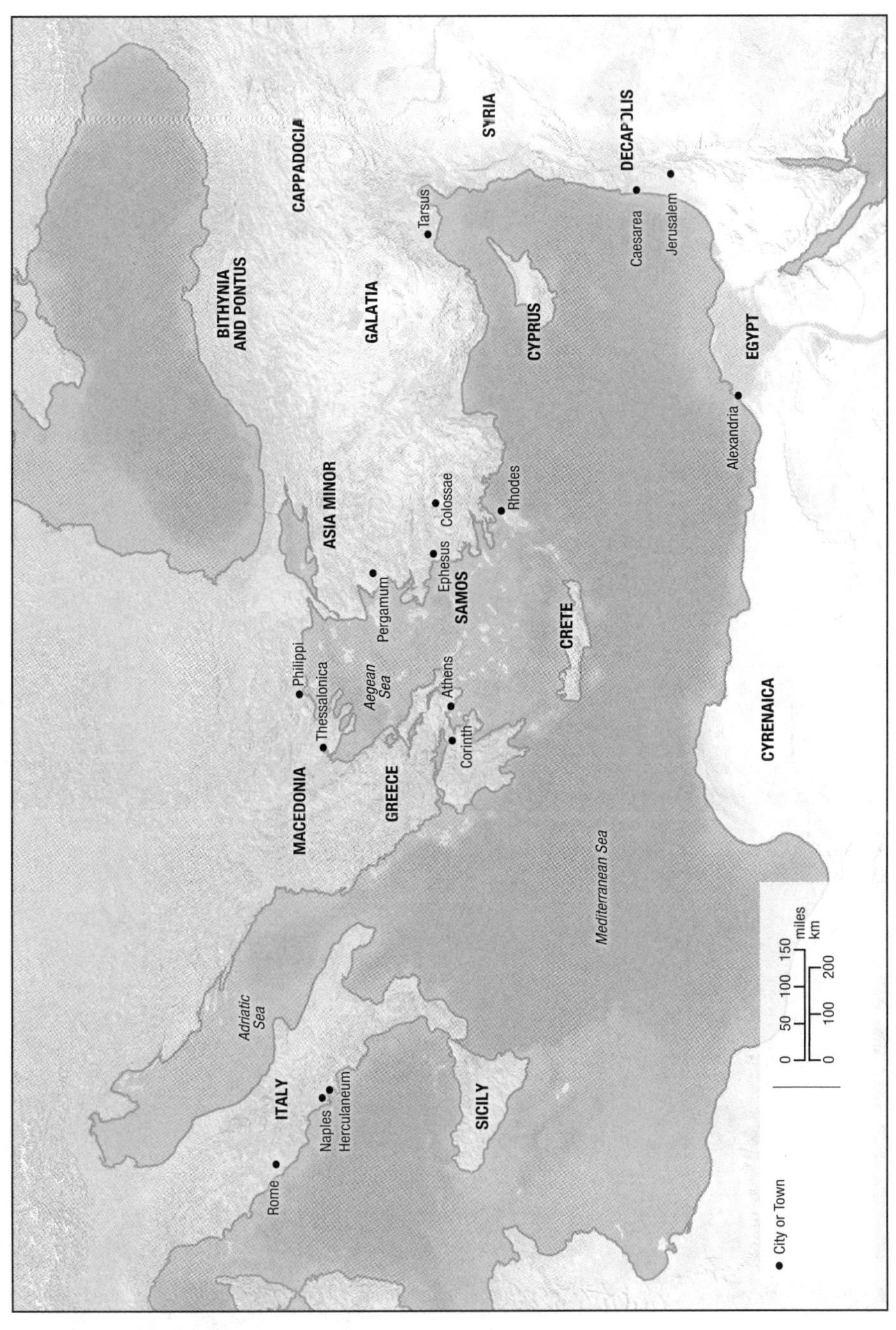

# Bibliography


Ahlholm, Tuuli. "Philosophers in Stone: Philosophy and Self-representation in Epigraphy of the Roman Empire." MPhil thesis, Oxford University, 2017.

Alexander, Loveday. "*IPSE DIXIT*: Citation of Authority in Paul and in the Jewish and Hellenistic Schools." Pages 103–27 in *Paul Beyond the Judaism-Hellenism Divide*. Edited by Troels Engberg-Pedersen. Louisville: Westminster John Knox, 2001.

———. "Paul and the Hellenistic Schools: The Evidence of Galen." Pages 60–83 in *Paul in His Hellenistic Context*. Edited by Troels Engberg-Pedersen. London: T&T Clark, 1994. Reprint, London: Continuum, 2004.

Allison, Justin. *Saving One Another: Philodemus and Paul on Moral Formation in Community*. Ancient Philosophy and Religion 3. Leiden: Brill, 2020.

Arnold, Bradley. "Αὐτάρκης in Stoicism and Phil 4:11." *Novum Testamentum* 59 (2017): 1–19.

Atkins, Christopher S. "Rethinking John 1:1: The Word Was Godward." *Novum Testamentum* 63 (2021): 44–62.

Balch, David L. *Greeks, Romans, and Christians: Festschrift in Honor of Abraham J. Malherbe*. Minneapolis: Fortress, 1990.

———. "The Neo-Pythagorean Moralists and the New Testament." *ANRW* (1992) 2.26.1:380–411. Part 2, Principat, 26.1. Edited by H. Temporini and W. Haase. New York: de Gruyter, 1989.

Barclay, John M. G., and B. G. White, eds. *The New Testament in Comparison: Validity, Method, and Purpose in Comparing Traditions*. London: T&T Clark, 2020.

Barnes, Nathan J. *Reading 1 Corinthians with Philosophically Educated Women*. Eugene, OR: Pickwick, 2014.

Betz, Hans Dieter. *Der Apostel Paulus und die sokratische Tradition: Eine Exegetische Untersuchung zu seiner Apologie 2 Korinther 10–13*. Beiträge zur historischen Theologie 45. Tübingen: J. C. B. Mohr, 1972.

Boys-Stones, George R. *L. Annaeus Cornutus:* Greek Theology, *Fragments, and Testimonia*. Writings from the Greco-Roman World. Atlanta: Society of Biblical Literature, 2018.

———. *Platonist Philosophy 80 BC to AD 250: An Introduction and Collection of Sources in Translation*. Cambridge Sourcebooks in Post-Hellenistic Philosophy. Cambridge: Cambridge University Press, 2018.

Brickhouse, Thomas C., and Nicholas Smith. *The Philosophy of Socrates*. Boulder, CO: Westview, 2000.

Briones, David E. "Why Can't We Be Friends? Paul and Aristotle on Friendship." Pages 36–49 in *Paul and the Giants of Philosophy*. Edited by Joseph R. Dodson and David E. Briones. Downers Grove, IL: InterVarsity, 2019.

Brisson, Luc. *How Philosophers Saved Myths: Allegorical Interpretation and Classical Mythology*. Translated by Catherine Tihanyi. Chicago: University of Chicago Press, 2004.

Brookins, Timothy A. *Corinthian Wisdom, Stoic Philosophy, and the Ancient Economy*. Society of New Testament Studies Monograph Series 159. Cambridge: Cambridge University Press, 2014.

———. *Rediscovering the Wisdom of the Corinthians: Paul, Stoicism, and Spiritual Hierarchy*. Grand Rapids: Eerdmans, 2024.

Bultmann, Rudolf. *Der Stil der Paulinischen Predigt und die kynisch-stoische Diatribe*. Göttingen: Vandenhoeck & Ruprecht, 1910.

Butts, J. R. "The Progymnasmata of Theon: A New Text with Translation and Commentary." PhD diss., Claremont Graduate School, 1986.

Colish, Marcia L. "Stoicism and the New Testament: An Essay in Historiography." *ANRW* 2.26.1:334–79. Part 2, Principat, 26.1. Edited by H. Temporini and W. Haase. New York: de Gruyter, 1989.

Cribiore, Raffaella. *Gymnastics of the Mind: Greek Education in Hellenistic and Roman Egypt*. Princeton, NJ: Princeton University Press, 2001.

Dautzenberg, G. "Die Freiheit bei Paulus und in der Stoa." *Theologische Quartalschrift* 176 (1996): 65–76.

Deming, Will. "Paul and Indifferent Things." Pages 384–403 in *Paul in the Greco-Roman World*. Edited by J. Paul Sampley. London: Continuum, 2003.

———. *Paul on Marriage and Celibacy: The Hellenistic Background of 1 Corinthians 7*. Society of New Testament Studies Monograph Series 83. Cambridge: Cambridge University Press, 1995; Grand Rapids: Eerdmans, 2004.

Despotis, Athanasios, and Hermut Löhr, eds., *Religious and Philosophical Conversion in the Ancient Mediterranean*. Leiden: Brill, 2022.

De Witt, Norman W. *St. Paul and Epicurus*. Minneapolis: University of Minnesota, 1964.

Dibelius, Martin. *An die Kolosser, an die Epheser, an Philemon*. Tübingen: J. C. B. Mohr, 1913.

Dillon, John. *Alcinous: The Handbook of Platonism: Introduction, Text and Commentary*. Oxford: Oxford University Press, 2003.

Divjanovic, Kristin. *Paulus als Philosoph: Das Ethos des Apostels vor dem Hintergrund antiker Populärphilosophie*. Münster: Aschendorff, 2015.

Dodson, Joseph R., and David E. Briones, eds. *Paul and the Giants of Philosophy*. Downers Grove, IL: InterVarsity, 2019.

———, eds. *Paul and Seneca in Dialogue*. Ancient Philosophy and Religion 2. Leiden: Brill, 2017.

Dodson, Joseph R., and Andrew W. Pitts, eds. *Paul and the Greco-Roman Philosophical Tradition*. Library of New Testament Studies 527. London: T&T Clark, 2017.

Downing, F. Gerald. *Cynics and Christian Origins*. Edinburgh: T&T Clark, 1992.

———. *Cynics, Paul, and the Pauline Churches*. New York: Routledge, 1998.

Dürr, Simon. *Paul on the Human Vocation: Reason Language in Romans and Ancient Philosophical Tradition*. Beihefte zur Zeitschrift für die neutestamentliche Wissenschaft 226. Berlin: de Gruyter, 2021.

Engberg-Pedersen, Troels. *Cosmology and Self in the Apostle Paul: The Material Spirit*. Oxford: Oxford University Press, 2010.

———, ed. *From Stoicism to Platonism: The Development of Philosophy, 100 BCE–100 CE*. Cambridge: Cambridge University Press, 2017.

———. "Gift-Giving and Friendship: Seneca and Paul in Romans 1–8 on the Logic of God's χάρις and its Human Response." *Harvard Theological Review* 101 (2008): 15–44.

———. *John and Philosophy: A New Reading of the Fourth Gospel*. Oxford: Oxford University Press, 2017.

———. *Paul and Philosophy: Selected Essays*. Wissenschaftliche Untersuchungen zum Neuen Testament 509. Tübingen: Mohr Siebeck, 2023.

———. *Paul and the Stoics*. Louisville: Westminster John Knox, 2000.

———, ed. *Paul Beyond the Judaism/Hellenism Divide*. Louisville: Westminster John Knox, 2001.

———, ed. *Paul in His Hellenistic Context*. Minneapolis: Fortress, 1994. Reprint, London: Continuum, 2004.

———. "Paul in Philippians and Seneca in *Epistle* 93 on Life after Death and Its Present Implications." Pages 267–84 in *Paul and Seneca in Dialogue*. Edited by Joseph R. Dodson and David E. Briones. Ancient Philosophy and Religion 2. Leiden: Brill, 2017.

———. "Paul, Virtues, and Vices." Pages 608–34 in *Paul in the Greco-Roman World*. Edited by J. Paul Sampley. London: Continuum, 2003.

———. "Radical Altruism in Philippians 2:4." Pages 197–214 in *Early Christianity and Classical Culture*. Edited by John T. Fitzgerald, T. H. Olbricht, and L. Michael White. Supplements to Novum Testamentum 110. Leiden: Brill, 2003. Reprint, Atlanta: Society of Biblical Literature, 2005.

———. "Setting the Scene." Pages 1–14 in *Stoicism in Early Christianity*. Edited by Tuomas Rasimus, Troels Engberg-Pedersen, and Ismo Dunderberg. Grand Rapids: Baker Academic, 2010.

———. "Stoicism in Early Christianity: The Apostle Paul and the Evangelist John as Stoics." Pages 19–43 in *Routledge Handbook of the Stoic Tradition*. Edited by John Sellars. London: Routledge, 2016.

Fiore, Benjamin. *The Function of Personal Example in the Socratic and Pastoral Epistles*. Analecta Biblica 105. Rome: Biblical Institute Press, 1986.

Fitzgerald, John T. *Cracks in an Earthen Vessel: An Examination of the Catalogues of Hardships in the Corinthian Correspondence*. Society of Biblical Literature Dissertation Series 99. Atlanta: Scholars, 1988.

Fitzgerald, John T., and L. Michael White. "*Quod est comparandum*: The Problem of Parallels." Pages 13–39 in *Early Christianity and Classical Culture*. Edited by John T. Fitzgerald, T. H. Olbricht, and L. Michael White. Leiden: Brill, 2003.

Galloway, L. E. *Freedom in the Gospel: Paul's Exemplum in 1 Cor 9 in Conversation with the Discourses of Epictetus and Philo*. Contributions to Biblical Exegesis and Theology 38. Leuven: Peeters, 2004.

Garcilazo, Albert V. *The Corinthian Dissenters and the Stoics*. New York: Peter Lang, 2007.

Gill, Christopher. "The School in the Roman Imperial Period." Pages 33–53 in *The Cambridge Companion to Stoicism*. Edited by Brad Inwood. Cambridge: Cambridge University Press, 2003.

Glad, Clarence. *Paul and Philodemus: Adaptability in Epicurean and Early Christian Psychagogy*. Supplements to Novum Testamentum 81. Leiden: Brill, 1995.

Gorman, Michael J. *The Self, the Lord, and the Other According to Paul and Epictetus*. Eugene, OR: Cascade, 2023.

Goulet, Richard. "Ancient Philosophers: A First Statistical Survey." Pages 10–39 in *Philosophy as a Way of Life: Ancients and Moderns; Essays in Honor of Pierre Hadot*. Edited by Michael Chase, Stephen R. L. Clark, and Michael McGhee. Oxford: Wiley-Blackwell, 2013.

———. *Dictionnaire des Philosophes Anciennes*. 7 vols. Paris: CNRS éditions, 1994–2018.

Goulet-Cazé, Marie-Odile. *Cynicism and Christianity in Antiquity*. Grand Rapids: Eerdmans, 2019.

Grant, Robert M. "The Wisdom of the Corinthians." Pages 51–55 in *The Joy of Study: Papers on New Testament and Related Subjects, Presented to Honor Frederick Clifton Grant*. New York: Macmillan, 1951.

Harris, William V. *Ancient Literacy*. Cambridge, MA: Harvard University Press, 1989.

Hatzimichaeli, Myrto. "The Texts of Plato and Aristotle in the First Century." Pages 1–27 in *Aristotle, Plato and Pythagoreanism in the First Century BC: New Directions for Philosophy*. Edited by Malcolm Schofield. Cambridge: Cambridge University Press, 2013.

Hine, Harry M. "Philosophy and *philosophi*: From Cicero to Apuleius." Pages 13–29 in *Roman Reflections: Studies in Latin Philosophy*. Edited by Gareth D. Williams and Katharina Volk. New York: Oxford University Press, 2016.

———. "Seneca and Paul: The First Two Thousand Years." Pages 22–48 in *Paul and Seneca in Dialogue*. Edited by Joseph R. Dodson and David E. Briones. Ancient Philosophy and Religion 2. Leiden; Boston: Brill, 2017.

Holladay, Carl R., John T. Fitzgerald, James W. Thompson, and Gregory E. Sterling, eds. *Light from the Gentiles: Hellenistic Philosophy and Early Christianity: Collected Essays, 1959–2012, by Abraham J. Malherbe*. 2 vols. Supplements to Novum Testamentum 150. Leiden: Brill, 2013.

Hubbard, Jeffrey M. "Paul the Middle Platonist? Exegetical Traditions on *Timaeus* 28c and the Characterization of Paul in Acts 17:16–31." *Harvard Theological Review* 115 (2022): 477–95.

Huttunen, Niko. *Paul and Epictetus on Law: A Comparison*. London: T&T Clark, 2009.

Inwood, Brad. *Later Stoicism 155 BC to AD 200: An Introduction and Collection of Sources in Translation*. Cambridge Sourcebooks in Post-Hellenistic Philosophy. Cambridge: Cambridge University Press, 2022.

Iribarren, Leopoldo, and Hugo Koning, eds. *Hesiod and the Beginnings of Greek Philosophy*. Mnemosyne Supplements 455. Leiden: Brill, 2022.

Jaquette, J. J. *Discerning What Counts: The Function of the* Adiaphora Topos *in Paul's Letters*. Atlanta: Scholars, 1995.

Johnson, W. A., and H. N. Parker, eds. *Ancient Literacies: The Culture of Reading in Greece and Rome*. Oxford: Oxford University Press, 2009.

Karamanolis, George. *The Philosophy of Early Christianity*. Ancient Philosophies. 2nd ed. New York: Routledge, 2021.

Kidd, I. G. *Posidonius, Volume 3: The Translation of the Fragments*. Cambridge Classical Texts and Commentaries. Cambridge: Cambridge University Press, 1999.

Kloppenborg, John S. "Disciplined Exaggeration: The Heuristics of Comparison in Biblical Studies." *Novum Testamentum* 59 (2017): 390–414.

———. *Excavating Q: The History and Setting of the Sayings Gospel*. Minneapolis: Fortress, 2000.

———. *The Formation of Q: Trajectories in Ancient Wisdom Collections*. Studies in Antiquity and Christianity. Philadelphia: Fortress, 1987.

Lee, Max J. *Moral Transformation in Greco-Roman Philosophy of Mind*. Wissenschaftliche Untersuchungen zum Neuen Testament 2/515. Tübingen: Mohr Siebeck, 2020.

———. "A Taxonomy of Intertextual Interactions Practiced by NT Authors: An Introduction." Pages 3–16 in *Practicing Intertextuality*. Edited by Max J. Lee and B. J. Oropeza. Eugene, OR: Cascade, 2021.

Lietzman, Hans. *An die Romer*. Tübingen: J. C. B. Mohr, 1906.

Long, A. A., and David Sedley. *The Hellenistic Philosophers*. 2 vols. Cambridge: Cambridge University Press, 1987.

Mack, Burton L. *The Lost Gospel: The Book of Q and Christian Origins*. San Francisco: HarperSanFrancisco, 1993.

Malherbe, Abraham J. "Determinism and Free Will in Paul: The Argument of 1 Corinthians 8 and 9." Pages 231–55 in *Paul in His Hellenistic Context*. Edited by Troels Engberg-Pedersen. Minneapolis: Fortress, 1994.

———. "Hellenistic Moralists and the New Testament." *ANRW* 2.26.1:267–333. Part 2, Principat, 26.1. Edited by H. Temporini and W. Haase. New York: de Gruyter, 1989.

———. *Moral Exhortation: A Greco-Roman Sourcebook*. Library of Early Christianity. Philadelphia: Westminster Press, 1986.

———. *Paul and the Popular Philosophers*. Minneapolis: Fortress, 1989.

———. *Paul and the Thessalonians: The Philosophic Tradition of Pastoral Care*. Minneapolis: Fortress, 1987.

Maso, Stefano. *Cicero's Philosophy*. Trends in Classics 3. Berlin: de Gruyter, 2022.

Moore, Christopher. *Calling Philosophers Names: On the Origin of a Discipline*. Princeton: Princeton University Press, 2020.

Morgan, Teresa. *Literate Education in the Hellenistic and Roman World*. Cambridge: Cambridge University Press, 1999.

Mussies, Gerard. *Dio Chrysostom and the New Testament: A Contribution to the Corpus Hellenisticum*. Studia ad Corpus Hellenisticum Novi Testamenti 2. Leiden: Brill, 1970.

Paige, Terrence. "Stoicism, *Eleutheria*, and Community at Corinth." Pages 180–93 in *Worship, Theology and Ministry in the Early Church*. Edited by Michael J. Wilkins and Terrence Paige. Sheffield: JSOT, 1992.

Petzke, Gerd. *Die Traditionen über Apollonius von Tyana und das Neue Testament*. Studia ad Corpus Hellenisticum Novi Testamenti 1. Leiden: Brill, 1970.

Rasimus, Tuomas, Troels Engberg-Pedersen, and Ismo Dunderberg, eds. *Stoicism in Early Christianity*. Grand Rapids: Baker Academic, 2010.

Rizakis, A. D., and S. Zoumbaki. *Roman Peloponnese I: Roman Personal Names in Their Social Context [Achaia, Arcadia, Argolis, Corinthia and Eleia]*. Meletemata 31. Athens: Research Centre for Greek and Roman Antiquity, 2001.

Rowe, C. Kavin. *One True Life: The Stoics and Early Christians as Rival Traditions*. New Haven: Yale University Press, 2016.

Sampley, J. P., ed. *Paul in the Greco-Roman World: A Handbook*. 2nd ed. Harrisburg, PA: Trinity Press International, 2016.

Sandmel, Samuel. "Parallelomania." *Journal of Biblical Literature* 81 (1962): 1–13.

Sassi, Maria Michela. *The Beginnings of Philosophy in Greece*. Princeton: Princeton University Press, 2018.

Schofield, Malcolm. *The Stoic Idea of the City*. Cambridge: Cambridge University Press, 1991.

Sedley, David N. "Philosophical Allegiance in the Greco-Roman World." Pages 97–119 in *Philosophia Togata*. Edited by Mirian Griffin and J. Barnes. Oxford: Clarendon, 1989.

Sellars, John. *Hellenistic Philosophy*. Oxford: Oxford University Press, 2018.

Sevenster, Jan Nicolaas. *Paul and Seneca*. Supplements to Novum Testamentum 4. Leiden: Brill, 1961.

Sharp, Matthew. *Divination and Philosophy in the Letters of Paul*. Edinburgh Studies in Religion in Antiquity. Edinburgh: Edinburgh University Press, 2022.

Shields, Christopher. *Ancient Philosophy: A Contemporary Introduction*. 2nd ed. New York: Routledge, 2023.

Smith, Jonathan Z. *Drudgery Divine: On the Comparison of Early Christianities and the Religions of Late Antiquity*. Chicago: University of Chicago Press, 1990.

———. *Map Is Not Territory: Studies in the History of Religions*. Chicago: University of Chicago Press, 1982.

———. "Re: Corinthians." Pages 17–34 in *Redescribing Paul and the Corinthians*. Edited by R. Cameron and M. P. Miller. Atlanta: Society of Biblical Literature, 2011.

Snyder, Gregory H. "'Not Subjects of a Despot': Stoics." Pages 14–44 in *Teachers and Texts in the Ancient World: Philosophers, Jews and Christians*. London: Routledge, 2000.

Stanton, G. R. "Sophists and Philosophers: Problems of Classification." *American Journal of Philology* 94 (1975): 350–64.

Stowers, Stanley. "Does Pauline Christianity Resemble a Hellenistic Philosophy?" Pages 81–102 in *Paul Beyond the Judaism-Hellenism Divide*. Edited by Troels Engberg-Pedersen. Louisville: Westminster John Knox, 2001.

Thorsteinsson, Runar M. "Jesus Christ and the Wise Man: Paul and Seneca on Moral Sages." Pages 73–87 in *Paul and Seneca in Dialogue*. Edited by Joseph R. Dodson and David E. Briones. Ancient Philosophy and Religion 2. Leiden: Brill, 2017.

———. *Jesus as Philosopher: The Moral Sage in the Synoptic Gospels*. Oxford: Oxford University Press, 2018.

———. "Paul and Roman Stoicism: Romans 12 and Contemporary Stoic Ethics." *Journal for the Study of the New Testament* 29 (2006): 139–61.

———. *Roman Christianity and Roman Stoicism: A Comparative Study of Ancient Morality*. Oxford: Oxford University Press, 2010.

Van der Horst, Pieter W. "Cornutus and the New Testament: A Contribution to the Corpus Hellenisticum." *Novum Testamentum* 23 (1981): 165–82.

———. "Hierocles the Stoic and the New Testament: A Contribution to the Corpus Hellenisticum." *Novum Testamentum* 17 (1975): 156–60.

———. "Macrobius and the New Testament: A Contribution to the Corpus Hellenisticum." *Novum Testamentum* 15 (1973): 220–32.

———. "Musonius Rufus and the New Testament." *Novum Testamentum* 16 (1974): 306–15.

Van Kooten, George. *Paul's Anthropology in Context: The Image of God, Assimilation to God, and Tripartite Man in Ancient Judaism, Ancient Philosophy and Early Christianity*. Wissenschaftliche Untersuchungen zum Neuen Testament 2/232. Tübingen: Mohr Siebeck, 2008.

Van Unnik, W. C. "Corpus Hellenisticum Novi Testamenti." *Journal of Biblical Literature* 83 (1964): 17–33.

von Dobschütz, Ernst. *Die urchristlichen Gemeinden*. Leipzig: J. C. Hinrichs'sche Buchhandlung, 1902.

Weiss, Johannes. *Der erste Korintherbrief*. Kritisch-exegetischer Kommentar über das Neue Testament (MeyerKommentar). Göttingen: Vandenhoeck & Ruprecht, 1910.

Williams, Gareth D., and Katharina Volk, eds. *Roman Reflections: Studies in Latin Philosophy*. New York: Oxford University Press, 2016.

Wilson, Annalisa Phillips. *Paul and the Jewish Law: A Stoic Ethical Perspective on His Inconsistency*. Ancient Philosophy and Religion. Leiden: Brill, 2022.

———. "Συνείδησις in Paul's Texts and Stoic Self-Perception." *New Testament Studies* 69 (2023): 182–94.

Windisch, Hans. *Der zweite Korintherbrief*. Göttingen: Vandenhoeck & Ruprecht, 1914.

# Modern Author Index

# Subject Index

# Ancient Sources Index

**Epictetus**

*Diatribes*